Melodies Unheard

PUBLISHING FOR THE WORLD
125 Years
THE JOHNS HOPKINS UNIVERSITY PRESS

JOHNS HOPKINS:
POETRY & FICTION

John T. Irwin
General Editor

Melodies Unheard

Essays on the
Mysteries of Poetry

ANTHONY HECHT

The Johns Hopkins University Press
Baltimore & London

© 2003 The Johns Hopkins University Press
All rights reserved. Published 2003
Printed in the United States of America on acid-free paper
2 4 6 8 9 7 5 3 1
The Johns Hopkins University Press
2715 North Charles Street
Baltimore, Maryland 21218-4363
www.press.jhu.edu

Library of Congress Cataloging-in-Publication Data

Hecht, Anthony, 1923–
Melodies unheard : essays on poetry and religion / Anthony Hecht.
        p.   cm.—(Johns Hopkins, poetry and fiction)
Includes bibliographical references and index.
ISBN 0-8018-6956-0 (alk. paper)
1. American poetry—History and criticism. 2. English poetry—History and criticism.
I. Title. II. Series.

PS305 .H43 2003
811.009—dc21
2002040579

A catalog record for this book is available from the British Library.

Pages 301–304 constitute a continuation of the copyright page.

To Christopher Ricks

*Sams writes that one section of the Humoreske [by Robert Schumann] is
written on three staves instead of two in order to set off the melody on a
separate staff of its own. But Sams never mentions that the third staff is
not intended to be played at all. There is one staff for the right hand,
one for the left, and a third between them for an inaudible music: in her
edition, Clara Schumann firmly marked this staff "not to be performed."
The melody (marked "Inner voice") is only to be imagined. What the
listener hears is an accompaniment which is clearly nothing more than
that, but which appears to echo and respond to an absent melody.*

—CHARLES ROSEN, *Romantic Poets, Critics, and Other Madmen*

. . . sweet instruments hung up in cases, that keep their sounds to themselves.

—*Timon of Athens* I.ii.98–99

*Rose-cheekt Lawra, come,
Sing thou smoothly with thy beawties
Silent musick, either other
Sweetely gracing.*

—CAMPION

*Heard melodies are sweet, but those unheard
Are sweeter, . . .*

—KEATS

Contents

Melodies Unheard

Introduction

Now in my eighty-first year, I have at long last learned a few things about myself that have gone with profit into the assembly of these essays and to the writing of them one by one. For many years I did regular book reviews, assigned by editors of literary journals, almost always about the work of my fellow poets and contemporaries. I didn't always admire everything I was asked to review, and I composed a few acidulous comments on some of these, couched, as I thought, in amusing or outright funny terms. I was probably able to half-absolve myself from the charge of cruelty on the grounds that I had been ordered to deal with works I didn't like and, in my own mind at least, to foist the blame, or some part of it, onto the editors I was hired to oblige.

I could have eased my conscience (if I'd felt the need) by citing John Ruskin, who observed that "very bad pictures may be divided into two principal classes—those which are weak and passively bad, and which are to be pitied and passed by; and those which are energetically or actively bad, and which demand severe reprobation."[1] It's just barely possible that such a distinction might be made about bad poetry, though in our days I think it would be harder. Poetry that is "energetically or actively bad" these days would be the kind seeking to be revolutionary, breaking all rules, defiant of normal canons of taste or morals, shocking, sensational, outraged and outrageous. The obvious problem is that very good poetry has been composed in this spirit; as has, alas, a lot of wretched poetry that is derivative, tedious, shrill, and without redeeming artistic value. And this, of course, is only one of the ways in which poetry can be bad. Long years of examining the work of other poets have taught me that not a few poets, under the pretext of freeing themselves from the bondage of prosodic and

---

1. Tim Hilton, *John Ruskin: The Early Years* (1985), 228.

formal considerations, have found in such manumission a convenient way to avoid the very obvious risks entailed by submission to form and meter: unskilled attempts are instantly to be detected, and on these grounds alone it is literally *safer* to play the poetic role of independent radical. (One such radical has recently affirmed that anyone who observes formal constraints is unambiguously a fascist.)

But the problem is far more complicated than any simple form-versus-freedom opposition. Poets can be bad, as they can be good, in any number of ways, and both the metered and meterless can exhibit emotional indiscipline, smug self-satisfaction, indolence of mind, and every kind of flaccidity. Too often such poems fail the way a joke badly told will fail: the teller sits back grinning in foolish triumph and still more foolish expectation of uproarious laughter, only to be greeted by embarrassed silence. And what does he do then? Why, he cheerfully seeks out the sort of audience who will share his special sense of humor, dismissing as dull-witted all those who failed to approve of his jest. He is sure to find a few more dull-witted than he, who will commend his skills be they never so little.

By now I have largely, almost entirely, put behind me that militant sort of "severe reprobation" Ruskin found it a moral imperative to administer; and I've done so with a sense of shame I was too young to feel at the time of commission but which has grown with maturity and resembles the same belated regret Ruskin felt for his early vituperations. It was Auden who first taught me that inferior poetic talents will fall by the wayside quite naturally in the course of time and that they need no vigorous dismissal or noisy exposure of their unworthiness.[2] I confess that this is not always easy to believe. It is especially difficult when I see poetic gifts of a very high order passed by and neglected while other poets, who are no more than unclothed emperors, are widely honored for their fine tailoring and natty style. It's easy to become annoyed when a poet of unchecked sentimentality or mindless elation passes himself off as an heir of Blake.

The unformulated urge to be "original" is easily satisfied with whatever passes for the "unconventional," which latter term all too easily becomes, with time, conventional itself. I know a writer who, as the author of sensational prose, looks for that same immediate shock effect in poetry, seek-

---

2. "Some books are undeservedly forgotten; none are undeservedly remembered." W. H. Auden, "Reading," in *The Dyer's Hand and Other Essays* (1962), 10.

ing flash and scandal, which is taken for novelty and intrepidity. Think only, for example, of those two artists who, in 1992, so troubled the National Endowment for the Arts, beleaguered as it was by that stern guardian of national morality, Patrick Buchanan. One of these was a "performance artist" whose skill it was to cover her naked body with chocolate while encouraging her audience to believe it was feces. The second was a photographer who took a notorious picture called "Piss-Christ." It presented a glass beaker in which a crucifix was submerged in a clear yellow fluid which might easily have been white grape juice but which the artist asserted was his own urine. What seems to me curious about this is that neither artist would succeed in procuring their desired effect of shocking the public without their own personal testimony to validate their deliberate vulgarity; in neither case could this have been determined without such certification. And this alone calls both "art works" into question.

It was soon after they met that Diaghilev issued to Cocteau the artistic injunction: *étonne-moi.* This was probably not the first time it was felt that an artist's duty is primarily, or entirely, to astonish. After all, astonishment results from the violation (the sometimes violent violation) of expectations. And this has been almost from the first the source of dramatic force and effect. Sophocles' *Oedipus* could head the list. For some, the formal aspects of lyric poetry—that a sonnet is composed of fourteen lines of (usually) iambic pentameter rhymed in a received way—were conventions from which it seemed overwhelmingly important to be freed. Paul Fussell Jr. observed that "much of the contemporary ambition to 'break out' of inherited metrical schemes, as if they were traps rather than opportunities, is distilled in the theory, and to some degree in the practice, of William Carlos Williams,"[3] who disdained sonnets and was very wary of iambic pentameter. To this degree he may be said to have been shrewd in his wariness: fixed poetic forms all too often become associated with conventions of feeling—the sonnet initially with love poetry—and it became easy to fall into habitual sentiments, familiar metaphors, and conventional symbols when adopting such a form. One need read through only a few of the numberless Elizabethan sonnet sequences to notice how wearily repetitive they can become. Even so, sometimes their formal constraints can add not only to a poem's elegance but to its persuasive music. Here, for

---

3. Paul Fussell Jr., *Poetic Meter and Poetic Form* (1965), 104.

example, are some lines by Giles Fletcher, boiled down by me, without loss to his content, from pentameter to tetrameter.

> If sad complaint would show my pain
> Or tears express my troubled heart,
> If melting sighs would pity gain,
> Or true laments but ease my smart;
>
> Then should my plaints all sounds surmount,
> And tears like seas flow from my eyes;
> Then sighs should far exceed all count
> And lamentations dim the skies.

Presumably there may be those who find these lines blameless if undistinguished, while clear enough in their sentiments. Some might even take some small pleasure in the careful parallelisms in the second stanza, each line of which carefully fulfills the hypothetical in the corresponding line of the first stanza. But the original, which has five feet instead of four in each line, speaks with an authority, a dignity, and a music my contraction altogether lacks.

> If sad complaint would show a lover's pain,
> Or tears express the torments of my heart,
> If melting sighs would ruth and pity gain,
> Or true laments but ease a lover's smart;
>
> Then should my plaints the thunder's noise surmount,
> And tears like seas should flow from out my eyes;
> Then sighs like air should far exceed all count,
> And true laments with sorrow dim the skies.

It is often held that fixed forms invite, and indeed encourage, prolixity; when there is no demand for any specified number of syllables, super-fluities can easily be spotted and eliminated. And to be sure, one of the most common blemishes of weak formal verse is its shameless collapse into padding. This is not true merely of poetry: the great music critic Donald Francis Tovey, in an article on Bruckner in the *Encyclopaedia Bri-*

tannica, fourteenth edition, reports that "one of the greatest living con-
ductors actually solemnized a Bruckner festival by producing the fifth
symphony with the omission of every alternate pair of bars throughout
whole sections! Gray's 'Elegy' has survived turning into octosyllables by
omitting an adjective in each line."

But we should immediately remind ourselves that formal conventions
are not the only, and perhaps not the most important, conventions. Conventions of morality, of political correctness, of intellectual attitudes, of
what may be called "styles of feeling," these and their diagrammatic oppo-
sites, adopted in militant rebellion, are as compelling in their convention-
ality as are heroic couplets. Since the beginning of the Romantic movement, since the era of Gray, Collins, Cowper, Burns, and Blake, what
counts in poetry above all else is *feeling,* and this becomes more pronounced
as time advances into modernism and postmodernism. Jacques Maritain,
the great neo-Thomist philosopher and aesthetician, for all his allegiance
to St. Thomas Aquinas, found himself writing in his magisterial work,
Creative Intuition in Art and Poetry (1953), that "poetic knowledge proceeds
from the intellect in its most genuine and essential capacity as intellect,
though through the indispensable instrumentality of feeling, feeling, feeling." And as if further to underline the force and authority of his repetitive
insistence, he proceeds in a note to cite Corot ("Be guided by feelings
alone") and van Gogh ("Is it not emotion, the sincerity of one's feelings for
nature, that draws us [?]") and Braque ("Emotion is the seed . . . the work
is the flower") and Hopper ("I believe that the great painters . . . have attempted to force this unwilling medium of paint and canvas into a record
of their emotions") and Matisse ("I am unable to distinguish between the
feelings I have for life and my way of expressing it") (119).

It is a matter of interest to me that all of M. Maritain's witnesses in this
matter are modern painters; not a Renaissance master among them. Nor
would any of the great Italian artists of earlier times have ever thought of
placing feeling high among their aims. As Francis Ames-Lewis makes
abundantly clear in *The Intellectual Life of the Early Renaissance Artist*
(2000), it was the primary ambition of painters, sculptors, and architects
of that period vigorously to distinguish themselves from mere artisans and
craftsmen; and to this end they gave much time and energy to the intellectual foundations of their labors, claiming for the artistic enterprise a
rank among the liberal arts, as distinct from the mechanical arts, with

which Plato had associated painting, along with the activities of doctors, farmers, and sailors. Concern for their own social and intellectual dignity, and therefore, for the respect they might deserve at the hands of powerful, rich, and well-educated patrons, led them to legitimize their profession by composing treatises such as we have from the hands of Alberti, Palladio, Serlio, Piero della Francesca (who wrote a learned discourse, *De Divina Proportione,* on the mathematical properties of Beauty), Leonardo, and Dürer, in which demonstration is made of the irrefragable principles upon which their work and the laws of perspective are based. "Feeling," as a central concern of the artist, is of no moment to any of these and is indisputably a more modern consideration. Even among the moderns it is often suspect as a gauge by whi̶c̶h̶ ̶ ̶ ̶ ̶effectiveness of a work may be judged. In a letter to Louise Co̶ ̶ ̶ ̶ ̶st 12, 1846, Flaubert wrote, "One m̶ ̶ ̶ ̶ ̶ ̶ ̶ ̶ ̶ ̶ ̶ ̶everything. Art is noth-

I̶ ̶h̶a̶v̶ ̶ ̶ ̶ ̶ ̶ ̶ ̶ ̶ ̶ ̶y indignation at the sort of poetry I don't like and have written less frequently about my contemporaries, with the exception of those I highly esteem. In the past these have included Robert Lowell, Elizabeth Bishop, Richard Wilbur, Joseph Brodsky, Richard Howard, James Merrill, Howard Nemerov, W. D. Snodgrass, and a few others; and in the present volume Wilbur and Bishop make their renewed appearances. But I have been a professor of English and American poetry as well as a poet and reviewer, and this fact has freed me a little from the parochialism the "poetry wars" so fruitlessly engender. To be sure, a number of these essays were commissioned for special occasions or publications; but they were all topics that enlisted my enthusiastic interest.

It's a matter of some curiosity to me to notice how far I have come, or into what hinterlands of error I have strayed, since my beginnings as an earnest "childe" of the New Critics, especially as one who affirmed their notion of a poem as *autotelic,* as containing within itself everything necessary to its complete and independent existence. This meant, particularly, the poem's absolute and perfect severance from historical and social contexts and the irrelevance to the poem of biographical data about its author. A poem, it was held, was about itself, a self-contained universe, fulfilling

---

4. *The Letters of Gustave Flaubert, 1830–1857,* ed. and trans. Francis Steegmuller (1979), 60.

all its own needs, a verbal utopia; and if, moreover, this were shown not to be so in some particular case, the poem was thereby proven to be faulty and inferior. In this, poetry distinguishes itself from criticism. As Eliot wrote in 1932, "No exponent of criticism . . . has . . . ever made the preposterous assumption that criticism is an autotelic activity," because criticism was then assumed to be about something other than itself: namely, the literary work under inspection. But in our day criticism can be practiced as among the most narcissistic, self-admiring activities, only marginally concerned, if at all, with a poem, novel, or play.

The first critic to deposit the seeds of doubt in my mind as to the utter independence of poetry from historical and biographical inquiry was William Empson, who was able to make a vivid case for the relevance of the English Reformation to some images in Shakespeare's Sonnet 73, "That time of year thou mayst in me behold." Indeed, his whole marvelous book *English Pastoral Poetry* (1938; in its English edition called *Some Versions of Pastoral*) is concerned with social and political issues. Empson, even so, exhibits at times a certain New Critical fastidiousness about just how much extraliterary data may legitimately be brought to bear on a poem in connection with a critical evaluation. In regard, for example, to some of the opening lines of *The Waste Land,* which I discuss in one of the following essays, he remarks, "The most surprising case comes at the start, the lady who went tobogganing with the Arch-Duke. I never felt sure about the discovery of Mr. Morris, that this bit is taken from the memoirs of Countess Marie Larisch, *My Past* (1913), because not one phrase from the book is echoed in the poem; but now Mrs. Eliot explains that the poet had met her, and was using her conversation."[5]

This is a puzzling passage. First, Mr. George L. K. Morris, whom Empson, Mrs. Eliot, and I all cite, dates the publication of the Countess's *My Life* at 1916. Since historical matters are at stake, accuracy is not a negligible consideration. But more important is the issue of what Empson meant. If he is saying, as it appears to me he is, that he "never felt sure" about Morris's discovery of a link between the book and Eliot's poem on the exclusive grounds that there are no verbal echoes of the book in the poem, then he seems to be setting a curious and narrow standard by which a critic could legitimately derive influence. In fact, Mr. Morris furnishes a

---

5. William Empson, *Using Biography* (1984), 189.

wealth of associated allusions and genealogical data richly to confirm his claim. But then Empson goes on to say that, unable as he was to detect any connection between book and poem, when later he read Valerie Eliot's note about the "archduke," a note published after Eliot's death and presumably based on a confidence shared up to that time only between husband and wife, Empson found this an authenticating and satisfactory resolution to the problem—though in legal terms it's no more than hearsay evidence. For my part, the Morris claim is more persuasive than the conversational certification.

But there's something in the same Empson essay on Eliot I find still more strangely unpersuasive. With an admirable loyalty to a man and poet he deeply and profoundly admires, Empson makes a strategic attempt to rescue Eliot from imputations of anti-Semitism, going so far as to quote Eliot's own disclaimer, which I supply more fully: "I am grieved and sometimes angered by this matter. I am not an anti-Semite and never have been. It is a terrible slander on a man. And they do not know, as you and I do, that in the eyes of the Church to be anti-Semitic is a sin"[6] (the person addressed in this declaration is the Rev. William Turner Levy).

Empson acknowledges that a problem does seem to exist, boldly quoting some truly repulsive lines that appeared in early drafts of *The Waste Land* but which were ultimately omitted. He calls these "exultantly rancorous" and undertakes to persuade us that the rancor is truly if covertly directed at Eliot's father, who had so designed his will as explicitly to keep Eliot's wife from obtaining any benefit of Eliot family inheritance in the event of the poet's death. Empson stakes out his claim in these terms:

> Eliot wanted to grouse about his father, and lambasted some imaginary Jews instead . . . Eliot's grandfather went to St. Louis as a missionary preaching Unitarianism, and incidentally founding a university there; Eliot's father continued to be a staunch Unitarian, while going into business. Eliot himself at Harvard read Sanskrit, a thoroughly Boston-Brahmin thing to do, and remarked soon after that it was almost impossible to be a Christian after studying the Far Eastern religions.

---

6. Ibid., 197. The Eliot disclaimer was reported by Robert Giroux in the *Washington Post Book World*, Dec. 18, 1988.

Unitarians describe themselves as Christians but deny that Jesus was God, whereas Eliot was beginning to feel a strong drag towards a return to the worship of the tortured victim. Now if you are hating a purse-proud business man who denies that Jesus is God, into what stereotype does he best fit? He is a Jew, of course; and yet this would be a terrible blasphemy against his family and its racial pride, so much so that I doubt whether Eliot ever allowed himself to realize what he was doing."[7]

I wonder how many readers will be persuaded by this attempt at exculpation. For my part, I am not one of them. "Rachel née Rabinovitch" who "Tears at the grapes with murderous paws" cannot easily be subsumed under the heading of purse-proud businessmen who deny that Jesus is God. Moreover, if as Jesus says in John 15:1 "I am the true vine, and my Father is the husbandman,"[8] if Jesus is emblematically "the fruit of the vine" and his blood the wine of the sacrament which he shares with his disciples at the Last Supper, saying "This is my blood," then someone who "tears at the grapes with murderous paws" is inescapably a Christ-killer, an all too familiar epithet of anti-Semitic abuse. If one were to add the testimony of the not inconsiderable number of those who report slanderous anti-Semitic remarks made by Eliot in the course of conversation—for example, "Eliot, who could be anti-Semitic, told [Stephen] Tennant that [Gertrude] Stein had 'a real look of the Ghetto'";[9] as well as Eliot's commendations of books by others, such as Djuna Barnes, who express unambiguous anti-Semitic sentiments—this not only weakens Empson's point but seriously undermines Eliot's claim that he was "not an anti-Semite *and never ha[d] been.*" I have added emphasis to the last four words because I will venture a guess that in due course, and especially after the widespread revelations of the hideous crimes of the Holocaust, Eliot might have had a change of mind, if not of heart, as Empson testifies that he did in regard to rejecting his early feeling that "it was almost impossible to be a Christian after studying the Far Eastern religions."

---

7. Empson, *Using Biography*, 197.
8. Throughout this volume, all references to the Bible are from the King James Version unless otherwise indicated.
9. Philip Hoare, *Serious Pleasures: The Life of Stephen Tennant* (1990), 256.

My New Critical apprenticeship meant that I was late in coming to a right appreciation of, for example, Northrop Frye, whose immense and almost visionary reach embraced far more than at first I could dream of assimilating with full comprehension. My heroes in the critical enterprise were originally such close readers as R. P. Blackmur on the shorter poems of Hardy, Rosemund Tuve on Herbert, Richard Ellmann on Yeats, William Empson on almost anything he examined with enough local concentration, Christopher Ricks on Keats and Tennyson. Accordingly, I was late in coming to value not only Frye but also Frank Kermode and Harold Bloom, who share with Frye a largeness of scope, a generosity of critical sympathies. And this, in turn, has meant that I have found myself appropriating whatever tools, methodologies, and critical strategies came to hand when engaged in composing these essays.

What, I have asked myself, is a critic trying to do? And there are plenty of answers. But perhaps we might begin with the urge governing Poe's Auguste Dupin: to solve a mystery. Not infrequently this means discovering that there was a mystery to be solved in the first place, because no one had noticed any need for scrutiny. Which is to say, the question of whether Auden is entitled to write, as he does in the poem "Under Which Lyre," of "the prig Prince Hal" will depend on varying ways of construing the dramatic structure of the Henry IV plays. In his essay "The Prince's Dog" he writes, "Seeking for an explanation of why Falstaff affects us as he does, I find myself compelled to see *Henry IV* as possessing, in addition to its overt meaning, a parabolic significance. Overtly, Falstaff is a Lord of Misrule; parabolically, he is a comic symbol for the supernatural order of Charity as contrasted with the temporal order of Justice symbolized by Henry of Monmouth."[10]

This is ingenious, artful, and not altogether to be trusted. Shakespeare's drama is not a morality play like *The Parliament of Heaven*, with such characters as Contemplation, Truth, Mercy, Justice, and Peace. And to impose upon the history play the methods of allegorical medieval drama is to mix genres in subtle and confusing ways, one of which is to deny the presence in the more modern play of character development, a denial central to Auden's contemptuous view of Prince Hal and his unqualified approval of Falstaff. Auden is deeply offended by Hal's brusk dismissal of Falstaff at

---

10. Auden, *The Dyer's Hand*, 198.

the end of the second play, a dismissal that has admittedly given serious pause to other commentators. He finds this sudden burst of self-righteous indignation "priggish" while finding Falstaff just as endearing as his own witty apologia in Part I ("Banish plump Jack and banish all the world," II. iv) makes him out to be.

All things considered, however, John Dover Wilson, in *The Fortunes of Falstaff* (1944), makes a more plausible case for the design of the plays, demonstrating the increasingly sinister and cold-blooded corruption into which Falstaff drifts, especially in Part II. To take but one detail, Wilson writes:

> The favorite way for a captain to make money, one notorious enough to receive special mention in an act of Parliament passed in 1557, was to enroll well-to-do men, known to be reluctant to serve, and then allow them to buy themselves out at the highest price they could be induced to pay. In the Coventry scene Falstaff confides to the audience that he has enlisted 150 "warm slaves" of this type, making over £300 on the lot; after which he has filled up his muster-roll by impressing another 150, whom he now commands, this time the sweepings of the highways and the prisons. "I did never see such pitiful rascals," protests the Prince, as they march into view; to which Falstaff retorts, "Tut, tut, good enough to toss, food for powder, food for powder—they'll fill a pit as well as a better." It is a famous piece of cynicism; but seriously intended. For he leads them into the hottest part of the battle of Shrewsbury, where all but three are killed, with the object, well understood by spectators of the time, of pocketing the pay of the dead. (84–85)

This cold-blooded war profiteering on the part of one who, in his apologia, did not scruple to call himself "valiant Jack Falstaff," but who had earlier played dead to avoid fighting and had hauled away the corpse of Hotspur, claiming to have beaten him in honorable combat, gravely compromises the "endearing" figure Auden would like to identify with "the supernatural order of Charity." There is, moreover, something dubious about Auden's weasel words "in addition to its overt meaning," because the two modes of reading the play are simply irreconcilable. It's not that Auden's theological terms do not belong to any study of Shakespeare, for I myself have made a claim for the application of just such terms in reading *Othello,* where I think it legitimate, but where Auden does not.

I argued in an essay on that play that one of the cruxes, construed either as "base Indian" or "base Iudean," should receive the latter reading, in which Othello, in his final speech and just before his suicide, identifies himself by this phrase with Judas Iscariot, and the pearl he throws away self-evidently with Desdemona but surely echoing the "pearl of great price," which signifies the kingdom of heaven in Matthew 13:46, and by which he acknowledges himself as one who has abjured Christ. There are those who are reluctant to identify Desdemona with Christ, almost entirely on grounds of gender. But I argue that she is, first and foremost, utterly blameless, as well as touchingly innocent as a character in this play. She dies, refusing to blame her murderer; and comes back to life after her death, repeating her refusal to blame, and, stunningly, taking all blame upon herself. To be sure, *Othello* is no allegory, but I would argue that Shakespeare, in this play so heavily laden with Christian language and symbolism, with mention of devils and angels, heaven and hell, not only permits but invites the reading I have offered. Yet in his *Lectures on Shakespeare,* Auden characterizes Desdemona as a "young schoolgirl who wants above all to be a grownup" and "a romantic girl going slumming." Doubtless there is behind this a desire to shock, especially to shock that New School for Social Research audience, who might well have been affronted to hear Desdemona's love for a black man characterized as "going slumming." But the temptation to shock is probably as great for the critic as for the poet. The editor of Auden's *Lectures on Shakespeare* (2000), Arthur Kirsch, in his excellent and judicious introduction, observes that "Auden's suspicion of romantic love . . . prevents him, both in his lecture on *Othello* and in his later essay on the play in *The Dyer's Hand,* from seeing the idealism, indeed scriptural idealism, of Desdemona" (xviii).

The need to take the intellectual atmosphere of historical periods into any account of texts belongs as much to scriptural interpretation as to poetry. In writing, as I do here, about St. Paul's Epistle to the Galatians, I have tried to take account of certain ancient views of slavery because (1) the metaphor of slavery resonates densely throughout the epistle, and (2) slavery and the liberation from slavery is a theme of the annual Passover service among Jews up to this very day; it would have been well known, as part of the Haggadah, the liturgy of the Seder service commemorating both the servitude and liberation of the Jews from Egyptian bondage, to a Pharisee such as Paul had been when his name was Saul— as well, of course, as after. Early in that religious service the words of Exodus 12:17 are spoken by the group in unison: "You shall keep the Feast of Unleavened Bread, for on this very day I brought your hosts out of Egypt. You shall observe this day throughout the generations as a practice for all time." And they recite Exodus 13:3, "Remember the day on which you went forth from Egypt, and from the house of bondage, and how the Lord freed you with a mighty hand." Neither can one fully come to terms with Shakespeare's *Sonnets* without considering the various views of the love one man may entertain towards another. Psychoanalytic interpretations of literary works (as well as of paintings, though far more rarely of musical compositions) are sometimes richly rewarding and valuable, if they are not insisted upon to the exclusion of anything else about the work. I hope I have employed such a perspective with suitable tact in my comments here on Elizabeth Bishop's poem "The Man-Moth."

The poet can often achieve powerful effects by implication, by innuendo, by pointed and dramatic omission of something we would have a right to expect. In Eliot's "The Journey of the Magi" we are invited to notice that the weary and despondent speaker who describes his arduous journey makes no mention whatever of the star that St. Matthew reports was the guide and sign that led the wise men to their destination. I have attempted elsewhere to account for this strange omission. I believe Robert Frost employs the same device in the poem I examine here, "The Wood-Pile."

I once had an academic colleague who had two sets of complete lecture notes, one of which he kept at home, the other in his office, so that if either place were to burn down he would still be able to teach his course in the history of the trans-Mississippi West. But never in the course of my entire teaching career did it seem remotely possible to settle on a set of notes and repeat what I had said about a poem or a play a year earlier. Such annual reconsiderations of mine were often inducements to publication, even as they were incitements to caution. Noticing, as I could not fail to do, that from year to year I found myself changing my mind about a certain text, I realized that setting things down in print smacked dangerously of asserting some rash finality of judgment, which I knew perfectly well was not likely to last long, if the past was any trustworthy indication. This by itself might have proven enough to prevent me from publishing my views about literary works, no matter how surely or with what joyful confidence in my discoveries I had come to see them. After all, I could remember a college roommate whose perfect certainty in his own opinions was unshaken even when those opinions lasted no more than a day. The essay in this book called "Paralipomena to *The Hidden Law*" represents my humble and candid revision of views and the acknowledgment of errors I had adopted in a 1993 book on Auden.

With time I came to see that the critics I most admired and valued were not prized by me for their invariable correctness or the degree to which they confirmed my own views—if these two categories are entirely distinct from one another. I found myself in vigorous disagreement with many of them, and often on important topics, as some of the essays included here will show. But I found that the critics I admired were ones of lively and original insights, however wayward I might find some particular judgment or attitude. The critics who have meant most to me are those who have broadened my ways of seeing both individual works and whole genres and types of writing, entire regions of thinking, sources of feeling, and especially social or historical conventions and rituals that so often lie immersed and unnoticed at the bottom of some work of literature. And while I know myself to be a poet first and only secondarily a critic, I dare to hope that some readers will find in this book some fresh thoughts and new ways of regarding a number of poems, some of them too well and some too slightly known.

But that's not quite the whole story. Playing Dupin has its gumshoe pleasures, but they are not entirely disinterested. No poet examines someone else's poem, especially a major poem or a large body of poetry, without hoping to learn something from such scrutiny; and, moreover, to learn something he can put to his own personal use. Shakespeare's *Sonnets* are instructive in matters of openness and concealment, matters with which most poets, even one so evasively shy as T. S. Eliot, must come to terms. The anxiety I seem to find in Robert Frost's poem was of a magnitude he must have wished to shield not merely, or even chiefly, from his reader, but from his wife and, still more, from his children. As for Sidney, the approaches to hysteria are not usually associated with his name or performance, both of which are conventionally sanitized by labels of civility, artifice, and pastoral innocence.

There is, in short, not a poem or sequence of poems dealt with here that

I have not found richly instructive in the course of learning my craft. And one need not turn for such instruction only to poets of the first order: Auden congratulated himself on the uses he could put to Hardy's poems, with which he was greatly pleased but which were not of a stature to daunt him. Henry Noel's poem helped me in something like the same way; and I would have delighted to include a discussion of Hardy, Philip Larkin, or Howard Nemerov (as in the past I ventured comments on Emily Dickinson, Robert Lowell, and Keats) if I could have found ways to conceal or disguise my fumbling depredations and pillagings. Trying to do what your betters have done is not merely humbling; while it may increase your admiration for them, you actually *do* learn something about the ways words are cobbled together, as well as what people entirely different from yourself once felt about both serious and trifling matters, about things that are of no great importance to the world in which you live but were once supremely important to others.

Mixed in with all this is old-fashioned technique, or craftsmanship. It is with wry regret that I call it "old-fashioned." The special skills that pleased me in poetry from the first were those I found in Donne and Herbert. Some of these were prosodic, and not to be minimized on that account. The deftness of those poets in the wielding of stanzaic forms was acrobatic, balletic, incredibly deft and agile, while being put to the most serious kinds of poetic service. No one, as far as I know, has actually noticed in print that Hopkins' poem "The Blessed Virgin Compared to the Air We Breathe" is a superb example of metaphysical technique, a metaphoric parallelism that runs with perfect application through 126 lines.

In any case, the poets and poems discussed here have been, among others, my instructors, and the essays that follow mean to express some measure of my indebtedness and gratitude.

PART I

Shakespeare and the Sonnet

It may be that the single most important fact about Shakespeare's *Sonnets*, at least statistically, is that they regularly outsell everything else he wrote. The plays are taught in schools and universities, and a large annual sale is thereby guaranteed for *Hamlet, Macbeth, Romeo and Juliet,* and *A Midsummer Night's Dream.* But the *Sonnets* are still more widely read. There are several diverse factions among their readership, many of which are not scholarly. Some people are eager for a glimpse into what they suppose is Shakespeare's private life; they hope for scandal. There are those who treat the *Sonnets* as biographical fiction; they yearn to decode the poems and reveal a narrative of exciting, intimate relationships. And there are readers whose overriding preoccupation with sexual politics makes them determined that no one shall view the *Sonnets* in any way that differs from their own.

In all likelihood, however, the largest group within this readership is made up of young lovers, for whom these sonnets compose a compact and attractive vade mecum. The poems speak directly to their condition, being rich and emotionally complex, and they describe states of perfect happiness but also submission, self-abnegation, jealousy, fear, desperation, and self-hatred.

It is possible to argue that there exists no work of comparable brevity and excellence that digests such intimate emotional experience. What is more, the *Sonnets* are written with an astonishing self-consciousness, a deep sense that love opens enormous vistas of novel reflection, not all of it flattering. Loving another human being, we find that our motives are no longer disinterested; everything we do or feel is no longer purely a personal matter but is strangely compromised by our relationship with this other person; our hopes and fears are generated not only by another but also by how we wish to be thought of and how we have come to feel about ourselves. Initially, when we fall in love, this does not appear as any sort of danger or, indeed, as anything to be deplored. Our own happiness seems enormously enlarged by being both shared with and caused by another. That is only the beginning of what, for a thoughtful person, becomes an increasingly complicated state of mind, with almost infinite permutations, most of them unforeseeable.

How do we react, for example, when the person we love commits a transgression that really wounds us? If the relationship is not immediately halted, it is necessary to palliate the fault, first and foremost to ourselves and then to the beloved. The simple first step is to fall back upon reassuring proverbial wisdom (To err is human, No one is perfect), and, while acknowledging our pain, to temper our feelings with the suspicion that, in our idolatry of the beloved, we may have imagined an impossible perfection which it would be ludicrous to expect anyone to live up to and which may itself have put an insupportable burden on the person we love. We begin to blame ourselves for what may have been unrealistic expectations. And if we are deeply enamored, we wish to spare the beloved any additional anguish of guilt that would be entailed by our explicit blame. Yet this kind of generous thinking can end in the danger of our viewing ourselves as supine and servile and lead to an active form of self-hatred. So to guard against that danger and against any tendency to blame the beloved, we may find ourselves determined to assert our unconditional love— which is, after all, as we desperately tell ourselves, what love ought to be— and to rebuke any third party who might criticize the beloved, a rebuke designed as much to confirm our own commitment as to silence the critic. I have known both heterosexual and homosexual instances of this kind of devotion, which, to an outsider, is likely to seem perverse, obstinate, and full of misery. Consider, for example, the following:

> No more be grieved at that which thou hast done:
> Roses have thorns, and silver fountains mud,
> Clouds and eclipses stain both moon and sun,
> And loathsome canker lives in sweetest bud.
> All men make faults, and even I in this,
> Authorising thy trespass with compare,
> Myself corrupting salving thy amiss,
> Excusing thy sins more than their sins are;[1]

---

1. A variant reading of this line is as follows: "Excusing thy sins more than thy sins are." See

For to thy sensual fault I bring in sense—
Thy adverse party is thy advocate—
And 'gainst myself a lawful plea commence:
Such civil war is in my love and hate
That I an accessory needs must be
To that sweet thief which sourly robs from me.

(Sonnet 35)

The first line presupposes a penitent attitude on the part of the beloved. Whatever the offence that is referred to as "thy sensual fault," it is clearly something that would cause a deeper sense of guilt than could be cleared away with a simple apology. What was done is serious enough for the speaker to think of himself as offering absolution—an absolution based on the universal imperfection of all sublunary, terrestrial things that figure in the catalogue of the following three lines. It should be noted that the moon and sun, beyond the orbit of imperfection, are not themselves contaminated but are viewed through imperfections nearer at hand. These imperfections are traditionally explained as a consequence of the fall from grace in the Garden of Eden and of man's first disobedience. (Milton himself was to write of that paradise, "Flow'rs of all hue, and without thorn the rose" [*PL*, IV.256]). This fallen world is thus a kind of paradox, where "loathsome canker lives in sweetest bud." What is being said here is complex. "Loathsome canker" is strong language, potentially wounding to the beloved: will it seem vengeful? The speaker may hope that its tone of indictment will be sufficiently mitigated by the description "sweetest bud." The fifth line is more tactful, and finds fault first of all with the speaker himself for so much as venturing to excuse the beloved and for doing so by means of metaphorical examples. There is good reason for him to apologize. The instances that he cites from nature are consequences of our fallen state and are now unalterable. To describe the faults of the beloved in the same terms is to risk saying something like: "There's no point in your apologizing, because you can't *help* doing what you do"—which makes the beloved a primitive or perverse creature and completely invalidates the sincerity of the grief mentioned in the first line. The speaker goes on, in the seventh and eighth lines, to balance any offence he may have given by

---

proclaiming himself the worse sinner of the two, both for making too much of the trespass in the first place and then for taking upon himself the role of the priest offering absolution, as if he himself were without taint.

The ninth line is pivotal and richly suggestive. William Empson has described it as containing at least three possible lines of thought: (1) "I bring in reason, arguments to justify [your sensual fault]"; (2) "I bring in feelings about it, feel it more important than it really was (and therefore excuse it more than it needs)"; (3) "I bring extra sensuality to it; I enjoy thinking about it and making arguments to defend it, so that my sensuality sympathizes with yours."[2] It can also bear this further meaning: "To the sensuality of your fault I bring in (to my regret) my own sensuality, which may well, alas, have been the initial cause of your arousal, though now it is not directed at me—in other words, I am myself the unwitting author of your new-found promiscuity."

Lines 10 and 11 are a very ingenious paradox:

> Thy adverse party is thy advocate—
> And 'gainst myself a lawful plea commence.

They may be a way of lessening slightly the gravity of the moral predicament in which both parties are now deeply enmeshed. But in addition, the paradox turns the whole focus of complaint and indictment against the speaker himself, leaving the beloved out of the picture to such a degree that with the twelfth line the love and hate are not merely balanced; we are entitled to feel that the *hatred* is as much self-directed as it is directed at the sensual fault of the beloved, and the *love* is that which is not only directed towards the beloved but generates the requisite (and, to the speaker, degrading) absolution. This "civil war" is, in Marlowe's words, an "intestine broil,"[3] and it is highly complex. (1) Love and hate are at war. (2) The speaker is at war with himself, as well as with the beloved. (3) He is furthermore at war with the impulses of war and the impulses of hate. This warfare may end in total disaster. It seems almost, in fact, on its way to that very end in the concluding couplet, which, among other things, seems to say that the very distraction of the speaker may be driving his beloved from

---

2. William Empson, *The Structure of Complex Words* (1951), 272–73.

3. Christopher Marlowe, *Hero and Leander*, I.251, in *Works*, 2:438.

him, or that his generous willingness to forgive transgressions has encouraged the beloved to feel that no harm has been done; and either alternative would be a highly undesirable state of affairs. These two possibilities are mutually exclusive, and this leaves the speaker in an agonizing and insoluble predicament.

What is finally so effective about this poem is its stunning dramatic power. It hovers among alternatives, all of them anguishing, delicate in its manoeuvring, tense in its anxiety not to place too much blame on the beloved but unable to conceal the torment from which the poem sprang. The "sweet" and "sour" of the last line echo the mixed imperfections that began the poem, in which the loathsome canker must find out and infect the sweetest bud.[4] The bitterness here is not wholly veiled by the cosmic explanation that *everything* is corrupt. The human drama is based on the terrible truth that thinking about and imagining infidelity is at least as poisonous as any proof of it, and as sickening to the contemplator. *Othello* and *The Winter's Tale* are extended illustrations of this, if any confirmation were needed. Moreover, the speaker's drama in Sonnet 35 is enhanced by our being allowed—indeed, virtually invited—to feel that he is discovering the complexity of his situation as the poem develops. The first line is grammatically and syntactically independent. It can be conceived as spoken in the uncomplicated spirit of charity, sympathy, and good will. The illustrative examples of imperfection in the lines that immediately follow are fairly conventional and might initially seem to confirm the permissiveness and generosity of the first line, did they not almost unwittingly introduce the appalling note of universal corruption. And from there on we move into increasing darkness and unending corridors of guilt.

It seems to me impossible not to find deeply moving and compelling the complicated and tormenting emotions latent in this poem, though it may be added that such riches are, or might be, implicit in any love poetry that is searching enough. In England in the 1590s there was a vogue of sonnet-writing in which poets admonished themselves, in the words of Philip Sidney, to look in their hearts and write.[5] Such introspection and honesty are not easy in any age, and it is the general consensus that, of all the sonneteers, Shakespeare was beyond question the

---

4. Compare Sonnet 94: "For sweetest things turn sourest by their deeds."
5. See the first sonnet in Sidney's *Astrophel and Stella*.

most penetrating. He was also the one who seemed most perfectly to adapt the form itself to his analytic or diagnostic and deeply dramatic purposes.

It may be as well at this point to say something about the sonnet as a literary form; this is not so simple a matter as commentators have supposed. In the 1870s Walter Pater argued that some parts of the early play *Love's Labour's Lost* resembled the *Sonnets:* "This connexion of *Love's Labours Lost* with Shakespeare's poems is further enforced by the actual insertion in it of three sonnets and a faultless song."[6] The song, of course, is the one that ends the play: "When daisies pied and violets blue." But as to the three sonnets, only two of them count as such by our modern and conventional definition; the third is a poem in tetrameter couplets twenty lines long. So it should be said here that there are at least two distinct definitions of the sonnet. One of them is not formally precise; it is given by the *Oxford English Dictionary* as simply "a short poem or piece of verse"—in early use especially, one "of a lyrical and amatory character." Though the *OED* calls this loose definition rare and indeed obsolete, it was current in English between 1563 and 1820, and it is worth remembering that Donne's *Songs and Sonets* (1633) contained not a single poem composed in the conventional fourteen-line form. Robert Giroux nevertheless continues to refer to *Love's Labour's Lost* as "the sonnet play." He would have done much better to have cited *Romeo and Juliet,* which employs far more sonnets, as well as sonnet fragments.[7] Indeed, Shakespeare seems in that play to have counted upon his audience's familiarity with some aspects of the sonnet form and with that form's association with amatory verse.

Under the formal modern definition, the sonnet is a fourteen-line poem, usually written in pentameter verse, though Sidney, for example, sometimes used hexameters, and there have been other variations. The fourteen-line sonnet can be divided into two sorts, the Italian or Petrarchan, on the one hand, and the Shakespearean, on the other. The Ital-

---

6. Walter Pater, *Appreciations* (1889), 167. A similar identification is made more recently by Robert Giroux, *The Book Known as Q* (1982), 140–41, citing Pater and referring to *Love's Labour's Lost* as "the sonnet play."

7. See Prologue to Act I; I.ii.45–50; I.ii.88–93; I.v.93–110; Prologue to Act II; V.iii.12–17; V.iii.305–10.

ian poet Petrarch (1304–74) did not invent the Petrarchan form; it was used earlier by Dante (1265–1321) and his circle, but Petrarch's use of this form of sonnet to celebrate his beloved Laura made it widely known, and it was much imitated, notably in France by Ronsard (1524–85) and Du Bellay (c. 1522–60). The Petrarchan sonnet is composed of an octave—an initial passage of eight lines, rhyming *abbaabba*—followed by a sestet—six lines requiring only that each line have a rhyming mate. In addition to the separation of octave from sestet by rhyme scheme, there is almost invariably a subtle but dramatic shift, a change of tone or point of view, introduced by the sestet and bringing to the poem a sort of "re-vision," or revelation. The severe restriction placed on the rhyming words in the octave—only two rhyme sounds for eight lines—is not difficult to overcome in Italian, which has an abundance of rhyming words; even though it is very much more difficult to deal with in English, the Petrarchan sonnet has become the preferred form, used by Milton, Wordsworth, and many more recent poets.

The Shakespearean sonnet, too, is named after its most famous practitioner, but as a form it was already firmly established, used by Shakespeare's predecessors and contemporaries, including Spenser, Surrey, Sidney, Giles Fletcher, Samuel Daniel, Michael Drayton, Thomas Lodge, Richard Lynche, William Smith, and Bartholomew Griffin. It consists of three quatrains rhyming *abab, cdcd, efef,* and concluding with a rhymed couplet, *gg.* This form is particularly easy to "catch by ear" and identify when spoken aloud. The final six lines of a sonnet, even though written in Shakespearean form, can become its sestet, and Shakespeare often seemed to think of his sonnets in terms of the Italian division, including the dramatic or rhetorical relationship of octave to sestet. This is clearly the case in Sonnet 35, discussed above, and Shakespeare enjoyed the rather luxurious advantage of being able to write his sonnets in the spirit of either the form named after him or the Petrarchan fashion,[8] as can be shown by comparing Sonnet 73 and Sonnet 18:

---

8. It should be added that, while these two canonical varieties of the sonnet predominate among Shakespeare's ventures in the form, there are individual sonnets that deviate from both; for rhetorical purposes, or under the pressure of overwhelming feelings, the "divisions" of some sonnets are at odds with both the Petrarchan and the Shakespearean conventions. See, for example, Sonnets 66, 145, and 154.

> That time of year thou mayst in me behold
> When yellow leaves, or none, or few, do hang
> Upon those boughs which shake against the cold,
> Bare ruined choirs, where late the sweet birds sang.
> In me thou seest the twilight of such day
> As after sunset fadeth in the west,
> Which by and by black night doth take away,
> Death's second self, that seals up all in rest.
> In me thou seest the glowing of such fire
> That on the ashes of his youth doth lie,
> As the death-bed whereon it must expire,
> Consumed with that which it was nourished by.
> This thou perceiv'st, which makes thy love more strong,
> To love that well which thou must leave ere long.
>
> (Sonnet 73)

This sonnet is a perfect example of the Shakespearean form. Three quatrains, each with its own governing figure of decline, serve as incremental parts of a discourse; each parallels and reinforces the others with beauty and delicacy of detail and describes the inexorable truth of the natural world's mutability. William Empson's imaginative account of the fourth line is famous:

there is no pun, double syntax, or dubiety of feeling, in

Bare ruined choirs, where late the sweet birds sang,

but the comparison holds for many reasons; because ruined monastery choirs are places in which to sing, because they involve sitting in a row, because they are made of wood, are carved into knots and so forth, because they used to be surrounded by a sheltering building crystallised out of the likeness of a forest, and coloured with stained glass and painting like flowers and leaves, because they are now abandoned by all but the grey walls coloured like the skies of winter, because the cold and Narcissistic charm suggested by choir-boys suits well with Shakespeare's feeling for the object of the Sonnets, and for various sociological and historical reasons (the protestant destruction of monasteries; fear of puritanism), which it would be hard now to trace out in their proportions; these reasons, and many more relating the simile to its place in the Sonnet, must all combine to give the line its beauty, and there is a sort of ambiguity in not knowing which of them to hold most clearly in mind.[9]

But these boughs are either themselves (by metaphoric transmutation) the bare ruined choirs, which shake against the "cold," used as a noun; or else "cold" is an adjective modifying bare ruined choirs themselves. This is not merely grammatical quibbling. Empson places a certain weight on the physical presence of a ruined church, cathedral, or monastery, and he derives from these stones a good deal of religious controversy and historical ferment, to say nothing of the putative narcissism of the beloved—an imputation expounded at greater length in "They That Have Power," an essay on Sonnet 94 in *Some Versions of Pastoral*.[10]

The decline of the year, of the day, of the fire, involving the repetition of autumnal, russet, and golden colors, even in the fire, is also graduated in brevity, gaining force thereby. The second quatrain is emotionally more ambiguous than the first, since death is explicitly mentioned, but its terrors are tempered by the soothing comparison with sleep, and more especially a sleep that "seals up all in rest." This note of tranquility is close to Macbeth's "Come, seeling night, / Scarf up the tender eye of pitiful day" (III.ii.46–47).[11] The four lines progress from twilight to dark, and we are permitted to regard that conclusion as either a consummation devoutly to be wished or else as the end of all the pleasures, beauties, and joys of this mortal world. But the final quatrain is dramatically and emotionally the most dense and meaningful. The fire, once brilliant, has dimmed; its ashes now serve to extinguish the very flame that, when those ashes were wood, they fed. What is implied, of course, is that the vigor and liberties of our youth are precisely what serve to bring us, by the excess of that youthful folly and energy, to our demise. We are thus self-executed. This is not altogether remote from the notion (to be found in Donne's "Farewell to Love") that every sexual experience

9. William Empson, *Seven Types of Ambiguity*, 2d ed. (1947), 2–3.
10. William Empson, *Some Versions of Pastoral* (1935), 89–115.
11. This is pointed out by Stephen Booth, ed., *Shakespeare's Sonnets*, rev. ed. (1978), 259.

abbreviates our lives by one day. This sense that youth, injudiciously or wantonly expended, brings about its own forfeiture, is restated in other terms in Sonnet 94, where Shakespeare writes of those who "rightly do inherit heaven's graces / And husband nature's riches from expense." These are people who maintain their youth and beauty seemingly forever because they are by temperament "Unmoved, cold, and to temptation slow."

And then we come to the deeply unnerving couplet. A number of critics have observed that "To love that well" means either to treasure your own youth or to love the poem's speaker, whose old age and imagined death have been the subject of this poem. Either alternative presents problems of emotional complexity. If the beloved is being instructed to husband his own youth and beauty, there is the double pathos of his being instructed by the decay of the poet before him and of the poet's making himself into a seemingly disinterested object lesson. In addition, this act of husbandry is cruelly doomed, since youth is something "thou must leave ere long." If, on the other hand, the beloved is being praised for the nobility of loving someone whom he is destined soon to lose, the poignancy is greatly increased, and the continued love, especially in the face of a ravaged lover, is quietly heroic. Something of the deep risk of all mortal attachments is expressed, and we once again realize that to avoid such attachments may be the safer and more prudent course, but it is not to live life to its fullest, whereas to love means to expose oneself to every possible kind of grief. On being told his newly married wife is dead, Pericles exclaims:

> O you gods!
> Why do you make us love your goodly gifts
> And snatch them straight away?
>
> (*Per.* III.i.22–24)

Something of Ben Jonson's anguished cry upon the death of his first son— "O, could I lose all father, now"—haunts the ending of the poem.

Sonnet 18 offers a direct contrast to Sonnet 73 in form and structure.

> Shall I compare thee to a summer's day?
> Thou art more lovely and more temperate:
> Rough winds do shake the darling buds of May,

And summer's lease hath all too short a date;
Sometime too hot the eye of heaven shines,
And often is his gold complexion dimmed;
And every fair from fair sometime declines,
By chance or nature's changing course untrimmed:
But thy eternal summer shall not fade,
Nor lose possession of that fair thou ow'st,
Nor shall Death brag thou wand'rest in his shade,
When in eternal lines to time thou grow'st.
So long as men can breathe or eyes can see,
So long lives this, and this gives life to thee.

(Sonnet 18)

This sonnet is decisively Petrarchan, notwithstanding its Shakespearean rhyme scheme. To begin with, it is rhetorically divided into octave and sestet, the change between the two parts balanced on the fulcrum of the word *but* at the beginning of the ninth line. The poem is widely and deservedly admired. Great riches of implication are packed into the interrogatory first line, which is a single sentence. A summer's day is itself full of meanings both lovely and ominous. It represents the season of growth, fertility, flowers, juvenescence, love, when days are not only luxurious in themselves but at their longest of all the seasons of the year. But that fact itself reminds us of a single day's brevity, no matter how long it lasts by count of daylight hours. We are already made conscious of the portents of decline and imperfection that are inevitably to follow. And how may it be said that some human being is "like" a summer's day? This person is declared to be superior to any of them, since even the best of them have their faults. There is, I think, a danger, in reading the octave, of forgetting that the descriptive terms drawn from the world of nature are metaphors for human imperfection and mutability. The third line, for example, is filled with the most delicate and tender solicitude for the fragility of beauty— and not just the beauty of buds. We are disposed to think of Hamlet's description of his father as "so loving to my mother / That he might not beteem the winds of heaven / Visit her face too roughly" (*Ham.* I.ii.140–42). Even the most seemingly benign forces of nature, the "eye of heaven," can induce drought and parch the skin; in Sonnet 62 Shakespeare describes himself as "Beated and chopped with tanned antiquity."

The octave concludes with a vital distinction between "chance" and "nature's changing course." Of these two forces, the latter is predictable, the former not; both are perilous. The sequential progress of the seasons is inexorable, and that it should present itself as a law of nature in the last line of the octave was implicit in the first line. But chance is another matter. In medieval times it was personified, notably by Boethius and Dante, as the pagan goddess Fortuna. Her vagaries and fickleness were proverbial, but a belief in her power provided a wonderful solution to an otherwise vexing theological problem. How could a beneficent and omnipotent God visit calamity or misfortune upon the meek, the pious, and the innocent? Speculation along these lines invited all the perils of heresy and atheism. But Fortuna, with her authority strictly confined to mundane and earthly matters, could be as capricious as she liked and thereby exculpate God from any charge of negligence or malignity. This solution can, however, be viewed in many ways, not all of them comforting. The licensed rule of chance, undiscriminating as death itself, was reassuring to those in unfavorable circumstances, as a guarantee that if things get bad enough they could only take a turn for the better. Kent reassures himself in this way—not altogether justifiably—when he is put in the stocks: "Fortune, good night; smile once more; turn thy wheel" (*Lear* II.ii.173). That turning of the wheel of chance also assured men that no temporal greatness was durable and that the mighty would surely fall. If this was a consolation to the powerless, it was a serious admonition to the powerful, urging clemency and charity upon them in that season when they were in a position to confer such favors. But when chance turns to havoc, as it does in Donne's *The First Anniversarie,* very little in the way of consolation or admonition is offered:

> 'Tis all in pieces, all cohaerence gone;
> All just supply, and all Relation:
> Prince, Subject, Father, Sonne, are things forgot,
> For every man alone thinkes he hath got
> To be a Phoenix, and that there can bee
> None of that kinde, of which he is, but hee.[12]

---

12. John Donne, *The First Anniversarie,* ll. 213–18, in *The Epithalamions, Anniversaries, and Epicedes,* ed. W. Milgate (1978), 28.

King Lear abounds in this sort of apocalyptic chaos of vanity and disorder, and it is this chaos that is quietly implied in Sonnet 18 by the word *chance.*

Then comes the brilliantly defiant sestet, in which the poet promises to immortalize his beloved in deathless verse. It needs immediately to be said that this is not personal vanity, or even a shrewd intuition on Shakespeare's part, but a poetic convention that can be traced back to classical antiquity. It can be found in Homer and Virgil, and J. B. Leishman noted that "passages on the immortalizing power of poetry are very frequent in Pindar's Odes."[13] This tradition was so strong among the Pléiade—the group of poets who acclimatized the sonnet form in France—that Ronsard in one of his sonnets threatened to withhold immortality from one particular unnamed lady unless she acceded to his decidedly carnal desire. The convention is to be found in Spenser's *Epithalamion:*

> Song made in lieu of many ornaments,
> With which my love should duly have bene dect . . .
> Be unto her a goodly ornament,
> And for short time an endlesse moniment[14]

and in Shakespeare's own Sonnet 55:

> Not marble nor the gilded monuments
> Of princes shall outlive this pow'rful rhyme.

If Shakespeare is undoubtedly invoking an ancient convention in asserting the poet's capacity to confer immortality, it is not the only convention he employs in his sonnets. We commonly assume that, whatever else love may be, it is at the very least a spontaneous and undeniable impulse, but it was not always thought to be so, and in the Renaissance, views about it were much more complicated. One modern critic has declared flatly: "L'amour? une invention du douzième siècle."[15] What could

---

13. J. B. Leishman, *Themes and Variations in Shakespeare's Sonnets* (1961), 27.
14. Edmund Spenser, *Epithalamion,* ll. 427–33, in *Works, Minor Poems,* 2:252.
15. Charles Seignobos, quoted by Maurice Valency, *In Praise of Love* (1961), 1. Much the same claim is made by C. S. Lewis, *The Allegory of Love* (1936), 2: "Every one has heard of courtly love, and every one knows that it appears quite suddenly at the end of the eleventh century in Languedoc."

seem more pedantically offensive to our habits of feeling and thought? But in classical literature, love is almost invariably regarded as an aberration, a dangerous taking leave of one's senses, most likely to lead to catastrophe and generally to be deplored. Many of the greatest Greek tragedies— *Oedipus Rex, Medea, Hippolytus, The Bacchae*—treat love as a tragic madness; so does Virgil in the episode of Dido in the *Aeneid.* The whole calamity of the Trojan war was brought about by a surrender to this insane impulse, which is treated in the *Iliad* as altogether unworthy and trifling in comparison with grave matters of war and heroism. The hero Odysseus, in the *Odyssey,* rejects all manner of solicitations from Calypso, Circe, and the Sirens; all these kinds of love are dangerous and to be avoided. Romantic love was historically a late development, which first manifested itself in Provence during the age of medieval feudalism, to which it bears a kind of metaphoric resemblance.

In the poetry developed by the troubadours and poets of Languedoc, the poet-lover always humbles himself in a submissive relationship to his beloved, a posture that duplicates the relation of a vassal towards his feudal lord. Indeed, as C. S. Lewis has pointed out, the lover addresses his beloved as *midons,* "which etymologically represents not 'my lady' but 'my lord.'" Lewis notes that "the lover is always abject. Obedience to his lady's lightest wish, however whimsical, and silent acquiescence in her rebukes, however unjust, are the only virtues he dares to claim."[16] He goes on to assert that "an unmistakable continuity connects the Provençal love song with the love poetry of the later Middle Ages, and thence, through Petrarch and many others, with that of the present day."[17] Anyone reading Shakespeare's Sonnet 57—"Being your slave, what should I do but tend / Upon the hours and times of your desire?"—would do well to remember the strength and antiquity of this tradition. It is a tradition virtually insisted upon in the final couplet of that sonnet:

> So true a fool is love that in your will
> (Though you do any thing) he thinks no ill.

This is more than merely abject; "true" in these lines means not only gen-

---

16. Lewis, *Allegory of Love,* 2.
17. Ibid., 3.

uinely and certifiably a fool but also "faithful." The implication is that fidelity not merely exposes one to folly but requires it.

These matters of tradition and convention lead us directly to the insoluble question of just what in the *Sonnets* may be said to be (as Wordsworth claimed they were)[18] a key with which Shakespeare unlocked his heart, and what may instead be attributed to a traditional posture belonging to the kind of fourteen-line love poem that he inherited. Are we to regard these poems as anything other than the surviving pages of an intimate diary, transcribing the poet's exact and authentic feelings on every topic he addresses? There are always readers who seek, not art, but something documentary and unassailably factual; when these two categories seem mysteriously intermingled, they will always prize the second over the first. Susan Sontag said that

> between two fantasy alternatives, that Holbein the Younger had lived long enough to have painted Shakespeare or that a prototype of the camera had been invented early enough to have photographed him, most Bardolators would choose the photograph. This is not just because it would presumably show what Shakespeare really looked like, for even if the hypothetical photograph were faded, barely legible, a brownish shadow, we should probably still prefer it to another glorious Holbein. Having a photograph of Shakespeare would be like having a nail from the True Cross.[19]

Those who cherish the *Sonnets* for their documentary value are inclined to dismiss as irrelevant, if not actually wrong, T. S. Eliot's pronouncement in "Tradition and the Individual Talent":

> the poet has, not a "personality" to express, but a particular medium, which is only a medium and not a personality, in which impressions and experiences combine in peculiar and unexpected ways. Impressions and experiences which are important for the man may take no place in the poetry, and those which become important in the poetry may play quite a negligible part in the man, the personality . . . One error, in fact, of eccentricity in poetry is to seek for new human emotions to express;

---

18. William Wordsworth, "Scorn not the Sonnet," a sonnet published in 1827.
19. Susan Sontag, *On Photography* (1977), 154.

and in this search for novelty in the wrong place it discovers the perverse. The business of the poet is not to find new emotions, but to use the ordinary ones and, in working them up into poetry, to express feelings which are not in actual emotions at all. *And emotions which he has never experienced will serve his turn as well as those familiar to him.* [My italics][20]

Those who reject this view insofar as it applies to the *Sonnets* most often declare that Eliot's formula is based on the nervous self-protection of an unusually fastidious and evasive man. But such an explanation fails to acknowledge that Eliot did very little more than reformulate some observations of Coleridge in *Biographia Literaria* (xv.2), so this view is not quite so idiosyncratic as has sometimes been asserted. Indeed, though the *Sonnets* were not published until much later, in 1598 Francis Meres, in *Palladis Tamia: Wit's Treasury,* already referred to the circulation of Shakespeare's "sugred Sonnets among his private friends,"[21] and it is reasonable to suppose that the poet would only have countenanced this kind of intimate distribution of his work if he felt it to be within the bounds of good taste. This is a question to which I shall return.

A word or two should perhaps be said here about meter and diction as they apply to these poems. Iambic pentameter—"When I do count the clock that tells the time"—is the most familiar metrical pattern in English verse. It is employed by Chaucer in *The Canterbury Tales,* by Shakespeare and Marlowe in their plays, by Milton, by Wordsworth, by the Victorians Tennyson and Browning, by Frost, Stevens, and the poets of today. It is the meter of most of the sonnets in English from Sir Thomas Wyatt to Richard Wilbur. Each line is composed of five feet, and each foot is composed, generally speaking, of two syllables, with the strong accent on the second of these, as in the naturally iambic words *today* or *because.* Any moderate acquaintance with the body of English poetry will so habituate a reader to this meter that it will become something that can be recognized involuntarily, as a dancer will recognize the rhythms of a waltz, a fox-trot, or a tango, each with its identifiable idiom and pattern. In the same way, a reader of poetry will in due course become habituated to the sound and

20. T. S. Eliot, *Selected Essays, 1917–32* (1932), 9–10.
21. E. K. Chambers, *William Shakespeare: A Study of Facts and Problems,* 2 vols. (1930), 2:194.

weight of a line of five iambic feet, though knowing that any given line will probably deviate in some regard from complete regularity. Such deviations are licensed by convention, and conventions change with the passing of time. Deviations of stress are useful and attractive for a number of reasons. They supply the rhythmical variety that is essential in a long poem or a five-act play. They make possible a flexibility of syntax and a directness of colloquial speech that a strictly regular meter would distort. They serve as a kind of counterpoint or syncopation, if the "ideal" pattern of the regular iambic line is kept in mind, varying from that ideal in the way a jazz musician will improvise riffs on an established harmony and measure, or the way Elizabethan composers wrote what were called "Divisions upon a Ground." As readers, we welcome the introduction of noniambic feet into a poem nominally iambic in character because we can hear in such poems the authentic sound of a human voice speaking in an idiom we can regard as reasonably "natural." There are many degrees and styles of such naturalness, and these, too, vary from period to period. But metrical flexibility allows a poet to avoid inverted word order and other peculiarities and permits the words of a poem to speak with a true sense of emotional urgency, whether of anger, rapture, grief, or devotion.

It must be said that Shakespeare's *Sonnets* are in general metrically regular, especially by comparison with the great liberties he took with meter in the later plays. He often uses feminine endings (an extra, unaccented eleventh syllable at the end of a line), and twelve of the fourteen lines of Sonnet 87 ("Farewell, thou art too dear for my possessing") end in this way, most of these endings being composed of the participial *-ing*.

Clearly, matters of meter are intimately connected with questions of diction, and the diction of Shakespeare's *Sonnets* is worth noticing for its comparative spareness and simplicity—a sometimes deceptive simplicity. It is as far from the harsh brass choirs of Donne's *Holy Sonnets,* on the one hand, as it is from the stately elegance and learning of sonnets by Spenser and Sidney, on the other. Just as Shakespeare made use of classical mythology only in the most chary and tentative way, so he employed a diction that distinguishes his work not only from that of his fellow sonneteers but also from the language of his own work as a dramatist, both early and late. Drama presents human beings speaking to one another in something approximating the manner of ordinary human discourse, whereas we often think of poetry as violating the normal modes of speech. Furthermore, one would suppose that when, in the course of his plays, Shakespeare turns to "heightened" forms of speech, he would reserve such heightening for the chief utterances of his major characters, as when Macbeth says:

> No; this my hand will rather
> The multitudinous seas incarnadine,
> Making the green one red.
>
> (*Mac.* I.ii.58–60)

But it is merely a nameless Second Gentleman, never to reappear, who observes at the beginning of the second act of *Othello:*

> I never did like molestation view
> On the enchafèd flood.
>
> (*Oth.* II.i.16–17)

That Shakespeare can allot language like this to persons of no dramatic consequence whatever means that he is not attempting, by such musical flourishes, to convey character, but is simply treating with exuberant and exploratory relish the resources of the English language.

The solid facts about the *Sonnets* that can be called undisputed are few. In 1599 William Jaggard published two of the sonnets (138 and 144) in a collection of poems called *The Passionate Pilgrim,* in which a number of other poems, some of them now firmly identified as being by other hands, were also attributed to Shakespeare. The 1590s were the time of the great vogue for sonnets in England, but Shakespeare's *Sonnets* did not appear until 1609, when they were published by Thomas Thorpe in a volume usually believed to have been unauthorized by Shakespeare. Thorpe possibly hoped to cash in, belatedly, on what was by then a waning interest in the form. His edition was mysteriously and indeed notoriously dedicated to "THE.ONLIE.BEGETTER.OF.THESE.INSUING.SONNETS.Mʳ.W.H.," and there has been a great deal of argument over this man's identity. There has been at least as much conjecture about the order of the poems as about the dedication, some critics proposing that they should be linked by rhyme or by words that connect one sonnet with another. Some of the sonnets are clearly linked in rhetorical structure as part of a developed argument; several in Thorpe's sequence are clustered round a specific theme. This order, fretted over and argued about, has not yet been superseded by any other that wins wide consent, and it has some elements of design and logic to recommend it. It is generally assumed that the first 126 sonnets are addressed to a young man; the remainder concern a woman. Both involve poems of unusual intimacy, sometimes openly bawdy and erotic in character, though the humor is similar to that of the off-color jokes that can be found in many of the plays. The poems concerned with the man are, for the most part, more respectful than those about the woman, but even the first group takes liberties that would be admissible between friends in the plays but are less likely between a poet and his titled patron—if indeed they are to be taken as addressed to the Earl of Southampton. Shakespeare had dedicated other poems to Southampton in words of conventional servility, though it has been correctly noted that the language Shakespeare used in his prose dedication of *The Rape of Lucrece* to Southampton is very closely echoed in Sonnet 26. Southampton, of course, is one of the leading candidates for the "young man"—along with William Herbert, Earl of Pembroke—among those who wish to decode the sequence into a personal narrative.

The question of the historical identity of the man is interestingly linked to another question. A group of the earliest sonnets in the sequence is concerned to urge the young man to marry and beget children who will perpetuate his beauty. "What man in the whole world," asks C. S. Lewis, "except a father or potential father-in-law, cares whether any other man gets married?" He regards this repeated recommendation of marriage as "inconsistent . . . with a real homosexual passion. It is not even very obviously consistent with normal friendship. It is indeed hard to think of any real situation in which it would be natural."[22] Lewis's remarks here seem amusingly suspicious of the benefits of marriage, since he finds it improbable that one friend should recommend it to another; but far more important is his comment that it is hard to think of a "real situation" in which such a recommendation would be natural. *Are* we to imagine a real situation behind the poems? Is Shakespeare always writing *in propria persona?* Some critics have proposed that these "marital" sonnets were commissioned to be passed on to the young nobleman as if coming from his mother.

The problem is not confined simply to the question of the young man's

---

22. C. S. Lewis, *English Literature in the Sixteenth Century Excluding Drama* (1954), 503.

identity or that of the so-called Dark Lady, who is the subject of the later sonnets. Some critics with a strong narrative bent have come up with a detailed plot of sexual betrayal and infidelity which supposes that Shakespeare is simultaneously attached both to the young man and to the woman and makes the fatal mistake of introducing them to each other, which leads, as in a third-rate film script, to their instant infatuation with each other, their abandonment of the playwright, and their exclusive erotic interest in each other. Followers of this line of argument suggest that Shakespeare acknowledged the double desertion in Sonnet 40—"Take all my loves, my love, yea, take them all"—and Samuel Butler adds the excruciating twist, perhaps suggested to him by Rostand's *Cyrano,* that some of the sonnets addressed to the Dark Lady were written by Shakespeare for the young man to pass on as his own.

There is at least one further major puzzle that seems beyond the reach of any solution. This has to do with the sexual orientation of the poet and the quality and degree of his intimacy with the young man. (The quality and degree of his intimacy with the woman is unambiguous.) About these matters almost no one feels neutral. Many of Shakespeare's plays have been construed to demonstrate an explicit or implicit homosexual bias on the playwright's part. The relationship between Horatio and Hamlet, between Antonio and Bassanio, and between Iago and Othello—to say nothing of Orsino's erotic interest in Viola disguised as a boy and played by a boy actor, as well as Olivia's interest in Viola, whom she thinks really is the boy she pretends to be, or the relationship between Falstaff and Hal[23]—all these seem homoerotic to some readers. And these arguments are invariably advanced by appealing to the "evidence" of the *Sonnets.*

There was an established tradition in Europe that placed a higher value on the love relationship between men than on love between the sexes. Towards the end of the *Morte D'Arthur* (bk. XX, ch. 9), Malory has King Arthur speak in a mood close to despair:

> "And therefore," said the king, "wit you well my heart was never so heavy as it is now, and much more am I sorrier for my good knights' loss than for the loss of my fair queen; for queens I might have enow,

---

23. See W. H. Auden, "The Prince's Dogs," in *The Dyer's Hand and Other Essays* (1962), 182–208.

but such a fellowship of good knights shall never be together in no company."[24]

Montaigne, in his essay "On Friendship" (by which he means the friend-ship between men), says something not dissimilar:

> To compare the affection toward women unto it [i.e., friendship], al-though it proceed from our own free choice [as distinguished from the bonds of child and parent], a man cannot; nor may it be placed in this rank. [Venus's] fire, I confess it . . . to be more active, more fervent, and more sharp. But it is a rash and wavering fire, waving and divers, the fire of an ague subject to fits and stints, and that hath but slender hold-fast [i.e., grasp] of us. In true friendship is a general and universal heat, all pleasure and smoothness, that hath no pricking or stinging in it, which the more it is in lustful love, the more is it but a ranging and mad desire in following that which flies us.[25]

"The exaltation of friendship over love was a widespread Neoplatonic commonplace . . . popularized in the writings of John Lyly"[26]—and not in Lyly's works alone, or in Montaigne's. There was the biblical story of David and Jonathan; the Homeric account of Achilles and Patroclus; the classical legend of Damon and Pythias; and, if more authority were needed, Aristotle's argument that relations between men who are friends must of necessity be closer than any possible relationship between men and women because men bear a closer resemblance to one another—an argument advanced in *The Merchant of Venice* by Portia herself in speak-ing of the "love" between Bassanio, her "lord," and his friend Antonio. There is, moreover, a theological basis for the devotion of Antonio and Bassanio to each other. The play pointedly confronts the Old Testament (Law) with the New Testament (Love), and the latter is figuratively dra-matized as an enactment of John 15:13: "Greater love than this hath no man, when any man bestoweth his life for his friends" (Geneva Bible). Such love is expressly "greater" than connubial love, and *The Merchant of*

---

24. Sir Thomas Malory, *Le Morte D'Arthur*, ed. Janet Cowan, 2 vols. (1969), 2:473.
25. *The Essays of Michael, Lord of Montaigne*, trans. John Florio (1603), 3 vols. (1928), 1:195–209.
26. See David Bevington, ed., *The Complete Works of Shakespeare* (1980), 1582.

Venice exhibits much wit in giving each a due and proportionate place in its dramatic fable.

Since it was at times a part of Shakespeare's poetic strategy to invert, parody, or burlesque sonnets in the conventional Petrarchan tradition—see, for instance, Sonnet 130: "My mistress' eyes are nothing like the sun"—it may be useful to illustrate this device by citing just such a model along with Shakespeare's irreverent treatment of the same conventions. The following sonnet by Sir Thomas Wyatt is in fact a translation of Petrarch's sonnet *In vita* CIX, "Amor, che nel penser mio vive e regna":

> The longe love, that in my thought doeth harbar
>   And in myn hert doeth kepe his residence,
>   Into my face preseth with bolde pretence,
>   And therin campeth, spreding his baner.
> She that me lerneth to love and suffre,
>   And willes that my trust and lustes negligence
>   Be rayned by reason, shame, and reverence,
>   With his hardines taketh displeasure.
> Wherewithall, unto the hertes forrest he fleith,
>   Leving his enterprise with payn and cry;
>   And ther him hideth, and not appereth.
> What may I do when my maister fereth
>   But in the feld with him to lyve and dye?
>   For goode is the liff, ending faithfully.[27]

This remarkable poem draws its central metaphoric structure from a tradition that reaches back to the *Roman de la Rose*, which had been partly translated into English by Chaucer. The image is that of a faithful knight dedicated to the service of love and obedient to the rebuke and correction of a sternly chaste but beautiful mistress, and thus destined to love and suffer simultaneously. But the image of knight-errantry, with all its military embellishments, goes back to the classical identification of love and war, the love of Venus and Mars, the proverbial association that links these forces in the expression "All's fair in love and war." Wyatt's translation of Petrarch is lovingly compounded of a double allegiance: to Love, the in-

---

27. R. A. Rebholz, ed., *The Complete Poems of Sir Thomas Wyatt* (1978), 76–77.

voluntary passion that shows itself like a banner in the flushed face of the lover in the first quatrain—and to the beloved, to whom the lover submits in meek obedience, shame, and contrition in the second quatrain. It then becomes the complex duty of the lover to be faithful both to his passion and to his mistress; his loyalty to the latter is expressed as a vassal's fidelity to his sovereign lord and a resignation to accept death itself if that should be called for.

This very set of metaphors—military in character, involving notions of fidelity to the point of death, loyalty, treason, betrayal, and triumph—figures, with deliberate allowance made for the irony of its deployment, in what is probably Shakespeare's most outrageously libidinous sonnet:

> Love is too young to know what conscience is,
> Yet who knows not conscience is born of love?
> Then, gentle cheater, urge not my amiss,
> Lest guilty of my faults thy sweet self prove.
> For thou betraying me, I do betray
> My nobler part to my gross body's treason:
> My soul doth tell my body that he may
> Triumph in love; flesh stays no farther reason,
> But rising at thy name doth point out thee
> As his triumphant prize. Proud of this pride,
> He is contented thy poor drudge to be,
> To stand in thy affairs, fall by thy side.
> No want of conscience hold it that I call
> Her "love" for whose dear love I rise and fall.
>
> (Sonnet 151)

It does not take a long acquaintance with this poem to realize that it is laden with puns, most of them leeringly sexual. Critics have ransacked the *OED* and precedents from Elizabethan literature in tracing the various meanings buried in this wordplay, but there has been very little agreement about whether this is to be regarded as a poem to be admired or simply a crude and embarrassing piece of youthful sexual raillery. Moreover, not only has the quality of the poem been left in doubt, but its meaning as well. For while the puns have been glossed, it is often left unclear which meanings apply to particular words as they make their multiple appearances from line to line. In addition, there has been little if any discussion of the rhetorical structure and premise of the poem.

It posits a dramatic context, an anterior situation, known to the person addressed, the beloved, and to be inferred by us, the readers. It is a defense against a prior accusation, a self-exculpation, a *tu quoque* argument, but presented in a spirit of bawdy good humor and free from any sense of guilt or of wounded feelings. Indeed, our whole task as readers is to determine the nature of the charge against which the poem has been composed as if it were a legal brief for the defense. The brief wittily employs all the ancient metaphors of vassalage and faithful military service, of warfare, treason, and triumph which had been part of the Petrarchan conventions but which are here adapted to carnal purposes where before they had served the most discarnate and spiritual ends.

The first two lines both contain the words *love* and *conscience*. To make any sense of them whatever requires a recognition that a different meaning applies to those words in each of the lines. "Love" in the opening line is Cupid, too young to know or care about the damage he inflicts with his weapons of bow and arrow (the military imagery of weapons is implied right at the start), too young to feel the pang of sexual arousal himself and thus unaware of the pain he causes others—hence, without conscience. But in the second line "conscience" as carnal knowledge is begotten by the passion of love (the root meaning here is *con scire,* "to know together," in the biblical sense: "And Adam knew Heva his wife, who conceiving, bare Cain" [Gen. 4:1, Bishops' Bible]). For reasons that I hope presently to make clear, I am at variance with critics who regard the phrase "gentle cheater" as an oxymoron, especially when they argue that "cheater" implies fraud, deceit, or infidelity. The *OED* cites these very lines to illustrate its first definition of *cheater:* "The officer appointed to look after the king's escheats; an escheator" (though this meaning became obsolete after the seventeenth century, when the modern sense implying "fraud" replaced it). An escheater was "an officer appointed yearly by the Lord Treasurer to take notice of the escheats in the county to which he is appointed, and to certify them into the Exchequer"; the office is therefore one concerned to demand forfeits from those who have defaulted from their obligations, usually financial. In the present case, the "gentle cheater" is an "assessor" of some sexual malfeasance, which the sonnet will shortly make somewhat clearer; and the epithet seems to be used without complication in an affectionate and jocular spirit.

The phrase "urge not my amiss" is densely compressed and probably cannot be construed in isolation from the line that follows: "Lest guilty of my faults thy sweet self prove." I would claim in defense of my reading of "gentle cheater" that it chimes harmoniously with "sweet self," as any suggestion of sexual treason would not. The third and fourth lines, taken together, are a central crux of the poem and can plausibly be interpreted in contradictory and mutually exclusive ways. If "urge" is understood as *incite*, we may read the lines as meaning: "Do not incite me to some known but unspecified offence (1) lest you be to blame for my fault by inciting me, or (2) lest you turn out upon further inquiry to be guilty of the very same fault yourself." If, on the other hand, "urge" means *accuse* or *allege*, the lines mean: "Do not charge me with this unspecified fault, lest in some way you turn out to be responsible for it." There is a further possible complication. In the seventeenth-century orthography of Thorpe's edition, the fourth line is printed: "Least guilty of my faults thy sweet selfe proue." And if *least* is taken in the modern sense, as distinct from a legitimate spelling of *lest*, the line would mean: "Distance yourself as emphatically as possible from my ways and errors." But this meaning cannot be fitted intelligibly into the rest of the sonnet.

All this leaves us tantalizingly uncertain about what the fault may be, though the entire remainder of the poem is devoted to it, in the form of a legal defense and exculpation, commencing with the first word of the fifth line—*for*—as the beginning of a demonstration and proof of innocence in regard to the charge. From the evidence of the argument for the defense, the charge appears ambiguously to be that the lover has either made sexual demands of too great and burdensome a kind or else is sexually backward, shy, and indifferent in performance.

The fifth line, with its punning use of "betraying" and "betray," is not without its own complexities and puzzles. It has been proposed by some critics that "betraying" means an overt act of infidelity and that what is being claimed is something like: "Every time you are unfaithful to me, I become sexually aroused." This seems to me at best unlikely, though it is of course possible. Far more plausible is the suggestion that "betraying" is used here to mean "seducing," as when Cleopatra says:

I will betray
Tawny-finn'd fishes; my bended hook shall pierce
Their slimy jaws; and as I draw them up,
I'll think them every one an Antony,
And say, "Ah, ha! y'are caught."

(*Ant.* II.v.11–15)

In contrast to "betraying," "betray" here means the treasonable conveyance of the soul ("my nobler part") to the gross and carnal powers of the body. The body itself commits treason by subverting the soul from its chief goal and purpose. The "I" in the fifth line betrays his own soul by subjecting it to the base authority of his body, so much corrupting the soul that it grants permission to the body to pursue its own lewd ends. And having gained this permission from the soul, the body seeks no further check upon its lusts (such checks as might be offered either by the soul or by outside authority), "But rising at thy name doth point out thee / As his triumphant prize." It should be noted here that the "I" who has been advancing the whole argument of the poem has, rather interestingly, disappeared in this description of the warfare between soul and body. This familiar convention of spiritual and bodily conflict dates back at least as far as St. Paul's Epistle to the Galatians 5:17: "For the flesh lusteth against the Spirit, and the Spirit against the flesh: and these are contrary one to the other" (Geneva Bible). This conflict was played out in such poems as Andrew Marvell's "A Dialogue between the Soul and the Body" and "A Dialogue, between the Resolved Soul and Created Pleasure,"[28] and may be found in other poems as well. In the present case, however, the conflict is circumvented or simply avoided by the total capitulation of soul to body.

The "rising" of the ninth line and the "pride" of the tenth refer to the tumescence of male sexual arousal; flesh is said to be "proud" when it swells. The wit here lies in the fact that this truth pertains equally to body and to spirit: a man swollen with pride is guilty of spiritual sin. But these acknowledgments of vigorous sexual reaction are now excused—and indeed glorified—as a testament to the obedience and duty of a vassal to his *midons,* his absolute sovereign, the disposer of his fortunes good and bad,

28. Elizabeth Story Donno, ed., *Andrew Marvell: The Complete Poems* (1972), 25–28 and 103–4.

his very life and death. It is *flesh* which is the subject of lines 8–14, and by *flesh* is meant the male sexual organ, which is personified as faithful even unto death, rising and falling at the behest of the beloved. For this reason it seems to me highly unlikely that the word "cheater" in the third line can contain any overtones of perfidy on the part of the beloved—a meaning which would involve the notion that the speaker is sexually aroused only by the infidelity of his beloved. This is, as I acknowledged, possible, though it raises the whole ludicrous puzzle of frequency. For a man to say of himself that he is instantly aroused by a woman's beauty is at least understandable. To defend his reputation by saying he is aroused only by infidelity on the part of the woman he loves must mean he is aroused at far less frequent intervals, as well as in more curious circumstances, and it becomes thereby a somewhat feebler defense.

There is much more to this sonnet than has been here too briefly summarized, but we must return to the nature of the "amiss" mentioned in the third line. Has the speaker been accused of sexual negligence, indifference, or impotence? Or of making too insistent carnal demands upon the beloved? The poem can, astonishingly, be read both ways, and in both cases the same argument for the defense works. If she has said to him that he has failed to gratify her sexual appetite, his response is that her "betrayal" or seductive looks instantly result in sexual arousal on his part, so he is blameless. If, on the other hand, she has accused him of being too insistent upon satisfying his own carnal appetites, his response is that she herself must be blamed for his behavior by the initial betrayal (i.e., seduction) that leads him to the further betrayal of his soul to his body. No doubt all this is forensic jesting, and the sort of banter not uncommon between lovers. Those who feel the point is overworked should consider once again how much in the way of traditional Petrarchan devices, metaphors of war and treason, images of vassalage and fidelity, are, as I think, brilliantly crowded into a mere fourteen lines. This may not be one of Shakespeare's greatest sonnets, but it is surely one of his wittiest.[29]

---

29. Anyone who wants to see how carefully constructed, how densely packed, a sonnet of Shakespeare's can be, and who would also like to see how a sensitive and painstaking reader with responsible critical intelligence can unpack those meanings and reveal the design, cannot do better than read Roman Jakobson on Shakespeare's Sonnet 129, in Roman Jakobson and Lawrence G. Jones, *Shakespeare's Verbal Art in "th'expense of spirit"* (1970).

Sonnet 151, though full of puns and complicated wordplay, is still a comparatively simple poem in terms of its tone, and it probably intends a simple and comparatively straightforward meaning, if only we were so situated as to know the nature of the "amiss" with which it is concerned. Far more complicated in terms both of tone and meaning is Sonnet 87:

> Farewell, thou art too dear for my possessing,
> And like enough thou know'st thy estimate:
> The charter of thy worth gives thee releasing;
> My bonds in thee are all determinate.
> For how do I hold thee but by thy granting,
> And for that riches where is my deserving?
> The cause of this fair gift in me is wanting,
> And so my patent back again is swerving.
> Thy self thou gav'st, thy own worth then not knowing,
> Or me, to whom thou gav'st it, else mistaking;
> So thy great gift, upon misprision growing,
> Comes home again, on better judgement making.
> Thus have I had thee as a dream doth flatter,
> In sleep a king, but waking no such matter.

The genius of this poem consists in its absolute command of tonal complexity throughout, by which it is left brilliantly ambiguous—through tact and diplomacy, with bitterness and irony, or with matter-of-fact worldliness—just which of the two parties involved is to be blamed for the impasse and end of what had once been a deeply binding relationship. The pretext of the poem is one of self-mortification characteristic of the traditional early love sonnets discussed above. The lover insists upon his own unworthiness, particularly as regards the exalted, unapproachable condition of the beloved. Although there is a pun on the word "dear" in the first line—a pun made the more explicit by the possibly commercial language of the second line—puns are not the building blocks of this poem as they are of others. The lover begins in what seems initially to be a spirit of generous renunciation: the line can mean both (1) "I am prepared to give you up" and (2) "I appear not to have much choice in the matter, so I am giving you up." Taken in conjunction with the first line, however, the second line of the poem seems to include or suggest the following possible meanings:

1. You know how much I love you.
2. You know how much you deserve to be loved.
3. You have a very high opinion of yourself.
4. You know how much others love you.
5. You know the value of the opinions of (a) me, (b) yourself, (c) others, (d) all of us.

The poem continues to manoeuvre between these modes of worldliness and unworldliness in a way that, by its skill, speaks of two different kinds of pain, and at the same time makes the pain almost tolerable by the sheer act of lively intelligence that went into the making of the poem, which is clearly no raw, unmediated transcription of experience. By the time we reach the end of the second line, the poem has begun to seethe with implied hostility, governed nevertheless by conventions of propriety and the decorum of charity. We cannot fail to notice the pervasive language of law and commerce, those two ledger-keeping modes of coming to terms with the world; and we cannot fail to feel the irony of the application of those modes to questions of love.

The speaker here seems to be giving the beloved a writ of freedom to depart, and justifying that departure by several different kinds of "reason," generally practical and intended as plausible. The words *estimate, charter, bonds, riches, gift, patent, misprision,* and *judgement* all speak, as might a shrewd auctioneer, from a market-place perspective. Beneath the surface of supposedly self-abnegating relinquishment, we detect a flavor of bitterness and scarcely repressed resentment. This may be most openly expressed, and at the same time best concealed, by the lines

> For how do I hold thee but by thy granting,
> And for that riches where is my deserving?

We do not love anyone on the basis of merit, or rank, or wealth, or for other worldly advantages. Love mixed with or tainted by calculation is highly suspect—is indeed not love at all. It follows then that if the beloved is willing to accept as a legitimate excuse for withdrawing from the relationship any of the various "worldly" and practical excuses proposed by the lover, then the lover cannot but conclude that the love has not been mutual, whatever he may have thought it to begin with; that the beloved, surveying the prospect or prospects, has both reason and right to seek elsewhere, since no real love seems to be involved. The very word "misprision" means both a misunderstanding or mistake and also a clerical error of the ledger-keeping sort. The final irony of the poem lies in the fact that both parties were deeply deceived—the beloved by either underestimating himself or overestimating the lover, and the lover by having believed that he was loved.

This mutual deception and self-deception are re-examined by Shakespeare in Sonnet 138:

> When my love swears that she is made of truth,
> I do believe her, though I know she lies,
> That she might think me some untutored youth,
> Unlearnèd in the world's false subtleties.
> Thus vainly thinking that she thinks me young,
> Although she knows my days are past the best,
> Simply I credit her false-speaking tongue:
> On both sides thus is simple truth suppressed.
> But wherefore says she not she is unjust?
> And wherefore say not I that I am old?
> O love's best habit is in seeming trust,
> And age in love loves not t'have years told.
> Therefore I lie with her, and she with me,
> And in our faults by lies we flattered be.

Sonnet 93 deals with the subject even more directly—"So shall I live, supposing thou art true, / Like a deceived husband?" Sonnet 138 is a private meditation, with no express addressee, and may perhaps exhibit a certain candor of insight that direct address might forbid in the name of tact. But each is concerned with love as illusion, as self-deception, as bitterly unreal—in ways that remind us that the world of *A Midsummer Night's Dream* is not altogether as taintless as it might at first appear.

This capacity for illusion and self-deception concerns not only matters of love but also our very sense of ourselves, of our worth—our self-image and self-respect. This issue raises its head in the sonnets about the "rival poet." These are usually regarded as a group made up of Sonnets 78–80 and 82–86. But even in so "early" a sonnet as the celebrated 29—"When in disgrace with Fortune and men's eyes"—we find the quatrain:

> Wishing me like to one more rich in hope,
> Featured like him, like him with friends possessed,
> Desiring this man's art, and that man's scope,
> With what I most enjoy contented least.

Such vulnerability, modesty, uncertainty, are touching in their own right, and a small solace to lesser poets in their moods of tormenting self-doubt.

I have earlier raised the topic of how literally and precisely we should allow ourselves to read these poems as documentary transcriptions of personal events. This calls for a few further words. A number of philosophers, beginning perhaps with Plato, have argued on a variety of grounds that poetry is a tissue of lies. This was Stephen Gosson's view in *The School of Abuse* (1579), and John Skelton, maintaining that religious poetry is "true," touches upon the same conventional topic when he asks:

> Why have ye then disdain
> At poets, and complain
> How poets do but feign?[30]

This view, that poets are only feigning, did not differ greatly from ideas that were forcibly advanced during the Enlightenment, when the domain of truth was confined more and more strictly to what could be known with scientific precision. It is a view still voiced in certain quarters to this day. But we may approach the question in another way, one that centers on the nature of poetic form and the demands it makes on the materials it must employ and put into artistic order. The raw materials of poetry can be recalcitrant; the demands of form can be severe. How are these conflicting elements to be reconciled? Here is W. H. Auden's especially persuasive answer to that question:

> In the process of composition, as every poet knows, the relation between experience and language is always dialectical, but in the finished product it must always appear to the reader to be a one-way relationship. In serious poetry thought, emotion, event, must always appear to

---

30. John Skelton, "A Replication Against Certain Young Scholars Abjured of Late," in John Scattergood, ed., *John Skelton: The Complete English Poems* (1983), 384.

dictate the diction, meter, and rhyme in which they are embodied; vice versa, in comic poetry it is the words, meter, rhyme, which must appear to create the thoughts, emotions, and events they require.[31]

If what Auden says is right (and it seems to me almost indisputable), then the question of the documentary nature of the *Sonnets* is largely irrelevant. This will no doubt leave some readers feeling cheated. But the *Sonnets* are, first and last, poems, and it should be our task to read, evaluate, and enjoy them as such. Devoted attention to each of them in its own right will yield striking discoveries. They are not all equally inventive or moving. Some are little more than conventional; others are wonderfully original and ingenious. Scarcely any lacks true merit, many of them are beyond compare, and in bulk they are without question the finest single group of sonnets in the language. They contain puzzles which will probably never be wholly answered, and this may be a part of their enigmatic charm. But most of all they speak with powerful, rich, and complex emotion of a very dramatic kind, and we cannot fail to hear in them a voice of passion and intelligence.

---

31. W. H. Auden, ed., *Selected Poetry and Prose of Byron* (1966), xix.

The Sonnet
Ruminations on Form, Sex, and History

SURVIVAL OF THE FORM

The survival of the sonnet form is astonishing. By comparison, the haiku, originating in the mid-sixteenth century, is a parvenu. There are, of course, a number of other forms with a long history—the ballade, the villanelle, the sestina, the canzone—but these have not enjoyed a continuous life. I can't think of one of them written in English in the entire seventeenth or eighteenth centuries. Like certain dance steps, they went out of fashion and were later revived. But from its inception the sonnet has enjoyed a continuous and vital existence. There are, I think, at least two reasons for this, one profoundly formal, the other intriguingly sexual. Let's save the sexy one for later.

In a conversation with a group of his friends, W. H. Auden once raised this puzzle of the sonnet's survival powers and asked us to speculate about how to account for it. He himself volunteered the very probing and suggestive notion that there must be manifest in the proportions of some familiar natural objects (say, the trunk of certain trees in relation to the crown of their branches and leaves) a ratio that corresponded in some way that we unconsciously recognized to the proportions of the two parts of a Petrarchan sonnet to one another, of the octave to the sestet, of eight to six. It was an absorbing puzzle, and no one, including Auden, was able, on the spur of the moment, to come up with any familiar instances of that proportional relationship. I thought about it for years, and eventually came to a tentative solution by way of that highly mathematical art, architecture, and one of its earliest and greatest theoreticians, Vitruvius.

I've written about this at some length in a book called *On the Laws of the*

Poetic Art, so I will offer here only a brief summary. Vitruvius, the leading architect of Augustan Rome, propounded the remarkable notion that great and enduring works of architecture, particularly temples, were based on the proportions, one to another, of their various parts in almost exact correspondence to the way the parts of the human anatomy are proportionally related in the body of what Vitruvius called "a well-shaped man." He worked out these relationships in elaborate fractions and in detail; and fourteen and a half centuries later his outline of them served as the basis of an illustration by Leonardo da Vinci of a naked man, inscribed inside a square and a circle, with two sets of arms and legs and with the center of the image the man's navel. It has become a very familiar iconic device.

Vitruvius was painstaking in his demonstration that these ideal human proportions, admired not only when encountered in fellow-humans but also in the greatest sculptures of ancient times, were the very proportions, recognized somehow unconsciously but kinesthetically and immediately, in those buildings that were most enduringly pleasing and elevating to contemplate. What he is saying is that our bodies react with excitement and with the sympathy of attraction to an edifice whose mathematical proportions we intuit as resembling what we would like to be at our best. This Vitruvian notion is made explicit use of in Yeats' late poem "The Statues."

I'd become familiar with these notions without ever so much as thinking of the sonnet form, and the connection did not occur to me for years until, well after Auden's death—I regret this, because I think he would have approved my small "discovery"—I began reading about architectural masterpieces of the Renaissance and visiting some of them. I was particularly drawn to the works of Palladio and to his extraordinary palazzo, the Villa Foscari, known as "The Malcontenta." It's worth quoting Rudolph Wittkower on Palladio's methods:

> The geometrical keynote is, subconsciously rather than consciously, perceptible to everyone who visits Palladio's villas and it is this that gives his buildings their convincing quality.
>
> Yet his grouping and re-grouping of the same pattern was not as simple an operation as it may appear. Palladio took the greatest care to employ harmonic ratios not only inside each single room, but also in the

relation of the rooms to each other, and it is this demand for the right ratio which is at the centre of Palladio's conception of architecture.[1]

In the Villa Foscari, if the rooms of the smallest width may be designated by the numeral 1, then the rooms across the whole villa, back, center, and front, are designed in the pattern 2-1-2-1-2 (where by 2 is meant twice the width of 1). Then, from back to front, the rooms' lengths are, respectively, $1\frac{2}{3}$, $2\frac{1}{3}$, and 2. To walk through the villa is to experience, as in many Palladian structures, a space at once serene and grand. But if, now, we formulate a relationship between the whole width and the whole length, we come to 8 × 6, or the very relationship in the two parts of the Italian sonnet.

I write this in perfect confidence that it will outrage certain readers, as well as writers, of poetry—those who believe that poetry is the immediate and spontaneous overflow of strong emotions, that it is entirely a matter of feelings, sensations, impulses, visceral promptings, and that nothing is more alien to it than mathematics and the rigidities of numerical proportions. But there must be some intelligible way of explaining why the Italian form (also called Petrarchan) endured with such Methuselan health, a matter that is only the more puzzling in that the English (or Shakespearean) sonnet (composed of three quatrains rhyming *abab, cdcd, efef,* and ending in a couplet, *gg*) is infinitely easier for us to write than its Italian forebear (with its octave rhyming *abbaabba*), in which only two rhyme sounds must serve for the first eight lines. English is not as rich in rhyme words as Italian, and so, while the form is easy and unforced in its original language, it risks becoming something of a tour de force in English. And yet, the sonnet in English from Wyatt and Surrey to Wilbur and Berryman has preferred this more demanding form.

THE FORM

As any form becomes canonical, it virtually invites experiment, variation, violation, alteration. In "Pied Beauty" Hopkins wrote what he called a "curtal," or abbreviated sonnet. Elizabeth Bishop first, and later Mona Van Duyn, wrote sonnets with strikingly short lines, Bishop beginning hers with the (complete) line "Caught—the bubble," Van Duyn calling hers "minimalist" sonnets. But these were neither the first nor the last to

---

1. Rudolph Wittkower, *Architectural Principles in the Age of Humanism* (1972), 72.

attempt such artistic parsimony and spare ingenuity. As far as I am aware, the first truly emaciated sonnet (with each line confined to a single syllable) was composed by Arthur Rimbaud.

Coucher Ivre

> Pouacre
> Boit:
> Nacre
> Voit:
>
> Acre
> Loi,
> Fiacre
> Choit!
>
> Femme
> Tombe,
> Lombe
>
> Saigne:
> Geigne.
>
> Clame!

Roughly rendered, this means: (The) Slob / Drinks: / (The) Pearl (of a girl) / Sees (what's coming): // (The) Bitter / Law (of gravity takes effect), / (The) Carriage / Collapses! // (The) Woman / Tumbles, / Loins // Bleed, / Whimpers. / Pandemonium!

The latest specimen in this frugal and demanding form that I know of is by Brad Leithauser and is titled "Post Coitum Tristesse: A Sonnet."

> Why
> do
> you
> sigh,
> roar,

fall,
all
for
some
hum-
drum
come
—mm?
Hm . . . [2]

All the evidence we have suggests that the canonical form was invented by Giacomo de Lentino, a member of the Sicilian court of the Emperor Frederick II and known as the Notary, possibly because he was empowered to act on the emperor's behalf in certain legal matters. We have, in any case, no earlier sonnets than his and those of his fellow courtiers, which date from the third decade of the thirteenth century, that is, not long before Dante and his circle of poet-friends took up the form in earnest. Originally, the Sicilian poets composed their fourteen-line poems in hendecasyllabics, that is, pentameter lines with feminine endings; and the octaves contained two identical quatrains of alternating rhymes: *abab, abab.* As Maurice Valency declares in his excellent study *In Praise of Love* (1961), "The sestet is usually distinguished logically from the octave; the musical volta was evidently accompanied by a turn of thought," and most poetry of the period was conceived as something either to be set to music or adapted to an already existent melody. The earliest sestets often divided into rhyming tercets but sometimes appeared as couplets: *cd, cd, cd.* As Valency observes, "The result is a relatively simple and flexible song form, learned and courtly in its association, but, unlike the majestic *canzone,* very suitable for casual rhyming."

That extra syllable at the end of each line is easier in Italian than in English, though Shakespeare manages to do it twelve out of fourteen times in his Sonnet 87, "Farewell, thou art too dear for my possessing," chiefly by the repeated use of participial endings. But when the French got hold of the form they cast it in alexandrines, ending not with an extra syllable but an extra foot. This is immediately evident in Ronsard's "Quand vous

---

2. Brad Leithauser, *Cats of the Temple* (1986), 20.

serez bien vielle, au soir, à la chandelle," as well as Du Bellay's "Heureux qui, comme Ulysse, a fait un beau voyage," though both poets also employed shorter lines for some of their sonnets. Probably in imitation, not of the Italians but of the French, the first of Sidney's sonnets in *Astrophel and Stella* is composed in hexameters, that is, alexandrines: "Loving in truth, and fain in verse my love to show." (Sidney, incidentally, carries off his alexandrine lines with enormous grace and skill, and in English this is no easy task; our language has been ill at ease with hexameters, which too often seem to us to deteriorate into doggerel or light verse:

Ballad by Hans Breitmann

Der Noble Ritter Hugo
    Von Schwillensaufenstein,
Rode out mit shpeer and helmet,
    Und he coom to de panks of de Rhine.

Und oop dere rose a meermade,
    Vot hadn't got nodings on,
Und she say, "Oh, Ritter Hugo,
    Vhere you goes mit yourself alone?"
                 [C. G. Leland]³

To our ears, the six-foot line breaks too easily into trimeters, and it may be for this very reason that when Renaissance translators cast about for English equivalents for the hexameters of Virgil and Ovid they came up with Surrey's pentameters and Golding's septameters: lines of five or seven feet that, being odd in number, won't fold squarely in the middle.)

THORPE'S DEDICATION

The dedication, by Thomas Thorpe, of his 1609 quarto edition of Shakespeare's *Sonnets*, is very familiar, and a source of endless, sometimes foolish, speculation. "TO.THE.ONLIE.BEGETTER.OF.THESE.INSVING.SON-NETS.MrW.H.ALL.HAPPINESS.AND.THAT.ETERNITIE.PROMISED.BY. OVR,EVER-LIVING.POET.WISHETH.THE.WELL-WISHING.ADVENT-

---

3. *The New Oxford Book of Light Verse*, ed. Kingsley Amis (1978), 111.

VERER.IN.SETTING.FORTH." G. Blakemore Evans, in the *New Cam-bridge Shakespeare* edition, paraphrases this as: "To the sole inspirer of these following sonnets, Master W. H., all happiness and that eternity promised by our ever-living poet [William Shakespeare], wishes the well-wishing adventurer [Thomas Thorpe] in publishing [these sonnets]."[4] But Evans is perfectly aware that any number of critics have proposed that for his word *inspirer* one could also advance the word *procurer*, since there seem to be grounds to suspect that the poems were published without the poet's consent, or even knowledge or supervision. The publisher, by this theory, would be dedicating his edition to that unnamed person who se-cured for him the copies of the poems that served his compositors. As for the candidates for Mr. W. H., Oscar Wilde, assuming that the dedication was Shakespeare's own, posited a young actor in Shakespeare's company, named, perhaps, Willie Hewes or Hughes. Other candidates are William Herbert, third Earl of Pembroke, and Henry Wriothesley, third Earl of Southampton ("his initials being reversed as initials sometimes were in prefatory matters," Evans observes). These persons all come under the heading and theory of "inspirer." As for "procurer," the list of candidates includes Southampton's stepfather and Shakespeare's brother-in-law. George Chalmers (1742–1825), a Scottish antiquarian, was the first person to propose that Thorpe's dedicatee, Mr. W. H., was the one who provided the publisher with the text of Shakespeare's sonnets. He also seems to have believed that, quite apart from any puzzles about the identity of Mr. W. H., the first 126 sonnets, seemingly addressed to a man, were in fact addressed to Queen Elizabeth, arguing that "Elizabeth was often consid-ered a man" and, as Sam Schoenbaum explained, "was termed a prince rather than a princess by Drant, Spenser, Ascham and Bacon."[5] In ad-dressing the Commons, she also spoke of herself as a "prince." In *The Civ-ilization of Europe in the Renaissance* (1944), John Hale describes the bur-dens of monarchy, and how irksome they were to a number of rulers of the period, reporting that "Elizabeth I told parliament in 1601 that 'to be a King and wear a crown is a thing more glorious to them that see it than it is pleasant to them that bear it'" (80). Clearly we are edging our way into the sexier aspects of the sonnet. And these aspects crop up right at the start

---

4. *The New Cambridge Shakespeare, The Sonnets*, ed. G. Blakemore Evans (1996), 115.
5. Samuel Schoenbaum, *Shakespeare's Lives* (1991), 168.

of the sonnet's literary life, though many regard Shakespeare's addresses to the young man as anything from embarrassing to needing to be explained away (hence Queen Elizabeth) or, contrarily, a major claim for the ranks of gays.

SEXUAL AMBIGUITIES

The sonnet came into existence during the feudal period, which was also the time of the flourishing of "courtly love," and these two forms, of literary and amatory art, bore a very strange resemblance to each other. The posture of a lover towards his lady was meant to be identical with that of a vassal towards his lord: a posture of absolute submission, even to the point of death. As C. S. Lewis points out in *The Allegory of Love* (1936), "The lover is always abject. Obedience to his lady's slightest wish, however whimsical, and silent acquiescence in her rebukes, however unjust, are the only virtues he dares to claim." Modern psychologists would regard such an attitude with suspicion and alarm; but there is more to come. The lover, Lewis goes on to explain, addresses his beloved as *midons*, "which etymologically represents not 'my lady' but 'my lord'" (2), implying any number of sexual complexities. If we encounter among Shakespeare's sonnets one addressed to "the master-mistress of my passion" (20), and find him abasing himself with the declaration, "Being your slave, what should I do but tend / Upon the hours and times of your desire" (57), we must ask ourselves whether he is following medieval conventions, expressing a personal psychological predisposition, or using the first of these as a pretext for the second. Though there is nothing in the way of solid evidence, this is clearly not a decision that should be allowed to rest on the personal whim or caprice of the reader.

This is only the beginning of the issue of sexual elements in sonnets. To be sure, as time went on, sonnets were employed for many topics that had nothing whatever to do with love in either its carnal or exalted forms. Milton's upon the massacre at Piedmont, Wordsworth's composed on Westminster Bridge, Keats' on Chapman's Homer or on the Elgin Marbles or to Sleep have nothing whatever to do with love or sex. Nevertheless, the form is still firmly associated with love, as Robert Frost knew when writing "The Silken Tent," with its very deliberate antique appurtenances. And one has only to consider the subjects of the English Renaissance sonnet sequences: after Sidney's *Astrophel and Stella*, Spenser's *Amoretti*, and

Daniel's *Delia,* we have Fulke Greville's *Caelica,* Giles Fletcher's *Licia,* Henry Constable's *Diana,* William Percy's *Sonnets to the Fairest Coelia,* Bartholomew Griffin's *Fidessa More Chaste than Kind,* and Robert Tofte's *Laura.* And from the time of Dante and Petrarch the sonnet was not just a form into which any subject might be poured but one so firmly identified with the amorous and the erotic that when Shakespeare arranges for Romeo and Juliet to speak to each other for the first time at the masked ball their exchanges are framed as discrete segments of sonnets. And in *Love's Labour's Lost,* Armado, confessing that he has fallen in love, exclaims, "Assist me, some extemporal god of rhyme, for I am sure I shall turn sonnet," that is, turn to the writing of sonnets.

THE PENALTY FOR SEXUAL PLEASURE

The third quatrain of Shakespeare's Sonnet 73 contains a curious, buried erotic note.

> In me thou seest the glowing of such fire
> That on the ashes of his youth doth lie,
> As the death-bed whereon it must expire,
> Consumed with that which it was nourished by.

In these lines the fire, once brilliant, has dimmed; its ashes now serve to extinguish the very flames that, when those ashes were wood, they fed. What is implied by this is that the vigor and liberties of our youth are precisely what serve to bring us, by the excess of that youthful folly and energy, to our demise. We are thus self-executed. This is very close to the idea John Donne expressed in his poem "A Farewell to Love," which concerns the diminishment of our lives by the length of a day each time we engage in sex.

> Ah cannot we,
> As well as cocks and lions jocund be,
> After such pleasures? Unless wise
> Nature decreed (since each such act, they say,
> Diminisheth the length of life a day)
> This; as she would man should despise
> The sport,

> Because that other curse of being short,
> And only for a minute made to be
> Eager, desires to raise posterity.

The Latin expression "omne animal post coitum triste," attributed alternately to Aristotle and to Galen, refers to postcoital sadness which was said to blight all creatures except, in one account, turtles, and in another, cocks and lions. A. J. Smith, in his excellent Penguin edition of Donne (1971), glosses this third stanza of the poem with this paraphrase: "Unless wise Nature ordained this disillusioning inadequacy of our sexual experience to stop us killing ourselves by repeated sexual acts, as we urgently seek to overcome the brevity of our own lives by begetting children." Aulus Celsus, a Roman encyclopedist of the reign of Tiberius, who wrote on a multitude of topics from agriculture and military science to jurisprudence, survives only in his medical books, for which he was known as the *Cicero medicorum.* This work, lost sight of during the Middle Ages, was rediscovered in the early Renaissance, and his medical views were highly respected. Among these was his declaration: "The ejaculation of semen is the casting away of part of the soul." In *The Unfortunate Traveler,* Thomas Nash writes, "The sparrow for his lechery liveth but a year."

MALE FRIENDSHIP AND LOVE

The sexual atmosphere in America at the start of the twenty-first century is both more open, with people emerging from their closets, and more embattled, with problems about military service and rancor from the religious right. In such circumstances it's difficult to try to imagine a society in which values differed greatly from our own. For a very long time, from antiquity up through the Renaissance, the friendship between men was regarded, on high authority, to be not merely the equal of but superior to the love between the sexes. Not just the dialogues of Plato, but Aristotle's *Ethics,* the biblical story of David and Jonathan, the Homeric account of Achilles and Patroclus, the classical legend of Damon and Pythias, Montaigne's essay on Friendship, Malory's *Morte D'Arthur,* all advance this idea. Shakespeare uses this idea very wittily in *The Merchant of Venice.* At the very moment when Portia and Bassanio plight their troth and agree to marry, Bassanio is urgently summoned to try to help his friend Antonio, who has been arrested for failure to keep his bond with Shylock. The two lovers, Portia and Bassanio, are therefore abruptly and shockingly parted at the very moment they become united. Act III, scene iv begins with Lorenzo commending Portia for her strength of character in being able to accept so gracefully the departure of the man to whom she has just given herself and all her considerable goods. She replies to him with a statement about the physical similarities of men to one another that has behind it the authority of Aristotle:

> I never did repent for doing good,
> Nor shall not now: for in companions
> That do converse and waste the time together,
> Whose souls do bear an equal yoke of love,
> There must be needs a like proportion
> Of lineaments, of manners, and of spirit,
> Which makes me think that this Antonio,
> Being the bosom lover of my lord,
> Must needs be like my lord. If it be so,
> How little is the cost I have bestowed
> In purchasing the semblance of my soul
> From out the state of hellish cruelty!

This argument of physical similarity will be used at the play's end as a bawdy jest when, about to wed Bassanio at last, Portia tells Antonio that if ever her husband breaks his oath in any way, she will call upon Antonio to take up all the offices and functions of her husband. But, on the serious side, Shakespeare has one more argument in behalf of the "superior" love of man for man, and it comes from Scripture, specifically from John 15:13, which in the King James translation goes, "Greater love hath no man than this, that a man lay down his life for his friends." The sensational trial scene in the play is a plain demonstration that Bassanio and Antonio are prepared to make precisely this Christlike sacrifice for one another. And the Gospel tells us unambiguously there is "no greater love." But apart from the Bible, there was established custom and patterns of behavior sanctioned by society. In *The Waning of the Middle Ages* (1954) Johan Huizinga tells us that

> even intimate relations in medieval society are rather paraded than kept secret. Not only love, but friendship too, has its finely made up forms.

Two friends dress the same way, share the same room, or the same bed, and call one another by the name of "mignon." It is good form for the prince to have his minion [*i.e.,* mignon]. We must not let the well-known case of Henry III of France affect for us the ordinary acceptance of the word "mignon" in the fifteenth century. There have been princes and favorites in the Middle Ages too who were accused of culpable relations—Richard II of England and Robert de Vere, for instance—but minions would not have been spoken of so freely, if we had to regard this institution as connoting anything but sentimental friendship. It was a distinction of which the friends boasted in public. On the occasion of solemn receptions the prince leans on the shoulder of his minion, as Charles V at his abdication leaned on William of Orange. To understand the duke's sentiment towards Cesario in *Twelfth Night* we must recall this form of sentimental friendship, which maintained itself as a formal institution till the days of James I and George Villiers. (54–55)

THE BODY/SOUL ANTAGONISM

Of all the Shakespeare sonnets, 151 ("Love is too young to know what conscience is") may be the bawdiest—some would say the crudest and most vulgar. Its erotic character is certainly beyond question. In a comic-erotic parody of the vassal's submission and fidelity to his *midons,* Shakespeare subordinates his soul to his body, and his body, synecdochically represented by his penis, is made subservient to the mistress to whom the poem is addressed. The sonnet depends on traditional, even biblical, contentions and competitions between the soul and the body, including St. Paul's formulation in Galatians 5:17, "For the flesh lusteth against the Spirit, and the Spirit against the flesh: and these are contrary the one to the other." Many poems, from medieval times forward, reflected this opposition. Negotiations between the realms of the body and soul, the carnal and the spiritual, as well as sometimes daring and dramatic substitutions of these domains one for the other, became a familiar literary device of the metaphysical poets and a staple of Baroque and Mannerist art of the Counter Reformation.

Initially, of course, the early Christian Church was eager to consecrate or sublimate all vestiges of pagan rites and rituals, associated as they had been with heresy and the gross appetites of the body. In that cause a number of ancient holidays were "baptized," or "christened," maintaining their original places in the seasonal calendar but altered by edict to a new character in the calendar of the church. For example, the Roman feast of Lupercalia, observed on the second of February, had been dedicated to the god Pan and was observed as a fertility festival, celebrating both the growing of crops and the sexual vitality of humans and the other creatures. The festival coincided with the resumption of work in the fields after the rigors of winter (which, in Italy, were milder and briefer than in the northern part of the United States). But in the year 492 Pope Gelasius I abolished the Lupercalia and substituted for it a sublimated version known as the *festa candelarum,* or Candlemas, dedicated to celebrating the Presentation of Christ at the Temple and the Purification of the Virgin Mary. Its ritual involved a procession of lighted candles meant to symbolize the light of the Divine Spirit.

But the negotiations, however much they may first have centered on the purification and consecration of what had formerly been carnal and pagan, in the course of time were found to flow in the reverse direction as well: that is, in behalf of the desacralization of the spiritual and the holy. Though he is no doubt being "playful and ingenious" in composing a lover's argument in a seduction poem aimed at the sexual conquest of a lady, Donne was following what had become established literary practice when he wrote, "Love's mysteries in souls do grow, / But yet the body is his book," as though the mysteries of the soul could best (perhaps only) be explicated by consulting the text of the body, and a strict respect for the spirit demanded that it be "incarnated" in the act of sexual union, thus "piously" mimicking the Incarnation of the Spiritual Godhead in the body of the person of Christ and through the agency of the Virgin's womb. Donne's metaphor turns the body into the Bible. Those who find this shocking, and possibly blasphemous, might do well to consult what Mario Praz has to say at the beginning of his chapter on "Richard Crashaw and the Baroque" in *The Flaming Heart* (1958):

> There exists in Rome, in the church of Santa Maria della Vittoria, a work of art which may be taken as the epitome of the devotional spirit of the Roman Catholic countries in the seventeenth century. Radiantly smiling, an Angel hurls a golden dart against the heart of a woman saint

languorously lying on a bed of clouds. [The Italian name for this work of art is *Santa Teresa in Orgasmo*.] The mixture of divine and human elements in this marble group, Bernini's Saint Teresa, may well result in that "spirit of sense" of which Swinburne, who borrowed the phrase from Shakespeare, was so fond of speaking. Spirit of sense as in that love song the Church had adopted as a symbol of the soul's espousals with God: The Song of Solomon, which actually in the seventeenth century was superlatively paraphrased in the *coplas* of Saint John of the Cross. Inclined as it was to the pleasures of the senses, the seventeenth century could not help using, when it came to religion, the very language of profane love, transposed and sublimated: its nearest approach to God could only be a spiritualization of the senses. (204)

Yet this was not a seventeenth-century innovation. Critics and scholars have pointed out that both the late medieval poets of southern France as well as Dante and Petrarch in Italy had spiritualized their love of women, often elevating the beloved to virtually discarnate conditions of perfection and abasing themselves with professions of profane desire. It has furthermore been observed that this adoration of the purified beloved incontestably owed much to the cult of Mariolatry. According to Teresa McLean, "*Amor* (love), *dilectio* (pleasure or delight), and *caritas* (charity) were the basic elements of monastic love, both fraternal and divine, in early medieval Europe, and become the elements of the courtly love cult which swept western Europe in the twelfth and thirteenth centuries, applying all the devices of the love for Mary in heaven to the love of a woman on earth."[6] The influence can be found as late as Baudelaire's "To a Madonna." As for Donne, he was able to bring the spiritual and the carnal into so close (and, for some, uncomfortable) a balance that he could end a sonnet of self-inquisition and acknowledged sinfulness with a prayer amounting to something like a desire for sexual violation (with a pun embodied in the word "ravish") in these words addressed to God: "Take me to you, imprison me, for I / Except you enthrall me, never shall be free, / Nor ever chaste, except you ravish me."

Something of the same unease or discomfort has disturbed at least some of the viewers of Bernini's angel and saint. While Hippolite Taine

---

6. Teresa McLean, *Medieval English Gardens* (1980), 131.

found this marble Teresa "adorable" in the religious sense of the word, Mrs. Anna Brownwell Jameson (1794–1860), whose writings are largely devoted to religious art, wrote, in *Legends of the Monastic Orders as Represented in the Fine Arts,* "All the Spanish pictures of S. Teresa sin in their materialism; but the grossest example—the most offensive—is the marble group of Bernini in Santa Maria della Vittoria in Rome. The head of S. Teresa is that of a languishing nymph, the angel is a sort of Eros; the whole has been significantly described as 'a parody of Divine Love.' The vehicle, white marble,—its place in a Christian church,—enhance all its vileness. The least destructive, the least prudish in matters of art, would here willingly throw the first stone."[7] Mrs. Jameson was not alone in finding a familiarly carnal aspect to Bernini's statue. Wittkower reports: "When the debonair Charles de Brosses, *président des parlements* of Dijon, wrote the memoirs of his Italian journey of 1739–40, he observed of Bernini's S. Teresa, considered the epitome of divine rapture, 'If this is divine love, I know it well.'"[8] But this complicated matter may perhaps best be summarized by a remark made in a letter by W. B. Yeats: "One feels at moments as if one could with a touch convey a vision—that the mystic vision & sexual love use the same means—opposed yet parallel existences."[9]

7. Mrs. Jameson is quoted by Augustus J. C. Hare, *Walks in Rome,* 2 vols. (1897), 2:30.
8. Rudolf and Margot Wittkower, *Born under Saturn* (1963), 180.
9. Letter of May 2, 1926, in Richard Ellman, *Yeats: The Man and the Masks* (1958), 260.

Sidney and the Sestina

Among the many charms of the fourteenth edition of the *Encyclopaedia Britannica*, few can match the pleasure of pure surprise and unexpectedness conveyed by the bold, unequivocal assertion: "The earliest sestina in English was published in 1877 by Edmund Gosse." In *The Countess of Pembroke's Arcadia* (1593) Sir Philip Sidney, usually credited with being the first to employ the form in English, introduces three sestinas, each distinctly different from the others. The first (70), beginning "Since wailing is a bud of causefull sorowe," is formally the most conventional, disposing its terminal words according to what have become orthodox permutations. This established form, which is commonly attributed to the invention of the troubadour poet Arnaut Daniel, was quickly imitated by, among others, Dante, whose sestina "to the 'stony lady, Pietra'" is a superb example of the form. William A. Ringler Jr., editor of the Clarendon Press edition of Sidney's *Poems* (1962), remarks that "the monotonous sevenfold repetition [if the final tercet is taken into account] of the same six words is appropriate to a song of mourning, though Puttenham, the only Elizabethan critic to recognize the form, commented that 'to make the dittie sensible will try the makers cunning'" (416).

I take these two points to be of the greatest importance and to be potentially self-contradictory. The sevenfold repetitions of the same terminal words does indeed invite a monotony that best accompanies a dolorous, despairing, and melancholy mood, such as would possess Dante's forlorn lover in his stony sestina. The repeated words, inexorable in their order, seem designed to convey a state of obsession, and of gloomy obsession especially. But what Puttenham calls "the makers cunning" may refuse to yield to that mood of solitary and redundant woe or may at the very least wish to vary it through the "cunning" of art. "To make the dittie sensible" is presumably to put those redundancies in a meaningful and effective order; but it may also mean "to create something that is acutely felt; markedly painful or pleasurable." And a number of poets have taken up the challenge of composing sestinas that defy the mood of desolation seemingly imposed by the rigid monotony of terminal repetition. One such poem is Pound's bravura "Sestina: Altaforte," which gleefully rejoices in violence and sanguinary enthusiasm, while another is Ashbery's comic "Farm Implements and Rutabagas in a Landscape." Such poems specifically repudiate the more familiar and lugubrious music of most sestinas.

The Sestina

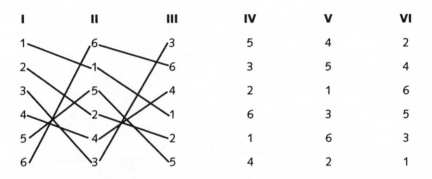

Fig. 1 The sestina, whose invention is commonly attributed to the troubadour poet Arnaut Daniel (c. 1180–1210), is composed of six stanzas of six lines each (hence its name) and is usually concluded by a tercet, three lines, each of which contains two of the six terminal words that end the lines throughout the poem. The permutations of these terminal words is rigidly and inflexibly fixed, and this diagram is meant to illustrate the pattern. Roman numerals indicate *stanzas;* arabic numbers represent the *words* that terminate individual lines. Once the six terminal words ending the six lines of the first stanza have been established, the order in which they will appear throughout the entire length of the poem is absolutely determined. Let *TW* represent *terminal word.* Then the *TW* of the final line of stanza I becomes the *TW* of the first line of stanza II. The *TW* of the first line of stanza I falls into second place in the next stanza. The penultimate *TW* (5) of stanza I becomes the third *TW* of stanza II, while the second *TW* of the first stanza takes fourth place in the second. Of the two remaining *TWs*, the latter (4) becomes the fifth of the following stanza, while the remaining *TW* (3) falls into last place in stanza II. The word order for the third—and all ensuing stanzas—is attained by deriving its *TW* order by repeating this exact reordering by which the second stanza was derived from the first. Observe that when the *TWs* of the final (VI) stanza are subjected to this reordering, they return to the order of the first stanza—1, 2, 3, 4, 5, 6—as Sidney's double sestina illustrates.

Of Sidney's two remaining sestinas in the *Arcadia*, one of them (76) departs from canonical form by employing rhymes, its first stanza's terminal words deployed in this order: *light, treasure, might, pleasure, direction, affection*. The subsequent stanzas redeploy these words according to the canonical system of sestinas, and the poem, in keeping with tradition, is mournful and valedictory throughout. T. S. Eliot, too, wrote a rhymed sestina, though, unlike Sidney's, his rhyming links did not occur within the limits of a single stanza. In "The Dry Salvages," third of the *Four Quartets,* Eliot rhymes all the first lines of his six stanzas with one another and proceeds to do the same with the terminal words of the five remaining lines. Again, the poem is mournful and even dirgelike.

Possibly inspired by Sidney's example, Spenser, in the mouth of August in *The Shepherd's Calendar,* included a sestina of his own, though varying the permutations of the terminal words in an original and unexceptionable order of his own. Both in its music and its substance, Spenser's poem seems to owe much to Sidney's pioneering efforts in the field, as Spenser's first stanza makes clear.

> Ye wasteful woods! bear witness to my woe,
> Wherein my plaints did oftentimes resound:
> Ye careless birds are privy to my cries,
> Which in your songs were wont to make a part:
> Thou, pleasant spring, hast lulled me oft asleep,
> Whose streams my trickling tears did oft augment.

The stanzas that follow faultlessly pursue the doleful tone that had become the ensign of sestinas and at which both Sidney and Dante had excelled. But as his scholiast, E. K., tells us, Spenser's August eclogue is indebted to another tradition as well: one that derives from Theocritus and Virgil, not because the classical poets wrote sestinas (which they did not) but because they wrote poems in the form either of debates or contests between competing shepherds, the competition sometimes judged by a third. In Virgil's Third Eclogue, Dameotas and Menalcas compete in a singing contest judged by Palaemon, while in the Fifth Eclogue Mopsus and Menalcas compete in mourning for Daphnis. In the Eighth Eclogue, Damon pines for Nysa ("Farewell, O / my woods. I'll hurl me into the

sea / From yonder peak") while Alphesiboeus pines for Daphnis. Theocritus, too, in his Sixth, Eighth, and Ninth Eclogues, presents competitions in song and in lyric devotion to a lost or absent loved one.

These independent traditions, of sometimes lighthearted and cheerful rivalry and competition between shepherds for excellence at song, and
the other, melancholy and painful song of lament that seemed especially
to belong to the sestina, are surpassingly braided, musically and dramatically intertwined in Sidney's masterful and brilliant double sestina, "Yee
Gote-heard Gods," one of the greatest achievements of English Renaissance poetry.

The Fourth Eclogues
71

Strephon   Klaius

Strephon   Yee Gote-heard Gods, that love the grassie mountaines,
Yee Nimphes which haunt the springs in pleasant vallies,
Ye Satyrs joyde with free and quiet forrests,
Vouchsafe your silent eares to playning musique,
Which to my woes gives still an early morning:
And draws the dolor on till wery evening.

Klaius   O *Mercurie,* foregoer to the evening,
O heavenlie huntresse of the savage mountaines,
O lovelie starre, entitled of the morning,
While that my voice doth fill these wofully vallies,
Vouchsafe your silent ears to plaining musique,
Which oft hath *Echo* tir'd in secret forrests.

Strephon   I that was once free-burges of the forrests,
Where shade from Sunne, and sport I sought at evening,
I that was once esteem'd for pleasant musique,
Am banisht now among the monstrous mountaines
Of huge despaire, and foule affliction's vallies,
Am growne a shrich-owle to myself each morning.

Klaius	I that was once delighted every morning,
	Hunting the wilde inhabiters of forrests,
	I that was once the musique of these vallies,
	So darkened am, that all my day is evening,
	Hart-broken so, that molehills seeme high mountaines,
	And fill the vales with cries in steed of musique.
Strephon	Long since alas, my deadly Swannish musique
	Hath made it selfe a crier of the morning,
	And hath with wailing strengh clim'd highest mountaines:
	Long since my thoughts more desert be than forrests:
	Long since I see my joyes come to their evening,
	And state throwen downe to over-troden vallies.
Klaius	Long since the happie dwellers of these vallies,
	Have praide me leave my strange exclaiming musique,
	Which troubles their daye's worke, and joyes of evening:
	Long since I hate the night, more hate the morning:
	Long since my thoughts chase me like beasts in forrests,
	And make me wish my selfe layd under mountaines.
Strephon	Me seemes I see the high and stately mountaines,
	Transforme themselves to lowe dejected vallies:
	Me seemes I heare in these ill-changed forrests,
	The Nightingales doo learne of Owles their musique:
	Me seemes I feele the comfort of the morning
	Turnde to the mortal serene of an evening.
Klaius	Me seemes I see a filthie clowdie evening,
	As soon as Sunne begins to clime the mountaines:
	Me seemes I feele a noysome sent, the morning
	When I do smell the flowers of these vallies:
	Me seemes I heare, when I doo heare sweete musique,
	The dreadful cries of murdred men in forrests.
Strephon	I wish to fire the trees of all these forrests;
	I give the Sunne a last farewell each evening;

I curse the fiddling finders out of Musicke:
With envie I doo hate the loftie mountaines;
And with despite despise the humble vallies:
I doo detest night, evening, day, and morning.

Klaius　　Curse to my selfe my prayer is, the morning:
My fire is more, than can be made with forrests:
My state more base, then are the basest vallies:
I wish no evenings more to see, each evening;
Shamed I hate my selfe in sight of mountaines,
And stoppe mine eares, lest I growe mad with Musicke.

Strephon　　For she, whose parts maintainde a perfect musique,
Whose beawties shin'de more than the blushing morning,
Who much did passe in state the stately mountaines,
In straightnes past the Cedars of the forrests,
Hath cast me, wretch, into eternall evening,
By taking her two Sunnes from these darke vallies.

Klaius　　For she, with whom compar'd, the Alpes are vallies,
She whose lest word brings from the spheares their
　　musique,
At whose approach the Sunne rase in the evening,
Who, where she went, bare in her forhead morning,
Is gone, is gone from these our spoyled forrests,
Turning to desarts our best pastur'de mountaines.

Strephon　　These mountaines witness shall, so shall these vallies,
and *Klaius*　　These forrests eke, made wretched by our musique,
(in unison)　　Our morning hymne this is, and song at evening.

Sidney's was not the first double sestina. He had for a model one published by Sannazaro in his *Arcadia* of 1502, as David Kalstone reminds us in his excellent book *Sidney's Poetry* (1965), where, among other valuable observations, he remarks, "Sidney had seen the possibilities in Sannazaro's organization of the sestina as a dialogue, employing pairs of stanzas, statement and response" (77). And explaining the dramatic context in which

Sidney's Strephon and Klaius render their joint poem, Kalstone declares, "The only shepherds not native to Arcadia, they are clearly to be distinguished from the rustics of the eclogues. They have come to the seacoast to mourn the departure of Urania for the island of 'Cithera'" (72). According to Ringler, "Strephon and his older friend Klaius" were "two gentlemen who had become shepherds because of their love for a maiden named Urania, 'thought a Shepherdes Daughter, but in deede of farr greater byrthe.' She never returned their affection, and some months previously had departed from Arcadia, leaving orders that they should remain there until they had received written instructions from her" (416). It is of supreme importance that "the island of 'Cithera' (Cythera) was reckoned as sacred to the goddess Venus, who was from thence surnamed *Cytherea*" and who rose, as some suppose, from the sea near its coast, near Laconia in Peloponnesus. The island was traditionally supposed to be joyfully devoted to the rites of Venus and to be a continuous festival of erotic pleasures. Strephon and Klaius, therefore, have specifically been denied entrance into the sacred domain of Requited Love.

Cithera, that realm of "gratified desire," to use Blake's words, has played a long and troubled role in the human imagination. It figures in a famous painting (or, rather, in two versions of one painting) by Jean-Antoine Watteau, called *Departure for the Island of Cythera*. One commentator, Michael Schwarz, notes:

> For the *Departure* Watteau brightened his palette, using pastel shades of pink and pale blue. Thin clouds and diaphanous veils of mist spread across the picture, increasing the delicacy of the pastel shades and making them glow even more intensely. Pairs of happy lovers are grouped around the boat. One cavalier is helping his lady to embark while she coquettishly tucks up her skirt. They are joined by a second couple, who go arm-in-arm, while others, who are seen approaching the boat, are indulging in friendly or amorous banter. The boat itself, which is enveloped in haze and surrounded by numerous putti, looks almost as if it had descended from the roseate heavens. These putti, the charming envoys of Venus, rise up high into the air as they sport and play with one another. The sailors, who were seen straining on their oars in the first painting of the *Departure*, were omitted from the later version so as not to mar the perfect serenity of the arcadian

setting. In this work, ancient mythology and eighteenth-century custom combine to form a world that appeared entirely real to Watteau's contemporaries. They themselves become dream figures and in Watteau's paintings they were able to enter into the lofty regions of the supernatural world previously denied to them. By daring to rise to these heights, by entering into this world of the imagination, they were able to transfigure their own everyday world. But would not this illusion be followed by profound melancholy? There is a hint of melancholy in all of Watteau's painting; it is one of the characteristic features of his style.[1]

In his brilliant and precocious survey of the tonal inflections and molecular linkages of English poetry, *Seven Types of Ambiguity* (1947), William Empson has set down with remarkable compression some of the wisest and most probing comments on Sidney's double sestina.

The poem beats, however rich its orchestration, [Empson declares] with a wailing and immovable monotony, forever upon the same doors in vain. *Mountaines, vallies, forrests; musique, evening, morning;* it is at these words only that Klaius and Strephon pause in their cries; these words circumscribe their world; these are the bones of their situation; and in tracing their lovelorn pastoral tedium through thirteen repetitions, with something of the aimless multitudinousness of the sea on a rock, we seem to extract all the meanings possible from these notions. (14–15)

He proceeds to show how richly and emotionally equivocal are those six terminal nouns, colored in each case by the speaker's state of mind, as they might reflect a former state of happiness or a present state of deprivation. "Mountaines," for example, can be great challenges to feats of strength but also a barrier, if not a weight beneath which one would be crushed to extinction. They can also become metaphorical "mountaines / of huge despair," and their metamorphosis from the literal to the figurative provides one of the most unnerving elements in the poem, as the distracted minds of the speakers seem to approach an almost suicidal phantasmagoria. In

---

1. Michael Schwarz, *The Age of the Rococo* (1971), 14–15.

the same way, *vallies* are protected and secure and yet are cut off from other, and perhaps better, kinds of life. Their lowness befits humility, but also the status of the unworthy. "Forrests" are places of danger, but a challenge to the courageous hunter, a place where stately cedars grow, where the mixed "musique" of Nightingales and Owles are both to be heard. "Morning" is the time of rising and hopefulness, unless you are so depressed that it can only renew the misery of the day before. "Evening" at least ought to bring rest after the labors of the day and the serenity of sleep after waking hours of misery, but evening is also a fading of light and hope as well, and Strephon claims that he has been cast "into eternal evening."

I have summarized here, far too briskly, the analysis Empson bestows on these six crucial nouns, demonstrating how slippery and unstable they become in a troubled mind. It is worth noting also that of the six, four are naturally mated pairs: morning is matched with evening, mountains with vallies. (Forests and music are not natural mates except by a pastoral extension; forests are places where shepherds dwell and, according to tradition, sing their songs to one another; music belongs to those pastoral songs but also to the more musical creatures of the forests, the nightingales. Used ironically, music is applied to the cacophony of owls or the painful groans of the tormented lovers.)

But there is something about this beautiful work of Sidney's that calls for further comment and, in my view, seems to challenge all the criticisms brought against it under the heading of *monotony*. Not that such a claim is baseless; Ringler, Empson, and I have used the word, which, given the mandatory repetition of six terminal words in an inflexible order, seems hard to avoid. But clearly one of the first resolves of any poet who sits down to compose a sestina must be the evasion, by whatever cunning at his disposal, of that imposition of monotony. The poet's job is somehow to divert us by his drama, his pathos, his crescendo of emotional forces and to encourage us to feel that in one way or another each succeeding stanza will provide some novelty or a wholly new perspective. Few readers have any patience for monotonous poetry, and good poets, of whom Sidney was certainly one, are perfectly aware of this.

We may usefully return to a remark of David Kalstone's quoted earlier: "Sidney had seen the possibilities in Sannazaro's organization of the sestina as a dialogue, employing pairs of stanzas, statement and response." Nothing, it seems to me, so characterizes Sidney's double sestina as the

careful (one may say "musical") parallelisms of its paired stanzas, and there
cannot be the least doubt that Sidney expected this to be noticed and ap-
preciated. The first two paired stanzas contain the same line ("Vouchsafe
your silent eares to playning musique"), which appears in the fourth line
of the first stanza and the fifth line of the second. It serves as a link between the speakers, Strephon and Klaius, but in each case the addressee is
different, Strephon addressing the earth deities, Pan, Priapus, nymphs,
and satyrs, while Klaius addresses the celestial deities, including Diana,
who is, poignantly, both goddess of the hunt, and thus protectress of the
shepherds, and also goddess of chastity and enemy of the love they both
profess. The fact that one addresses earthly, and the other, heavenly deities
may be seen as either something that divides them or, more probably, as
two aspects of prayer that together embrace the entire cosmos.

The second pair of stanzas begin with identical wording: "I that was
once." They also contain two lines which, while not identical, bear a close
resemblance to one another. The third line of the first of these two stanzas
("I that was once esteem'd for pleasant musique") resembles the third line
of the next stanza ("I that was once the musique of these vallies"). The two
stanzas, moreover, describe the transformation of the two speakers from a
former freedom, happiness, and capacity for musical performance to a present state of utter despondency, wretchedness, and complete remove from
that realm of music that both belonged to the pastoral life and betokened
the harmonies of nature and of love. The parallelisms are worth a moment's
thought. The second speaker, always Klaius, does not seem intent on best-
ing his companion in misery by outstripping Strephon in the severity of his
complaints. This is not a competition in who suffers most or who can utter the most miserable complaint. The paired stanzas are instead like musical variations on each other, and the parallelisms can suggest that Klaius
quite humbly takes his cue from the speech of Strephon that precedes his
own. This will be especially striking in the next two stanzas.

The first, fourth, and fifth lines of both the fifth and sixth stanzas begin "Long since," and both speakers are now concerned to explain that
they have been languishing in the depths of misery for some time.
Strephon's music has turned "deadly" and "Swannish," indicating not
only his expectation of an imminent death but also that one who was
"once esteem'd for pleasant musique" is now incapable of anything but
unmelodious complaint. Klaius, too, confesses that "the happie dwellers

of these vallies, / Have praide me leave my strange exclaiming musique."
The two pastoral swains have lost possession of the one art that most
characterized their profession. It is just possible that Sidney is making a
subtle joke at his own expense—or at the expense of the traditional dolorous monotony of sestina writers. In any case, these two stanzas have
become profoundly more "inward," describing states of mind that are
neurotic, self-tormenting, and virtually suicidal. They are preparing us
for the even more hallucinatory stanzas that immediately follow.

The seventh and eighth stanzas are rich in parallelisms. The first, third,
and fifth lines of both stanzas begin with almost identical phrases, subtly
varied. The first of the stanzas offers them as "Me seemes I see," "Me seemes
I heare," and "Me seemes I feele," while the following stanza alters the sequence to "see," "feele," and "heare." These stanzas are morbidly surrealis-
tic, reminding one of the weird and primitive terrors in the paintings of
Piero di Cosimo. All the familiar values have been transvalued; nothing is
stable or familiar; the minds of Strephon and Klaius are profoundly disoriented and given over to a morbidity that is the more frightening in that we
have seen it grow in intensity right before our eyes in the course of the poem.

The ninth and tenth stanzas are the most violent in their self-
condemnation. The first line of the ninth ("I wish to fire the trees of all
these forrests") is echoed but altered in the tenth's second line ("My fire is
more, than can be made with forrests"). The ninth's second line ("I give
the Sunne a last farewell each evening") is restated in other terms in the
tenth stanza's fourth line ("I wish no evenings more to see, each evening").
These two stanzas are, in their way, more terrible than the immediately
preceding ones, since they have abandoned the protective devices of hal-
lucination and are now coldly and self-condemningly analytical. Someone
who can say unflinchingly, "I doo detest night, evening, day, and morning," has covered all possibilities and left himself nowhere to exist. And
someone who says of himself that I "stoppe mine eares, lest I growe mad
with Musicke" has acknowledged that the single most powerful and celestial cure for the soul not only avails him nothing but drives him to further disorder. This important reference to music as that harmonious and
reconciling power that was thought to operate throughout the universe,
presented as unavailing at the end of the tenth stanza, leads now to the un-
folding of the mystery: the revelation in the final two full stanzas of the
source and cause of all this disorder.

Both Strephon and Klaius begin "For she," but Strephon continues with the musical metaphor that closed the previous stanza: "For she, whose parts maintainde a perfect musique." Her "parts" are certainly bodily parts, assembled in a perfect proportion. They are also her attainments, as "a woman of parts." But they are of course the musical parts of a composition scored for the interweaving and combination of several musical "parts," as in a madrigal or motet. Both Strephon and Klaius, in praise of their departed mistress, return once again to images of utter perfection, to the very sovereign "music of the Spheres," but only at the end to contrast that perfection to the desolation in which both of them now must, as it seems, forever abide.

I should like to claim that the poem escapes, at least to some degree, the charges of tedium and monotony by virtue of the intensifying psychological drama it presents, and through the pairing, yet the distinct separateness of the two speakers, who seem to take up cues from one another, to enhance and embroider upon the other's statements. No doubt this point must not be made too forcefully. The terminal words are, if anything, more insistently repetitive in a double sestina than in a single one. And yet I can't imagine anyone wishing this poem to be shorter than it is. It fills out all its stanzas with richness and variety; its tone is not merely dolorous but terrifying, unbalanced, and in fact not so remote from that self-disgust that characterizes certain late-nineteenth- and early-twentieth-century poems.

But if this poem, and some other sestinas, can be defended against accusations of monotony, it is more difficult, I think, to protect them from the claim that they tend to be dramatically static. They present a frame of mind, sometimes an interestingly disturbed frame of mind but usually an obsessed one, which tends to harp on the same sad theme, varying it in certain ways but never departing from it, bound to it by the shackles of those six terminal words. Indeed, something about those compulsory repetitions seems to prohibit the possibility of a sestina developing in the way other kinds of poems do. A familiar lyric freedom is curtailed, richly detailed descriptions are pretty firmly excluded, narrative development, above all, is difficult to accommodate. The resources of the sestina seem astonishingly circumscribed.

But if these seem to be characteristic limitations imposed by the form itself, we are entitled to be the more delighted, impressed, and gratified when we find some poet intelligent and ingenious enough to overcome them. And such triumph over the form has been attained not once but twice by Elizabeth Bishop, in two sestinas which otherwise bear very little resemblance to each other.

A Miracle for Breakfast

At six o'clock we were waiting for coffee,
waiting for coffee and the charitable crumb
that was going to be served from a certain balcony,
—like kings of old, or like a miracle.
It was still dark. One foot of the sun
steadied itself on a long ripple in the river.

The first ferry of the day had just crossed the river.
It was so cold we hoped that the coffee
would be very hot, seeing that the sun
was not going to warm us; and that the crumb
would be a loaf each, buttered by a miracle.
At seven a man stepped out on the balcony.

He stood for a long minute alone on the balcony
looking over our heads toward the river.
A servant handed him the makings of a miracle,
consisting of one lone cup of coffee
and one roll, which he proceeded to crumb,
his head, so to speak, in the clouds—along with the sun.

Was the man crazy? What under the sun
was he trying to do, up there on his balcony!
Each man received one rather hard crumb,
which some flicked scornfully into the river,
and, in a cup, one drip of the coffee.
Some of us stood around, waiting for the miracle.

I can tell what I saw next; it was not a miracle.
A beautiful villa stood in the sun

And from its doors came the smell of hot coffee.
In front, a baroque white plaster balcony
added by birds, who nest along the river,
—I saw it with one eye close to the crumb—

and galleries and marble chambers. My crumb
my mansion, made for me by a miracle,
through ages, by insects, birds, and the river
working the stone. Every day, in the sun,
at breakfast time I sit on my balcony
with my feet up, and drink gallons of coffee.

We licked up the crumbs and swallowed the coffee.
A window across the river caught the sun
as if the miracle were working, on the wrong balcony.

This extraordinary, elusive, but mesmerizing poem has something of
the nature of a parable about it. Shy of making anything that might be
taken for grandiose religious claims, Bishop wryly referred to it as "my De-
pression, or Bread Line poem." But however much it may apply to enfee-
bled social programs for the poor, it also clearly seems like a secular equivalent of the Feeding of the Multitudes and of the Eucharist. The mystery
of the poem (an analogy, perhaps, to the mystery of the Feeding or the Eucharist) resides in that completely unexpected vision of wealth and comfort
embodied in the "beautiful villa that stood in the sun." Its "galleries and
marble chambers," its "baroque white plaster balcony" make it sound positively Spanish or Italian in its luxury and altogether alien from the vague,
unspecified, but generally bleak setting of the rest of the poem. The "vision," for that's what it is, of a palatial glamour is attained by the minute,
close-up inspection of a crumb of bread that was handed out in the Bread
Line. As I have commented elsewhere, "The complex intricacies of the 'architecture' of the risen dough, its baroque perforations, corridors, its struts,
ribs and spans of support, all form the 'beautiful villa' with the 'white balcony.' And this bread, and the vision it provides, have come into existence
by the miraculous and infinitely patient workings of that evolutionary process that Darwin (one of Miss Bishop's favorite writers) and other natural-

ists have so painstakingly recorded. The process itself is awesome enough to be characterized, not improperly, as a 'miracle.'"[2]

But the chief point about this sestina is that it is composed as a kind of narrative. It begins at six o'clock in the morning; a crowd has gathered, waiting to be fed; the first ferry of the day had only just crossed the river. It is depressingly cold out. At seven a man appears on the balcony; a servant joins him, handing him "the makings of a miracle." The man proceeds to distribute individual crumbs and drops of coffee. How are we to make sense of the dispensing of these Loaves and the Fishes? In any case, action is going on by specific stages, as in a religious ritual. And this action precipitates a "vision" and concludes on a note of cheerful, contented comfort and serenity. The familiar bane of "monotony" and "stasis" has been triumphantly overcome. As it is once again in another Bishop sestina.

Sestina

September rain falls on the house.
In the failing light, the old grandmother
sits in the kitchen with the child
beside the Little Marvel Stove,
reading the jokes in the almanac,
laughing and talking to hide her tears.

She thinks that her equinoctial tears
and the rain that beats on the roof of the house
were both foretold in the almanac,
but only known to a grandmother.
The iron kettle sings on the stove.
She cuts some bread and says to the child,

It's time for tea now; but the child
is watching the teakettle's small hard tears
dance like mad on the hot black stove,
the way the rain must dance on the house.
Tidying up, the old grandmother
hangs up the clever almanac

2. Anthony Hecht, *Obbligati: Essays in Criticism* (1986), 123.

on its string. Birdlike, the almanac
hovers half open above the child,
hovers above the old grandmother
and her teacup full of dark brown tears.
She shivers and says she thinks the house
feels chilly, and puts more wood in the stove.

It was to be, says the Marvel Stove.
I know what I know, says the almanac.
With crayons the child draws a rigid house
and a winding pathway. Then the child
puts in a man with buttons like tears
and shows it proudly to the grandmother.

But secretly, while the grandmother
busies herself about the stove,
the little moons fall down like tears
from between the pages of the almanac
into the flower bed the child
has carefully placed in front of the house.

Time to plant tears, says the almanac.
The grandmother sings to the marvelous stove
and the child draws another inscrutable house.

Superficially, nothing much happens in this little drama with its two
characters who don't interact in any dynamic way on the wet September
afternoon they share. But their situation and their setting is laden with
omens and portents. The grandmother not only weeps in the very first
stanza but must also struggle to conceal her tears from the child. Something predestined governs the season of the tears, as of the rainy weather,
and the recurrent cycles of the year return annually to the anniversaries of
past events. Conspicuous by their absence from this poem are the inter-
vening generation between child and grandmother; where are the parents?
The drawing of a house by a child is regarded as an expression of a desire
for security, though this child seems touchingly unaware that anything is
out of order. The almanac prophesies tears to come, presumably when the

child is old enough to understand what the grandmother already knows and is trying to conceal. The drama is the more poignant and terrible for being so carefully understated and evaded. Were the parents killed in some accident? How long ago? Did they die in some other terrible way? The poem allows us a terrifying latitude in which to let our imaginations range. The almanac, half open, is even likened to a bird, traditionally a prophetic creature. The drama is the more eloquent for its spareness. But the point is that a story has been unfolded in a way that is not usually to be found in a sestina.

We may take the story as a poetic fiction, and it stands up with perfect form and as much clarity as the situation permits. But biographers have been diligent in pointing out that Elizabeth Bishop's father died in 1911, when she was eight months old. His death so deeply disoriented his wife, the poet's mother, that she was in and out of hospitals and rest homes for the next five years, after which, in 1916, she was permanently hospitalized in Nova Scotia, and Elizabeth never saw her mother again, though her mother lingered on as a patient until 1934. There was a time when I felt that this documentary information was required for a full understanding of the poem. I no longer think so. The poet has created a heartrending drama, from which she has deftly removed herself except as the artificer of the work. And it remains to be said that the challenge she has set for herself is the more demanding in that this poem is composed in tetrameter, rather than pentameter, lines, thus making even tighter than usual the constrictions of the six-linked chain of terminal words she has bound herself with.

Let me cite one more, this one by James Merrill, that clearly defies the lugubrious, monotonous, static condition usually associated with sestinas.

Tomorrows

The question was an academic one.
Andrey Sergeyvitch, rising sharp at two,
Would finally write that letter to his three
Sisters still in the country. Stop at four,
Drink tea, dress elegantly and, by five,
Be losing money at the Club des Six.

In Pakistan a band of outraged Sikhs
Would storm an embassy (the wrong one)
And spend the next week cooling off in five
Adjacent cells. These clearly were but two
Vital details—though nobody cared much for
The future by that time, except us three.

You, Andrée Meraviglia, not quite three,
Left Heidelberg. Year, 1936.
That same decade you, Lo Ping, came to the fore
In the Spiritual Olympics, which you won.
My old black self I crave indulgence to
Withhold from limelight, acting on a belief I've

Lived by no less, no more, than by my five
Senses. Enough that circus music (BOOM-two-three)
Coursed through my veins. I saw how Timbuctoo
Would suffer from an undue rainfall, 2.6
Inches. How in all Fairbanks, won-
der of wonders, no polka would be danced, or for

That matter no waltzes or rumbas, although four
Librarians, each on her first French 75,
Would do a maxixe (and a snappy one).
How, when on Lucca's greenest ramparts, three-
fold emotion prompting Renzo to choose from six
Older girls the blondest, call her *tu,*

It would be these blind eyes hers looked into
Widening in brief astonishment before
Love drugged her nerves with blossoms drawn from classics
Of Arab draughtsmanship—small, ink-red, five-
Petalled blossoms blooming in clusters of three.
How she would want to show them to someone!

But one by one they're fading. I am too.
These three times thirteen lines I'll write down for
Fun, some May morning between five and six.

I think there can be no denying that this brilliant, quasi-inebriated poem is crowded with incident: so much for the charge that sestinas are doomed to be static. Just what all the activities add up to is open to some conjecture, though apparently the speaker regards himself as someone gifted with "second-sight" and concludes by foretelling the composition of the poem he has just finished. There is a wonderful mixture of milieux, events, of the fictive and the seemingly factual, astonishingly disparate and unrelated characters (we learn no more of Andrée Meraviglia, Lo Ping, or Renzo than of Eliot's Mr. Silvero, Madame de Tornquist, or Fräulein von Kulp) as if in a sort of hashish trance, yet with enough tantalizing detail (the Chekhovian particulars of the first stanza seem comfortingly familiar) to persuade us, however briefly, that we are in a world we ought to recognize. This is emphasized by the curious historical context provided for some of the events; dates, statistics are urged upon us. And these historical and factual details have a bearing, however obscure, on the whole notion of futurity (the poem is titled "Tomorrows"), of "second-sight," and the significance of all events, whether large or small, real or fictive, since even fictive worlds are made to resemble the one we commonly think of as "real." All this is accomplished with a bravura sense of ridiculousness, though not, I would claim, with frivolity. The question of how much we think we understand our lives and the lives of others and the course of history itself lurks among the interstices of this poem.

It hardly seems necessary to defend the poem against the charge of lugubriousness, so I turn directly to the indictment of monotony, commonly brought against sestinas because of the inexorable repetitions of the terminal words. Merrill has ingeniously taken the first six ordinals for this purpose, but he has escaped his fetters by the ingenious use of homophones, homonyms, word fragments and hyphenation, and various sorts of wordplay. In the last line of the third stanza he forms the sound of *five* by borrowing the *f* at the end of "belief" and joining it to "I've." This is neither unprecedented nor irresponsible. In the 32nd stanza of Hopkins' great and deeply serious poem "The Wreck of the *Deutschland*," the poet rhymes "unconfessed of them," with "the breast of the" and borrows the needed *m* sound from the word that begins the following line, "Maiden." To be sure, when Hopkins takes this kind of "liberty" it is done in behalf of the pulse and pressure entailed by a lyrical rapidity of action and meditation, which makes use of free-flowing enjambments. Merrill, too, has his enjambments ("won-/der of wonders"), but they are dictated by easy colloquial speech rather than by Hopkins' kind of agitation. No doubt a certain lightness of tone and intention is a necessary ingredient in Merrill's versatility, but it may be claimed that he has for once emancipated the sestina from some of the bondage traditionally imposed upon it. He serves cheerfully to remind such commentators as Ringler, Empson, and others that monotony, obsession, and gloom are not the destined trademarks of all sestinas.

At the same time, the possibilities Merrill discovers in no way offer disrespect to the still more virtuosic achievements of Sidney's great double sestina. Sidney's world in the *Arcadia* was a world he shared in part with Ariosto and many other writers of pastoral romance, in which the lament of the forlorn lover enjoys a long and honorable history. The "tradition" of frustrated and unreciprocated love was popular in the Middle Ages and is to be found in Wyatt and Surrey as well as in the belated "Definition of Love" by Marvell. Great as was the pain described by these poets, it was thought to confer the spiritual benefits of mortification, and "the poets in the circle of Charles D'Orléans," Huizinga tells us, "compared their amorous sadness to the sufferings of the ascetic and the martyr. They called themselves 'les amoureux de l'observance,' alluding to the severe reforms which the Franciscan order had just undergone."[3] Writing of this tradition from its medieval origins, Maurice Valency observes, "Love was . . . a special hazard of the poet's trade, for it was chiefly out of the pain of love that poetry was made. The symptoms of love-illness, *hereos*, Chaucer called it, were often described; from the *Viaticum* of Constantious Africanus in the eleventh century to Burton's *Anatomy* in the seventeenth, the love-syndrome varied little. In the initial stages the symptoms were not unbecoming—sleeplessness, loss of appetite, loss of flesh, and the characteristic pallor of the lover, together with love of solitude and a tendency to weep, particularly when music was played. But, we are told, unless the disease was cured, it became dangerous—the lover might pass into a melancholy, waste away, and die."[4] And these are the perils to which, in his *Arcadia*, Sidney exposes Strephon and Klaius. They were the perils of an abundant literature.

---

3. Johan Huizinga, *The Waning of the Middle Ages* (1954), 111.
4. Maurice Valency, *In Praise of Love* (1961), 154.

On Henry Noel's "Gaze Not on Swans"

Gaze Not on Swans

Gaze not on swans in whose soft breast
A full hatcht beauty seems to rest,
Nor snow which falling from the sky
Hovers in its virginity.

Gaze not on roses though new blown
Grac'd with a fresh complexion,
Nor lilly which no subtle bee
Hath rob'd by kissing chemistry.

Gaze not on that pure milky way
Where night vies splendour with the day,
Nor pearls whose silver walls confine
The riches of an Indian mine:

For if my emperesse appears
Swans moultring dy, snow melts to tears,
Roses do blush and hang their heads
Pale lillyes shrink into their beds;

The milky way rides past to shrowd
Its baffled glory in a clowd,
And pearls do climb unto her eare
To hang themselves for envy there.

So have I seene stars big with light,

Proud lanthorns to the moone-ey'd night,
Which when Sol's rays were once display'd
Sunk in their sockets and decay'd.

I first came upon this lovely lyric in the five-volume anthology *Poets of the English Language,* edited by W. H. Auden and Normal Holmes Pearson, where it is attributed unambiguously to William Strode. So much did I delight in it that I eventually found a copy of the *Poetical Works of William Strode* (1907), edited by Bertram Dobell, who is by no means as confident as the anthologists regarding the poem's authorship. Indeed, Dobell says, "The only authority for attributing the lines . . . to Strode, is that the poem is mentioned in Dr. Grosart's list of his poems. It, however, is included in [Henry] Lawes' 'Ayres and Dialogues' where it is assigned to Henry Noel, who would seem therefore to have the best claim to it" (129). I am persuaded by the judgment of Dobell, the opinion of Lawes, and my own instincts gained from reading the whole of Strode's poetic output, in the course of which he never rises to anything like the level of this extraordinary poem. (Neither, for that matter, do any of the poems confidently attributed to Edward De Vere, Earl of Oxford, approach the qualities of the songs, poems, or plays of Shakespeare, though obstinate Oxfordians continue to suppose the former wrote the works of the latter.)

Yet, remarkable as it is, this poem belongs to a little genre of elaborate quatrain-verse compliments to ladies that would include a number of other graceful and elegant poems: Thomas Carew's song "Ask me no more," Sir Henry Wotton's poem in praise of Princess Elizabeth, daughter of King James, who married the Elector Palatine in 1619, "You meaner beauties of the night," and Sir Francis Kynaston's "Do not conceal thy radiant eyes." These poems, all extravagant praises of a woman's beauty in grand and hyperbolic terms, go out of their way to ring changes upon the commonplace similes, the conventional imagery, that crop up in so much Elizabethan and Jacobean poetry, and venture instead upon a more daring originality and a more arresting kind of metaphor. Three of four of them (those by Carew, Kynaston, and, as I now think, Noel) are framed rhetorically as injunctions: "Ask me no more," "Do not conceal," "Gaze not on swans," while Wotton's poem quivers with aristocratic disdain for the presumptions of the natural beauties of the universe. Beyond this point their rhetorical strategies vary, and in my view Noel's is the most imaginative, subtle, and satisfying.

In its first stanza, the "full hatcht beauty" of swans is itself nearly miraculous, suggesting, first, the purity and cleanliness of a birth that emerges unsoiled from within the solid confines of an eggshell, and the sort of birth unique to Athena, come forth full-blown and mature from the brow of Zeus. The swan's "soft breast" has all manner of feminine, erotic, maternal associations, and its whiteness does not even require mention, though it is obviously meant to chime with the whiteness of the snow mentioned in the third and fourth lines. That this snow "hovers in its virginity" betokens its lightness, its vulnerability, its purity, and its danger of imminent extinction.

It may be precisely the mutability of the snowflake's existence that suggests to the poet those twin emblems of female beauty, the rose and the lily, that trace their way back to the Song of Songs, and became standard symbols of feminine beauty, found in such lyrics as Campion's "There is a garden in her face, / Where roses and white lilies grow." Though conventional (the rose was regarded as the most perfect of flowers and associated with the Blessed Virgin, as well as with the royal English houses of York, Lancaster, and Tudor, while the lily was associated with the royal dynasties of France and with Christ as a descendant of Kings David and Solomon), the very word *complexion* in connection with the rose summons not only something like the epidermal beauty of a woman but "the combination of qualities in a certain proportion" (*OED*) that would make it the most perfect, and regal, of flowers.

The "kissing chemistry" of the bee suggests the amorous, yet pure, sexual activity of pollination, the delicacy of the bee's address to the flower's nectar, a chemistry that will convert this precious fluid into the honey of the hive. Between humans, of course, kissing would accelerate the "chemistry" of mutual attraction, but even in the purer context of bee and flower a slight residue of the voluptuous lingers on. There remains a question about the word "rob'd," which can be (for want of certainty) construed as either "robbed" or "robed," and can be made sense of either way. The lily is robbed of its nectar by the bee, but it is also robed in its glory (Matt. 6) by the bee's chaste sexual offices. If "no subtle bee" has performed this office, the chastity of the lily remains intact, and its beauty must be attributed to more supernatural causes.

The Milky Way is described as "pure" (and in this it resembles all the preceding imagery) because the stars are the visible signs of the angelic hosts of heaven. (Looking up at a starlit night, Hopkins exclaims, "O look at all the fire-folk sitting in the air!") It is, in the words of another poet, a *via lactaea*, suggestive of heavenly nourishment and supernatural abundance, and the first two lines of the third stanza equate it with, as well as distinguish it from, the splendor of the day. As for the pearls in the following lines, they, too, are biblical in the freight and wealth they carry, recalling the pearl beyond price (Matt. 13); yet at the same time the pearl was regarded as one of the few adornments of the otherwise naked Venus in her role as goddess of profane love. The pearl is here brilliantly described as hiding its full value invisibly within its exterior walls, and in fact the nacreous luster of pearls derives from its capacity at once to absorb and to reflect light, and its interior layers of accretion are the central ingredients of its beauty and worth. It should go without saying that in Elizabethan and Stuart times the richest of gems were all thought to come from the Orient, and this is why Columbus undertook to find a new route there, and believed he had succeeded.

We have now considered three stanzas, each with a double, or mated, set of subjects: swans and snow in the first, roses and lilies in the second, stars and pearls in the third. There now follow two (not three) stanzas in which the beauty of all six emblems mentioned is disqualified when contrasted with the sudden appearance of "my emperesse." It is of no great consequence whether this woman is indeed an empress or simply the empress of the poet's heart. On what authority I do not know, Dobell, who lists the poem under "Doubtful Pieces" as regards attribution, nevertheless gives it the title of "On His Mistresse." But we must recall that the word *mistress* had many meanings in Renaissance parlance, some of them utterly devoid of any sexual overtone; a mistress was one who could command any service from her devotee, and Wotton's poem is called "On His Mistress, the Queen of Bohemia" and was composed in a spirit of perfect propriety. In stanzas four and five all the beauties that have been listed now wilt, wither, withdraw in shame or, finally, brilliantly, commit suicide out of envy. The bloom and health of the rose is, by juxtaposition with the woman's beauty, converted to a blush of embarrassed mortification; the lilies, by the same shaming context, are forced to withdraw into their beds as George Herbert observed: "as flowers depart / To see their mother-root, when they have blown; / Where they together / All the hard weather, / Dead to the world, keep house unknown." And the Milky Way, which earlier had vied with the splendor of the day, now hastens to veil itself. The pearls become the sacrificial, self-immolated adornments of the woman, as pearls traditionally bedecked Venus herself and certain royal ladies, prominently including Elizabeth. (The royal portraits of the queen almost invariably present her as adorned with a very firmament of pearls.) I have never ceased to admire the asymmetry in which the six admonitions of three stanzas are justified in two. This swift triumph of demonstration represents an easy and perfect confidence. But more importantly, it leaves a final stanza for the clinching, irrefutable analogue.

The last stanza seems to me a triumph. Its excellence consists in a brilliant, delicate balance and combination of ingredients, all at the service of a grand concluding fanfare of praise, as undeniable as a sunrise. The stars are "big with light" in several senses, and it is important, I think, to discover these ways gradually, by gradation, in the order they are likely to occur. First, they look big in darkness because, as Gilbert Murray reports Epicurus observing, "the Sun was probably about as big as it looked, or perhaps smaller; since fires at a distance generally look bigger than they are."[1] The stars also look big because of the pride attributed to them in the second line of the stanza. There they dignify themselves as guides, indispensable cicerones to the Cyclopean, one-eyed, "moone-ey'd" night. The stars are proud of their torch-bearing, illuminating office and are swollen with pride. The night, being one-eyed, requires guidance, and when full the moon resembles a single ocular pupil, especially of someone made at least partially blind by cataracts. The word "sockets" in the final line is meant first of all to recall the "lanthorns" of the second line. The first three definitions of "socket" in the *Oxford English Dictionary* are all mechanical in character, and the third is: "The part of a candlestick or chandelier in which the candle is placed." If we can assimilate, as I think we are expected to do, the idea of lanterns to the sockets of candlesticks, the sudden presence of the sun in the third line both overwhelms the light of the candles

1. Gilbert Murray, *Five Stages of Greek Religion* (1955), 108.

and melts them by its warmth, and both powers account for the candles' sinking and decaying. But the last line seems also to convey an almost grotesque memento mori flavor, and in this it recalls the first line of the stanza. Those stars were "big with light" as a woman is said to be "big with child." But the potentially rich pregnancies of starlight, when overpowered by the birth of a new sun at dawn, are effaced, doomed, and destroyed, as night itself becomes the skull of what had been a dazzling nocturnal beauty. The sovereignty of the newborn sun is inaugurated by the skeletal diminution of the old, inferior order.

I remember once recommending this poem to a lady who was generally skilled in reading poetry, taught it, and whose approval I thought it reasonable to count upon. She was repelled by the last stanza, and could find in it nothing but the image of a skull from which the eyes and flesh had withered away. I think this reading, while probably present in some latent way, is meant to be altogether secondary to the sense of the socket as receptacle to a candle, and we are meant chiefly to envision the melting of wax and effacing of candlelight by the superior brilliance and warmth of the sun. For me, in any case, the poem works like a charm.

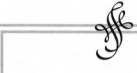

PART II

Technique in Housman

A. E. Housman continues to fascinate us, both as a poet and as a man, separately and jointly. He has been made the subject of a play by Tom Stoppard, and in a poem W. H. Auden called him "the leading classic of his generation." Though this is too little known, he was the author of some brilliant and uniquely funny light verse, of which one of the lesser known deserves quotation but demands a small explanatory note. It seems intended as a dig at Henry Wadsworth Longfellow, and more specifically at that poet's "Excelsior," and, still more specifically, at Longfellow's rather pretentious account of what he thought his poem was doing. The poem was intended, Longfellow wrote, "to display, in a series of pictures, the life of a man of genius, resisting all temptations, laying aside all fears, heedless of all warnings, and pressing right on, to accomplish his purpose. His motto is Excelsior—'higher.' He passes through . . . the rough cold paths of the world; . . . disregards the happiness of domestic peace and sees the glaciers—his fate—before him. He disregards the warning of an old man's wisdom and the fascinations of woman's love."[1]

There's much more silliness to Longfellow's explanation, but what I have provided will go some way to justifying the following lines by Housman.

> The shades of night were falling fast,
>   And the rain was falling faster,
> When through an Alpine village passed
>   An Alpine village pastor:
> A youth who bore mid snow and ice
>   A bird that wouldn't chirrup,

---

1. H. W. Longfellow, from a letter to C. K. Tuckerman.

And banner with the strange device—
    "Mrs. Winslow's soothing syrup."

"Beware the pass," the old man said,
    "My bold, my desperate fellah;
Dark lowers the tempest overhead,
    And you'll want your umbrella;
And the roaring torrent is deep and wide—
    You may hear how loud it washes."
But still that clarion voice replied:
    "I've got my old galoshes."

"Oh, stay" the maiden said, "and rest
    (For the wind blows from the nor'ward)
Thy weary head upon this breast—
    And please don't think I'm forward."
A tear stood in his bright blue eye,
    And he gladly would have tarried;
But still he answered with a sigh:
    "Unhappily, I'm married."

(An index of Housman's mischief in this poem may be seen in the fact that the odd-numbered lines are almost exact duplications of Longfellow's poem, and Housman's ridicule has been confined correctly to the even lines.) Housman failed his final examinations as an Oxford student but went on to become a professor of Latin at Cambridge, where he was celebrated for the savagery of his attacks on other classicists. This testiness was even exhibited in discourse with people he had nothing especially against. Lunching at Cambridge with André Gide in 1917, Housman amiably began the conversation with, "Comment expliquez-vous, M. Gide, qu'il n'y a pas de poésie française?"[2] He was also, as has now become well known, a tormented closet homosexual who had the profound misfortune to fall in love with an undeviatingly heterosexual fellow undergraduate. He was a textual scholar of abstruse and difficult ancient poetry (Greek as well as Latin) who wrote verses of a deceptive simplicity, most of them

2. *Anthologie de la Poésie Française*, ed. André Gide (1949), viii.

sorrowful and tragic in character and tone. Others labeled him a Stoic, but
he denied this, declaring instead, "In philosophy I am a Cyrenaic or ego-
istic hedonist, and regard pleasure of the moment as the only possible motive for action. [This sounds oddly like Walter Pater.] As for pessimism, I
think it almost as silly, though not as wicked, as optimism. George Eliot
said she was a meliorist: I am a pejorist"[3] (that is, someone who believes
the world is steadily getting worse). Thomas Hardy felt compelled to defend himself against the same charges, writing in his "Apology" to *Late
Lyrics,* "What is to-day, in allusions to the present author's pages, alleged
to be 'pessimism' is, in truth, only . . . 'questionings' in the exploration of
reality, and is the first step toward the soul's betterment, and the body's
also."

There is danger in a too-facile identification of Housman's tragic tone
with the notion of his projection of his own unhappiness upon the young
men whose misfortunes compose the substance and drama of much of his
poetry; and to think of his own frustrated sexual longings as either exor-
cised or obscurely gratified by the premature deaths of those who serve as
his (usually) nameless heroes. But in fact he based his poems, even down
to elegiac moods of lamentation, on a pastoral tradition of simple pleasures and perennial misfortunes that was essentially a classical inheritance
and that can no more surely be said to mask feelings of his own than can
the poems of Theocritus, Moschus, Bion, or Virgil. As a prefatory verse
to *More Poems* (1936), Housman wrote, shrewdly though not at his best,

> They say my verse is sad: no wonder;
>   Its narrow measure spans
> Tears of eternity, and sorrow,
>   Not mine, but man's.
> This is for all ill-treated fellows
>   Unborn and unbegot,
> For them to read when they're in trouble
>   And I am not.

I want to examine two fine and characteristic poems of Housman, with
particular attention to their technique. Technical skill counts importantly

---

3. Quoted in W. H. Auden, *Forewords and Afterwords* (1973), 327.

in Housman's poems, their language constrained by deliberate simplicity, their rhymes almost pedestrian, or never experimental. Yet subtleties of nuance, the delicate inflections of meaning, are obtained in his poems by unobtrusive but elegant technique. The first poem is number XX from *Last Poems.*

> The night is freezing fast,
>   To-morrow comes December;
>   And winterfalls of old
> Are with me from the past;
>   And chiefly I remember
>   How Dick would hate the cold.
>
> Fall, winter, fall; for he,
>   Prompt hand and headpiece clever,
>   Has woven a winter robe,
> And made of earth and sea
>   His overcoat for ever,
>   And wears the turning globe.

Among the pleasures of the first stanza are what may be thought of as the asymmetrical relations between the syntax and the poem's stanzaic form. Both stanzas are composed of six trimeter lines, rhyming *abcabc,* with a feminine ending for the second and fifth lines. The rhyme scheme, visually emphasized by the indentations of the second, third, fifth, and sixth lines, presents a musical group of three lines matched by three others. But the syntax of this first stanza is divided into three units of two lines each. The first two lines form a unit that concludes with a semicolon; so do the next two; and the final two end with a period. These contrasting, almost competing, designs are part of a complex, disorienting music that will express itself in what is almost cosmic dislocation by the time the poem ends.

But to stick to the first stanza, "fast" can mean both *rapidly* and *firmly;* when something is frozen fast it is unbudging. Yet night is destined to get still colder, because December has not yet begun. There is worse to come. "Winterfalls" is the poet's coinage, not a dictionary word, presumably allowable on the precedent of *nightfall,* which perhaps it subliminally recalls, not only by way of justification but also as a tonal element. Lines three and four concentrate the "freezing" element of the opening, multiplying and intensifying it by repetition of who knows how many previous winters. The final two lines are full of eloquent and quiet suggestion. We are invited into a special confidentiality when we hear the diminutive "Dick," as though sharing privileged intimacy with the speaker, who, in his preoccupation, may have forgotten that we don't know the man in question; or he may be speaking to himself, unaware that we are overhearing him. Anyway, after the comparative impersonality of the first four lines, the introduction of "Dick" in what seems an ambiguously wistful context shifts and narrows the focus of our attention. There is calculated mystery about the recollection of "How Dick would hate the cold." That detail, recalled in isolation, could mean that the speaker has lost track of Dick, that Dick has moved away. It may even recall the frigidity of Shakespeare's "When icicles hang by the wall, / And Dick the shepherd blows his nail." At all events, Dick is associated with something of the past, linked in the speaker's mind with winter.

The second stanza, following the same formal pattern of rhyme and meter, is nevertheless syntactically completely different from—and directly contrasted to—the first. It is composed of two units separated by a semicolon. And setting aside for the moment the first three words, it is a fluent, single, graceful movement towards its virtually orchestrated finale. Let us first consider those opening words: "Fall, winter, fall." They recall "winterfalls" from the first stanza. They further suggest that for Dick, who so hated the cold, there were no balms or comforts in spring and summer; with him they counted for nothing.[4] In his view there was only winter and the promise of winter. Facing such inexorable repetitions of misery, Dick has, at least symbolically, taken things into his own hands. Because no one else has helped him, he has become his own tailor, making himself a "robe" (a noble garment) that is also an "overcoat" (sensible protection from the cold). These vestments are made of earth and sea, and now he "wears the turning globe." Because he has made raiment for himself of the whole world, this clothing imagery demands that we think of him as *at the center* of the world, with the world draped upon and around him, because we

---

4. Richard Wilbur has plausibly suggested to me that "Fall, winter, fall" may be voiced in the imperative mood, as an intemperate petition, meaning, "Go ahead; do your worst."

are at the center of the clothes we wear. This has the effect of making him the world's new axis. And whereas we are in the habit of thinking of the world as turning upon an axis that passes through its center, now we must revise that idea or substitute for it another in which the world pivots upon a small point near its surface, and the entire universe is unbalanced thereby. We may assimilate this dislocation of the universe to the profound effect Dick's death has had upon the speaker or simply to the sheer power of metaphor. But we are not yet done with the metaphors and symbols of this second stanza.

I said earlier that Dick had, at least symbolically, taken things into his hands by making the world his clothing, robe and overcoat. But he has been complimented on his cunning and skill ("Prompt hand and head-piece clever"), and there is at least the possibility that he literally took things into his own hands by committing suicide—though this is only the most extreme possibility. The locution may be quite innocent as when, in "To an Athlete Dying Young," Housman writes, "Smart lad, to slip betimes away / From fields where glory does not stay." Here we are clearly to understand an ironic compliment to the wit and shrewdness of one who has been clever enough to die young. This would be no more than a conventional classical notion to be found, among other places, in Herodotus' account of the views of Solon, wisest of the Greeks, in discussion with the fabulously wealthy King Croesus. The king asked his visitor who was the happiest man he had ever seen, expecting to be told it was no other than Croesus himself. Instead Solon answered with the names of two unknowns, "two young men of Argos, Cleobis and Biton." These he singled out because after the two had performed an act of piety and great exertion, their mother prayed to the goddess Hera that they be rewarded with "the greatest blessing that can fall to mortal man," whereupon, Solon reported, they fell asleep in the temple of the goddess and never woke again, "a heaven-sent proof of how much better it is to be dead than alive."

In Housman's poem we are allowed to suspect that the pangs of winter are more than simply seasonal discomforts; they stand for the inexorable miseries of which the Greek tragedians, Sophocles in particular, made noble and complaining music, asserting that the best of fates is never to have been born and the next best is to die young. This is the view of the chorus of old men in *Oedipus at Colonus* (composed when Sophocles himself was ninety). Speaking of the plight of Oedipus, they declare: "A whole winter of miseries now assails him, / Thrashes his sides and breaks over his head."

I find Housman's poem strong and effective, and I find its music compelling. But there is another poem that aimed at the same sort of music—with almost the same rhymes and intending something of the same effect, though patently without Housman's success. I will quote its first stanza.

> I cannot but remember
>   When the year grows old—
> October—November—
>   How she disliked the cold!

This comes from a seven-stanza poem that repeats this stanza at its end. It is by Edna St. Vincent Millay. It was not based on Housman's, having been published in 1917, whereas his appeared in 1922. And it would be foolish to think he had been influenced by her; they seem only to have come up with a few of the same elements, but his were worked out with infinitely more care and art. Her poem, published in *Renascence and Other Poems* under the title "When the Year Grows Old," is feeble and sentimental to an embarrassing degree. The woman in Millay's poem simply dislikes cold weather, thereby missing out on the beauties of winter:

> Oh, beautiful at nightfall
>   The soft spitting snow!
> And beautiful the bare boughs
>   Rubbing to and fro!
>
> But the roaring of the fire
>   And the warmth of fur,
> And the boiling of the kettle
>   Were beautiful to her.

There are many ways to distinguish between the techniques of Housman's poem and Millay's, but I will settle for a simple one. Hers contains six exclamation points; his none.

The other poem by Housman I want to discuss is number XV from the same book. He has given it a title: "Eight O'Clock."

He stood and heard the steeple
    Sprinkle the quarters on the morning town.
One, two, three, four, to market-place and people,
    It tossed them down.

Strapped, noosed, nighing his hour,
    He stood and counted them and cursed his luck;
And then the clock collected in the tower
    Its strength, and struck.

The time of the title is the hour of execution, and the poem's drama, moving from the simple and passive "He stood and heard" to the more conscious and active "He stood and counted," is an incremental, almost minuscule development. This slight shift reflects other slight shifts from the first to the second stanza; yet slight though they be, they are decisive. In a poem in which *time* is the governing instrument of drama, it should not surprise us to have metrical skills commanding our attention, and Housman is abrupt and forceful in his use of meter, stretching regularity to its limits. The two stanzas are formal duplicates of each other, but meter and metaphor make all-important distinctions.

    The first lines of both stanzas are meant as trimeters with feminine endings—it is likely that *hour* is meant to be disyllabic because of its rhyme with *tower* though British speech slurs *tower* to a single syllable; however, we have the precedent of the first stanza to justify our supposition.[5] The first of these lines is conventional: two iambs and an amphibrach. Yet the first line of the second stanza, with its initial three strong accents, is a bold stroke, and unsettling. We have, to a degree, been prepared for it, but it startles nevertheless. We had best, however, return to the beginning and

---

5. The *OED* declares *hour* to be monosyllabic, though it allows *tower* to be either one or two syllables. It was Housman's virtually unfailing practice to make his stanzas uniform in regard to both rhyme and meter, so that a given line with a feminine ending in one stanza would require conformity in the corresponding lines of all other stanzas. But Housman seems to wish to have it both ways in regard to the *hour / tower* rhyme. In number XV of *More Poems* he could write:

    Tarry, delight, so seldom met,
        So sure to perish, tarry still;
    Forbear to cease or languish yet,
        Though soon you must and will.

take note that as far as the "action" of the poem is concerned, it is an un-
equal contest between the man and the clock. He can do nothing but
stand, count, and curse. The behavior of the clock, by contrast, is more
varied, interesting, and powerful. In the first stanza, it "sprinkles" the
quarters on the morning town. The verb is lustrous, beneficent, fertile. (It
must, alas, be pointed out that "quarters" had for Housman no monetary
significance, which is a wholly American association. No small coins are
being dispersed.) The "quarters" are the quarter-hours, and if, as seems
implied, we are hearing Westminster chimes, each quarter will be indicated by a four-note musical phrase—sixteen notes altogether for the full
hour—and enough for a generous sprinkling. The town is identified as the
"morning town" because the hour is 8:00 A.M., not specified in the title but
the canonical hour of executions, with its own brutal judicial irony, bringing the beginning of everyone else's day into opposition with the end of
the condemned man's life. The buried sense of *mourning* lies dimly audible to the imagination. And then come two spondees, tolling the death
of the condemned. They are powerful, relentless, equal in emphasis, and
they disrupt the generally iambic character of the poem's otherwise conventional meter. They are, nevertheless, still quarter-hours, "tossed" down
as though they were some largesse, as indeed to all but the condemned
they are.

In the first stanza the clock's location is "the steeple," with its sacred associations of piety and prayer. The spondees of the first stanza serve as
prelude to the three strong beats that begin the second stanza, and the alliteration of "noosed" and "nighing" connects them as though the very
rope of his execution was drawing the condemned man towards his destined end. The first stanza had carefully numbered the quarter-hours—
four of them—and now in the second stanza what the condemned man

---

> By Sestos town, in Hero's tower,
>   On Hero's heart Leander lies;
> The signal torch has burned its hour
>   And sputters as it dies.

Here lines 1 and 3 of the first stanza demand that *tower* / *hour* be reckoned as monosyllables.
But in the poem under discussion these words occupy the positions given to *steeple* / *people* in
the first stanza; and Housman's practice strongly suggests that he wanted these lines to end on
unaccented syllables.

counts is not the four quarters, which, in Westminster fashion, went before as musical prelude, but the eight strokes, cold, unmusical monotones, denoting the hour of eight. We do not hear them, as we heard the quarters. Yet to him they are clearly audible. "His luck" is a richly ambiguous phrase, allowing us enormous interpretive options. Is he cursing the fact that he was caught? That he might have been betrayed by a confederate? That he was, as many of the underprivileged feel, "born to lose"? That society and its punitive instruments, courts and laws, were stacked against him? That others, even more criminal than he, get away with their crimes every day with impunity? *Luck* is a casual word, covering everything from Karma, Destiny, and Fate to trifling happenstance and coincidence. And on the scaffold such distinctions may seem trifling in themselves.

And then we come to two decisive, final lines of the poem that ring with absolute authority. This is due to several causes: (1) The benign and revered steeple of the first stanza has been transformed into the "stronghold, fortress, or prison" that the *Oxford English Dictionary* supplies as the second definition of *tower*. All churchly hints of absolution and redemption have been thrust aside by this substitution. (2) The almost muscular convulsion and unnatural word order of "the clock collected in the tower its strength" involves a conspicuous awkwardness. This is not the awkwardness of someone who is not at home in the language. It is the contorted, purposeful reordering of words to allow the sentence to mount towards its climactic point of force—which is not "tower" but "strength," galvanized in preparation for the last two words of the poem. (3) The alliteration in the last line connects that "strength" with a stroke, a striking that so decisively ends the poem as to make us feel it is not the hour alone that has been struck but the man himself. The striking, moreover, seems directed at the condemned in part because there is no mention of an executioner or hangman. There is only the solitary criminal, listening, counting, and cursing. To be sure, people were mentioned in the first stanza. Perhaps they will be witnesses to the execution. But they seem removed from him, both because they are unmentioned in the second stanza and because they seem to be placed below him, since the steeple sprinkles its notes "down" on them and because scaffolds and gallows are always raised above the heads of the multitude to afford a suitable view of the spectacle. (4) The word "struck" carries the more force by contrast with the gentle verbs "sprinkled" and "tossed" in the first stanza. (5) Finally, "struck" rhymes with "luck," as though some fateful complicity were at work to bring about, not justice, but a destiny as inevitable and irresistible as Time itself, to be gainsaid by no man. If there is no hangman, perhaps we may obscurely discern, by means of the strap and the noose, that thread of life dealt with at their own caprice by those blithe and indifferent ladies, Atropos, Clotho, and Lachesis, the Parcae, the Unappeasable Ones. However that may be, Housman's metrical and musical powers have endowed his poem with a chilling closure and finality.

On Hopkins'
"The Wreck of the Deutschland"

—for Eleanor Cook

So much thoughtful and brilliant commentary about Hopkins' great poem has been published that nothing much might be hoped for in the way of further enlightenment. My comments are accordingly a set of localized observations on a well-known and well-annotated poem about which, for all that, I hope to provide some innovative observations; and I suspect that at least one point I mean to raise will be met with anything from resistance to outrage. My intention, however, is not to be shocking but to seek clarification, even in the swampy realm of conjecture about the possibility that the text of the poem as we have come to know it is, quite simply, faulty and imperfect.

The poem is divided into two parts, and while the stanzas of both parts appear identical, they are not. In Part One, the first line of each stanza is a dimeter line, while in Part Two that first line becomes a trimeter. The rest of the lines in both parts are clearly meant to be identical in length as far as sprung rhythm, with its lavish admission of unaccented syllables, will allow; and the rhyme scheme of the elaborate stanza—*ababcbca*—remains consistent throughout.

A great part of the power and impetuosity of the poem is created by bold enjambments ("Thou mastering me / God!"), which serve not only to confer emphasis when desired but also to lend the whole poem a kind of headlong breathlessness that belongs to the twin dramas that lie at the poem's core. The enjambments affect not only the rapidity of movement

---

Gerard Manley Hopkins (1844–89) is technically a nineteenth-century poet. However, his poems were first assembled and edited with notes by Robert Bridges in 1918; a second edition, with an Appendix of Additional Poems and a critical introduction by Charles Williams, was published in 1930. Accordingly, Hopkins' true role and influence as a poet lies firmly in the twentieth century.

but the very sound of the lines, including the rashness and daring of some of the poet's rhymes. Hopkins himself called this device "rove over," and his friend and first editor, Poet Laureate Robert Bridges, explains, "This expression is used here to denote the running on of the sense and sound at the end of a verse into the beginning of the next."[1] For example, in the fourteenth stanza the word "leeward" (line 1) is made to rhyme with "drew her" (line 3), the final *d* sound required for a genuine rhyme borrowed from the first letter of the word *Dead,* which begins the fourth line. Lest we think this an idle and incidental trick, the same kind of borrowing occurs in the thirty-first stanza, where "unconfessed of them" (line 4) is rhymed with "breast of the" (line 6), the requisite *m* sound appropriated from the word *Maiden,* which begins the seventh line.

This extraordinary, libertarian way with rhyming might seem artificial if employed for less serious reasons than obtain in this poem. It requires, at the very least, that the reader's (or the reciter's) ear remain attentively alert. The question of whether these meticulous formalities can truly be detected in an oral presentation is not easily answerable. But surely, there are many kinds of highly charged poetry, some of them nearly impenetrable, that do not yield themselves to full apprehension until after much scrutiny and many readings. (The compositors of the First Quarto of *King Lear* were apparently unable to distinguish Shakespeare's prose from his verse.)

As to the twin dramas, I take it that the two parts of the poem are related to each other, not with the first as prologue or introduction to the second but because both are about conversion: Part One is about the personal conversion of Hopkins himself, and Part Two about the prayed-for, hoped-for conversion of England to its early and ancestral faith. Moreover, I would claim (being led to this conclusion by Louis Martz, though he makes no such claim himself) that in Part Two Hopkins is engaged in that aspect of the Ignatian *Spiritual Exercises* known as composition of place, through which he tries his best to imagine and to reconstruct in the most careful possible detail the actual scene of the catastrophe of the *Deutschland,* the suffering of the great crowd of passengers and crew, and of the martyr-nuns as particular emblems of salvation.

---

1. *Poems of Gerard Manley Hopkins,* ed. Robert Bridges (1930), 100.

Richly enmeshed with both familiar and unfamiliar Christian paradoxes, the poem also keeps in play the four elements (air, earth, fire, and
water) and is filled with allusions to the conundrum of unmerited suffering, as biblically exemplified by Job. God is seen in the very first stanza as
both the maker and unmaker of man, and Christ as both Redeemer and as
ultimate Judge. Moreover, the wind that becomes the source and power of
the storm has behind it the ambiguous words of John 3:8: "The wind
bloweth where it listeth, and thou hearest the sound thereof, but canst not
tell whence it cometh or whither it goeth. So is everyone that is born of the
Spirit." The wind, which is spirit, the breath of God, was breathed into
Adam, conferring life; but it is no less the whirlwind out of which God
speaks to Job, the sign of the destructive powers later to be described in
Revelation. In the first stanza God is called "Lord of living and dead," and
these two constituencies, one vastly larger than the other, are both subject
to a Judgment of which the initial version was the Fall, with its penalty of
the calamities of this life, and of which the final version is yet to come.

Hopkins' conversion from Anglicanism to Roman Catholicism was in
certain ways a painful experience, both for him and for John Henry Newman, whose counsel he had sought and who, in due course, received him
into the Roman Church. They were both concerned, among many necessary considerations, about the great pain this conversion was infallibly destined to cause Hopkins' parents, both of them devout Anglicans. The bliss
that might be expected of conversion—the embracing of a newfound clarity, certainty, sanctity, and hope—cannot but be tainted to some degree if it
must come at the price of the suffering of others. Paddy Kitchen, one of
Hopkins' biographers, writes that about October 8, 1866, "Hopkins returned to Oxford and wrote to his parents about his decision. On 15 October he reported to Newman that their replies had been so 'terrible' he could
not read them through more than once. They begged him to wait until after he had taken his degree . . . In answer to a plea by Manley Hopkins [the
poet's father] to consider the family estrangement his conversion would
cause, he replied that he had had months to think over everything." Not the
least part of his parents' pain was caused by their being among the last to
learn of his decision. His father wrote, "All we ask of you is for your own sake
to take so momentous a step with caution & hesitation; have we not a right
to do this? Might not our love & sorrow entitle us to ask it? & you answer

by saying that as we might be Romans if we pleased the estrangement is not of your doing. O Gerard my darling boy are you indeed gone from me?"

Not only was this something that greatly distressed young Hopkins in his spiritual quest, but he acknowledged it as part of the paradox of any such conversion. When (st. 2) he declares "I did say yes / O at lightning and lashed rod," he is speaking of the Passion of Christ, the torment of the flagellation, the lightning of the storm that accompanies the earthquake at the moment of Christ's death on the cross (Matt. 27), and his saying yes is both and simultaneously a confession of faith and a willingness to accept the benefits derived vicariously from the suffering and death of another. Conversion for Hopkins means fully to apprehend the terrible price of his own salvation, which is likened to the terrors of Jonah, who called, in the words of Psalm 130, "Out of the depths I have cried unto thee, O Lord." There may also be an allusion, more deeply hidden, to the more familiar Psalm 23, "Thy rod and thy staff they comfort me": the rod for correction, the staff for guidance, both for better care of the flock, though one gives pain while the other does not. The pain that his conversion gave the parents he deeply loved was inextricable from Hopkins' sense of the emotional paradoxes in which his faith was fixed. It may be that the biblical passage that most explicitly concerns the pain and breach of family feeling that may be engendered by conversion is Luke 14:25–26. "And there went a great multitude with him: and he turned, and said unto them, If any man come to me, and hate not his father, and mother, and wife, and children, and brethren, and sisters, yea, and his own life also, he cannot be my disciple."

From the Jonah of the second stanza Hopkins moves smoothly to the Noah of the third, with its echoes of Psalm 139, which describes an action that runs through the entire poem: of being cast down only to be raised up again, as Noah was both tested and saved by the Deluge. *Spell* in this stanza rhymes with *tell,* and both words, but especially the second, are central to the poem. *Tell* means, of course, recount; but it also means to acknowledge, confess (as in a confession of faith), and to know, identify, and locate—"They could tell him for hours" (st. 16); "a virginal tongue told" (st. 17). Hopkins' heart is "carrier-witted," equipped by instinct to come "home," like Noah's dove. But Hopkins is not content to think of conversion as simply instinctual, though it is at least partly that. For him faith is both instinctive impulsion and rational assent, and in the very last stanza of Part One he compares, without discredit to either, the sudden "as once at a crash" conversion of St. Paul and the "lingering-out sweet skill" of religious controversy and philosophic calm that characterized the conversion of St. Augustine. In a paper written for Walter Pater at Oxford, Hopkins, in the words of Paddy Kitchen, declared "that although those without leisure or education to reason out their beliefs must rely on the impulse of faith, it is imperative that everyone else's beliefs are grounded 'on the same kind of truths' as those which Plato and Aristotle explored."[2]

Hopkins' ability to extrapolate Christ from the starry heavens in the fifth stanza ("I kiss my hand / To the stars, lovely assunder / Starlight, wafting him out of it") is certainly meant to recall Psalm 19: "The heavens declare the glory of God; and the firmament showeth his handiwork. Day unto day uttereth speech, and night unto night showeth knowledge. There is no speech nor language where their voice is not heard." This audible and visible presence of God in the universe is nevertheless contrasted in the very same stanza with God's seeming absence at certain times, especially in times of great stress (Psalm 22, which is the cry from the cross). This is "His mystery," the "glory in thunder," and the mystery of his purpose when he seems to be absent. "Verily thou art a God that hidest thyself, O God of Israel, the Savior" (Isa. 45:15).

The sixth, seventh, and eighth stanzas are connected in thought, logic, and syntax. The "it" in the penultimate line of the sixth stanza refers back to "His mystery" and declares that this mystery, which is nothing less than the providential purpose of God, is expressed in the history of mankind, beginning with the Creation, and obscurely understood by the early prophets. But its true meaning began to be made manifest with the birth of Christ and shall only eventually become clear and intelligible at the end of time, with the Apocalypse. The apocalyptic ending and clarification are already symbolically revealed in the paradoxical joys and sorrows of the life and death of Christ, the beginning and the end, the Alpha and Omega of the Word that spells the Truth. So that, in stanza 8, when the poet says "We lash with the best or

---

2. Paddy Kitchen, *Gerard Manley Hopkins* (1978), 86.

worst / Word last!" that word is, in both cases, *Christ!* used either as prayer and blessing or, blasphemously, as execration. So powerful and all-embracing is that Word that it can express the whole meaning of the history of mankind and the purpose of God, as the whole poem is designed to declare. But in the twenty-second stanza and the twenty-ninth, as well as in the symbolic incapacity to articulate that is dramatized in stanza 28, the Word, as in John's Gospel, becomes the theological center of the poet's concerns. In his biography of Hopkins, John Pick quotes from an unpublished manuscript of the poet's to this effect: "God's utterance of himself in himself is God the Word, outside himself it is the world. This world then is word, expression, news, of God. Therefore its end, its purpose, its purport, its meaning, is God, and its life or work to name and praise him."[3]

Stanza 7 begins with the birth of Christ and is filled with Christian paradox, being no simple Christmas pageant in a manger with docile beasts, humble kings, and friendly shepherds. All the anguish, the pain, and the suffering that were to come not only were implicit in the birth but, by traditional belief, were also known to the Virgin at the very moment of the Annunciation. This impossible mixture of gladness and misery, horror and grace, is a necessary fusion of Christian elements. And it has a meaning, which is the meaning of the mystery. This is, that neither pain nor bliss is allotted to us by heaven in direct response and accordance to our merits but instead is meant to teach us both the joy of Christ's birth and the anguish of his Passion. Christian doctrine (and this poem is filled with its echoes) is full of paradoxes ("Warm-laid grave of a womb-life grey," st. 7; "Thou art lightning and love, I found it, a winter and warm; / Father and fondler of heart thou hast wrung: / Hast thy dark descending and most art merciful then," st. 9).

But while paradoxes are often entertained merely as intellectual puzzles—If God is omnipotent, can he create a stone so heavy that he can't lift it?—Hopkins is more earnestly concerned with those paradoxes that are chiefly emotional in character, and of these there are two in particular that concern him, and they are related. The first is the paradox of the Fortunate Fall, which, concerned with a strangely remote event, can seem like

3. John Pick, *Gerard Manley Hopkins: Priest and Poet* (1966), 49.

an intellectual puzzle. But the second, and more pressing one from the poet's point of view, is the cost in suffering and anguish of others—first of all on the part of the Sacrificial Christ, but then on the part of his own parents—which must serve as the ground for his bliss and his salvation. These emotional paradoxes are a part of what constitutes the Christian "mystery,"[4] and they are spoken of in precisely these terms when, in *Murder in the Cathedral*, Eliot has Thomas Becket, nearing the hour of his expected assassination, preach a Christmas service that begins,

> Dear children of God, my sermon this Christmas morning will be a very short one. I wish only that you should meditate in your hearts the deep meaning and mystery of our masses of Christmas Day. For whenever Mass is said, we re-enact the Passion and Death of Our Lord; and on this Christmas Day we do this in celebration of his birth. So that at the same moment we rejoice in his coming for the salvation of men, and offer again to God His Body and Blood in sacrifice, oblation and satisfaction for the sins of the whole world . . . Beloved, as the World sees, this is to behave in a strange fashion. For who in the World will both mourn and rejoice at once and for the same reason? For either joy will be overborne by mourning, or mourning will be cast out by joy; so it is only in these our Christian mysteries that we can rejoice and mourn at once for the same reason.

Within the body of Hopkins' poem this paradox of feeling as emblematic of the Christian "mystery" is represented in stanza 20 by the fact that the town of Eisleben (frozen life) was both the birthplace of the

---

4. In his *Life of St. Francis of Assisi* (1248), Thomas of Celano, recounting the crucial "vision of the Man in the Likeness of a Crucified Seraph," vouchsafed to the saint "while he was living at the hermitage which was called Alverna," describes this very mixture of commingling of emotions in a language that at certain moments seems to echo Luke's account of the Annunciation: "When the blessed servant of the Most High [i.e., Francis] saw these things, he was filled with the greatest wonder, but he could not understand what this vision should mean. Still, he was filled with happiness and he rejoiced very greatly because of the kind and gracious look with which he saw himself regarded by the seraph, whose beauty was beyond estimation; but the fact that the seraph was fixed to a cross and the sharpness of his suffering filled Francis with fear. And so he arose, if I may so speak, sorrowful and joyful, and joy and grief were in him alternately. Solicitously he thought what this vision could mean," and presently the marks of the stigmata appeared on his body.

detested Luther, Catholicism's foe, and the site of the convent where St. Gertrude dwelt in the thirteenth century, while, as the poem goes on to observe, "Abel is Cain's brother and the breasts they have sucked the same."

What this sequence of three stanzas (6–8) asserts is the pivotal importance of the paradox/mystery involved in the anguish and bliss of Christian doctrine as it manifests itself in personal life, as irrefutably as the fresh burst of juice from fruit pierced by the teeth and released into the savoring mouth. It is a sensation that is undeniable: simply and unequivocally *there*. That biting into the fruit should remind us that Christ is variously symbolized as a grape-cluster and as the fruit tasted by Adam and restored to the Tree of Knowledge (the cross) by Christ. He is present in the wine and wafer of the Eucharist, and therefore the taste that can "flush the man, the being with it . . . Brim, in a flash, full" (st. 8) is the savor of divinity. And of suffering, as expressed in Hopkins' "Barnfloor and Winepress":

> Terrible fruit was on the tree
> In the acre of Gethsemane;
> For us by Calvary's distress
> The wine was rackèd from the press;
> Now in our altar-vessels stored
> Is the sweet vintage of our Lord.

The final stanza of Part One is a prayer in behalf of everyone, but as single individuals. It is that each and every one should come to acknowledge the power and love of God, whether through anguish (as being wrought upon at a forge, coerced, bent to the Supreme Will) or through gentleness and love (as Spring steals imperceptibly through in its slow progress): and these two ways to God are seen as analogues not merely to the different conversions of Paul and Augustine but to the paradoxically opposed yet identical means of violence and bliss, suffering and joy that form the basis of Christian "mystery."

Part Two is both a detailed account of the maritime disaster and a meticulous application of those mysteries that find glory in suffering and life in death. It opens with Death speaking, as in those medieval poems about the Dance of Death. Here Death enumerates the modes by which he makes himself known to mankind: sword, flange, rail, flame, fang, and flood. These are all modes for the execution of the martyrs. Despite their numbers and their fame, and the very fact of death surrounding us at every side, we contrive somehow to forget it and to imagine that we are deathless. This willful ignorance is both perverse and humanly necessary. To imagine oneself immortal is certainly folly, and spiritually impious; to dwell, however, undeviatingly upon the hour of our death is to repudiate and undervalue life itself and thereby to commit an equal and alternative impiety. This dilemma is not unrelated to the kinds of paradox and mystery that have been adumbrated in Part One. And so Hopkins takes passing note of the irony (st. 14) that, instead of "a reef or a rock," the ship was destroyed by a sandbank ("I am soft sift / In an hourglass," st. 4), a yielding and pliant obstacle that ought not to have proven fatal.

If Part One was private and inward, Part Two is public and outward, and with stanza 12 a recital of historical events begins. Part One is concerned with the microcosm of the individual soul; Part Two with an enlargement of that purview to include "two hundred souls in the round," the crew and passengers of the *Deutschland*. But before the poem concludes, these twin perspectives give way before a vision of what is, for Hopkins, the macrocosm, the fate and future of mankind and the restoration to England of its ancestral faith. Stanza 12 also begins the composition of place, the devotional attempt to realize imaginatively in all its particularity, the time, place, and conditions that obtained on the night and morning of December 7, 1875, when the disaster occurred.

I want to turn directly to a crucial part of the scene that Hopkins reimagines, stanza 16, for it is here that I suspect a flaw. But before presenting my conjecture, a word is required about the provenance of the poem. The original holograph has been lost, presumably forever. But before it was lost, Robert Bridges, Hopkins' editor, made a copy. Moreover, Bridges reports that though Hopkins himself "kept no copy," he "made both corrections of copy and emendations of the poems which had been copied . . . by me."[5] In addition to this, "Another transcript, now at St. Aloysius' College, Glasgow, was made by the Rev. F. Bacon" from the holograph, but without any of the emendations Hopkins adopted in Bridges' copy. The two versions were then collated, providing what

5. *Poems of Gerard Manley Hopkins*, 103–4.

Bridges calls "one true reading." So I must point out immediately that any flaw I seem to find must have survived the careful copying of Bridges as later overseen and corrected by Hopkins himself, and checked against an alternate copy. I am fully aware of the audacity of my proposal, but I will advance it nevertheless.

16

<blockquote>
One stirred from the rigging to save
The wild woman-kind below,
With a rope's end round the man, handy and brave—
He was pitched to his death at a blow,
For all his dreadnought breast and braids of thew:
They could tell him for hours, dandled the to and fro
Through the cobbled foam-fleece. What could he do
With the burl of the fountains of air, buck and the flood of the wave?
</blockquote>

What for years of studying and teaching this poem has puzzled, irked, and provoked me is the end of the sixth line, "dandled the to and fro," as if there were such a thing as an unhyphenated "to-and-fro." *Dandle* is a transitive verb, meaning "to lift up and down on one's knee; to fondle; to pamper" (*OED*). In any case, it requires an object, and the only one the poem seems to supply is "to and fro." My solution to this problem is derived from the single source that Hopkins used as the basis of his spiritual exercise and from which he adopted the very words *to and fro:* the account of the event that appeared in the *London Times* on December 11, 1875. There it was reported that the captain of the *Deutschland* "(British built, and working for the North German Lloyd's Company on the Bremen— New York route) lost his bearings and the ship went aground on the shifting sands of the Kentish Knock." The *Times* proceeds to give details, some so grotesque Hopkins must have found them repellent and omitted them from his account.

At 2 A.M., Captain Brickenstein, knowing that with the rising tide the ship would be waterlogged, ordered all the passengers to come on deck . . . Most of them obeyed the summons at once; others lingered below till it was too late; some of them, ill, weak, despairing of life even on deck, resolved to stay in their cabins and meet death without any further struggle to evade it. After 3 A.M. on Tuesday morning a scene of horror was witnessed. Some passengers clustered for safety within or upon the wheelhouse, and on the top of other slight structures on deck. Most of the crew and many of the emigrants went into the rigging, where they were safe enough as long as they could maintain their hold. But the intense cold and long exposure told a tale. The purser of the ship, though a strong man, relaxed his grip, and fell into the sea. Women and children and men were one by one swept away from their shelters on the deck. Five German nuns, whose bodies are now in the dead-house here [Harwick] clasped hands and were drowned together, the chief sister, a gaunt woman 6 ft. high, calling out loudly and often 'O Christ, come quickly!' till the end came. The shrieks and sobbing of women and children are described by survivors as agonising. One brave sailor, who was safe in the rigging, went down to try to save a child or woman who was drowning on the deck. He was secured by a rope to the rigging, but a wave dashed him against the bulwarks, and when daylight dawned his headless body, detained by the rope, was seen swaying to and fro in the waves. In the dreadful excitement of those hours one man hung himself behind the wheelhouse, another hacked at his wrists with a knife, hoping to die a comparatively painless death by bleeding.

What I propose is that "dandled the to and fro" ought to be read "dandled there to and fro." This is, of course, to claim that (1) Bridges miscopied the text, that (2) when Hopkins made his corrections and emendations he failed to notice the error, and that (3) when the Rev. Geoffrey Bliss, S. J., collated the emended Bridges text with the one made by the Rev. F. Bacon the fault once again passed unnoticed, producing what Bridges calls the "one true copy." All this seems highly unlikely, of course. On the other hand, the text as it stands is nonsense, and the *Times* account of the man's body, "swaying to and fro in the waves," is consistent with my proposal. The only reason I have raised this small point is that no commentator I have seen has ventured to take any notice of the matter or remark on the line.

Though composition of place demands focused concentration, it does not forbid application of the facts observed to the person of the meditator himself. The scene of the disaster, beginning with stanza 12, continues unflinchingly through the stanza I have just quoted (16) and continues beyond (17) until, abruptly, the poet challenges his curious and complex feelings about what he is contemplating. The tone of stanza 18 I take to be—at least in its opening lines—sardonic and suspicious, as if to say, tauntingly, "So you find yourself touched, do you, by your comfortable and removed contemplation of the suffering of others? Moved enough, are you, to sit down to write poetry, in the face of the protracted misery and death of others?" The tone of suspicion and reproach lingers through the stanza, reappears in stanza 24, and at some level it must have had something to do with the pain Hopkins felt he had caused his parents.

Yet there is another way to read the stanza, not unrelated to the one I have just offered, but without its obvious note of contempt. It is made most explicit in the final line's question, "What can it be, this glee?" To be sure, the words that immediately follow ("the good you have there of your own?") seem full, once again, of suspicion and self-accusation. But *glee* is an unexpected word, not easily applied to someone exempt from danger or engaged in writing a poem, much less to someone contemplating the suffering of others, unless that someone were an unembarrassed sadist. The whole stanza, I think, is a living, immediate experience of the Christian mystery of self-contradictory emotion.

In any case, after the final words of stanza 17 ("a virginal tongue told") stanza 19, returning to the scene after the interruption of the eighteenth stanza, begins, "Sister, a sister calling." There will now follow almost five full stanzas before the "tongue" that "told" (tolled) in stanza 17 actually speaks in stanza 24. And no sooner does she speak ("Christ, come quickly") than the poet asks, thoughtfully (in the first line of stanza 25), "what did she mean?" He proposes two answers and dismisses them both. The first, the desire for martyrdom, is something, as the poet wryly observes, that the apostles themselves had no appetite for or confidence in (Matt. 14:25–33). The second is a prayer for a quick death and end of life. This second possibility seems to the poet more plausible on the ground that we instinctively think of a future time that is better, since in bad weather we naturally dream of spring; so that, even more plausibly, a devout soul will think of the treasures of heaven (I Cor. 2:9) in moments of travail. But in stanza 27, this answer, too, is rejected. (I must add parenthetically that the fourth line of stanza 25, "Breathe, body of lovely death," has for my ear a distinct echo of Whitman's "Come lovely and soothing death," line 135 of "When Lilacs Last in the Dooryard Bloom'd.") But the main point is that, having dismissed two conjectural answers to his own question, "What did she mean?" he turns, in stanza 28, to a sort of incoherent, fragmentary, garbled set of attempts at expression that give the effect of something stunning and inexplicable. Naturally enough, this has invited the most varied and reckless suggestions, the best known of them being that the nun who speaks has been granted a vision of Christ himself and that the poet has so thoroughly identified with her that he has joined in her vision, which, as *vision,* is an experience untranslatable into words.

I should like to propose the virtual opposite. What is the meaning of the prayer, "Christ, come quickly"? My answer is that the prayer is made in response to a promise repeated at least four times in the Book of Revelation (3:11; 22:7, 12, and 20).

> Behold, I come quickly: hold that fast which thou hast, that no man take thy crown.

> Behold, I come quickly: blessed is he that keepeth the sayings of the prophecy of this book.

> And behold, I come quickly; and my reward is with me, to give to every man according as his work shall be.

> He which testifieth these things saith, Surely I come quickly. Amen. Even so, come, Lord Jesus.

The last of these quotations is the penultimate verse of Holy Scripture. But it is not only the end of the Bible; it is the escatological end of human and divine destiny. And in the end is the beginning: Alpha and Omega, *principium et finis,* the name and the incarnation of divinity *qui fuit, est, et erat.*

> Thus saith the Lord the King of Israel, and his redeemer the Lord of hosts; I am the first, and I am the last; and beside me there is no God.
> (Isaiah 44:6)

John to the seven churches which are in Asia: Grace be unto you, and peace, from him which is, and which was, and which is to come.

(Rev. 1:4)

I am Alpha and Omega, the beginning and the end, saith the Lord, which is, which was, and which is to come, the Almighty.

(Rev. 1:8)

And he said unto me, It is done. I am Alpha and Omega. I will give unto him that is athirst of the fountain of the water of life freely.

(Rev. 21:6)

There is a related or analogous passage in II Cor. (1:20) that invites notice:

For all the promises of God in him are *yea,* and in him Amen, unto the glory of God by us.

By some, those promises are construed as the Old Testament, while the Amen is the New Testament. But a claim can also be made that the promises are both the prophecies and potentialities which come to fulfillment, neither at the birth of Christ, nor at his death, but at the end of time. (Also, that "*yea*" recalls Hopkins' claim, "I did say yes / O at lightning and lashed rod.") But most apposite, of course, are those verses that begin John's Gospel: "In the beginning was the Word," and that Word in John's Greek is *logos:* (1) the rational principle that governs and develops the universe, and (2) the divine word or reason incarnate as Jesus Christ.

All this bears upon the unanswered question, "What did she mean?" After having proposed two provisional answers and having dismissed them, Hopkins, in stanza 28, adopts the rhetorical figure of aposiopesis, in which the speaker suddenly halts as if unable or unwilling to proceed. Puttenham offers five reasons for employing the figure: because nothing further needs to be said, to express shame, to express fear, to express a threat, or to express a moderation of anger. He doesn't mention the reason for Hopkins' use of it here, which is to express absolute awe. What the nun means by her prayer involves the whole history and destiny of mankind, the supreme will of God, the purpose, beginning, and end of everything as embodied, from the first, and forever, in the Word.

> Wording it how but by him that present and past,
> Heaven and earth are word of, worded by
>
> (st. 29)

As poet, as priest, as believer, Hopkins' devotion to the amplitude and
plenitude of the Word can, in a happy paradox, leave him nearly speech-
less. And this is because, as stanza 9 has already declared, what he is trying
to articulate is "Beyond saying sweet, past telling of tongue." And yet,
through the veil of mystery, it is known, as is the God he praises, who
"heeds but hides, bodes but abides" (st. 32).

The final stanza I take to be a prayer for the reconversion of Britain to
the Roman Catholic faith and the return to "English souls" of their true
Christ-King. I want to focus attention on the poem's final line, which
commentators have sidled past with easy nonchalance, as though it mer-
ited no special notice and were limpidly clear. But, for one thing, in a
poem whose stanzas uniformly end with hexameter lines, this one, with
its insistent series of nouns, has eight strong beats. Then, too, readers have
been genuinely puzzled by the accumulation of possessives and uncertain
what to make of them. Here is the line, which refers to Christ.

Our hearts' charity's hearth's fire, our thoughts' chivalry's throng's Lord.

For clarification's sake, these possessives can be diagrammed as a set of
concentric circles enclosed within one another; which is to say that of the
first group of four nouns, *heart* becomes the largest and outermost circle,
containing within it, in diminishing order, *charity, hearth,* and *fire.* And,
for purposes of simplification, it can be claimed that the words are about
the fire of the heart (hence the possessive), a warmth expressed in charity
to be found at the hospitality of the hearth.

By the same token, the simplification of the second set of nouns speaks
of the Lord of thought. And the two contrasted, or juxtaposed, lists of
nouns speak, therefore, of two, perhaps different, perhaps twinned, modes
of apprehending the Divine: through emotion's impulse (the heart) and
through the rational mind (thought), as Hopkins had observed in the paper he wrote at Oxford for Walter Pater.

But something else is implied as well by the two lists. The second one
includes *chivalry* and *throng;* and we immediately notice that whereas the

first list is private, interior, and personal, the second is public, social, and communal. (*Chivalry* has Jesuit connections, St. Ignatius Loyola having been a soldier who had converted military valor into inward discipline; *throng*, or crowd, being the large-scale magnification of social conventions and religious devotion implied in *chivalry*.) Hopkins is neither the first nor the last to insist that religious experience must be at once both private and public. For the utterly private experience could fall into the potential error of unauthenticated "vision-feelings" "in the solar plexus" in the words of Auden's Herod, "induced by undernourishment, angelic images gener- ated by fevers or drugs, dream warnings inspired by the sound of falling water."[6] And, on the other hand, rote observance and numb conformity to ritual presents the alternate peril of being numbered among the scribes and Pharisees, "whited sepulchres, which indeed appear beautiful out- ward, but are within full of dead men's bones" (Matt. 23:27). Hopkins' prayer in this last stanza is addressed to the chief nun. It is a prayer in be- half of the whole community of England, for their return to the old faith and to God's service. It is based on the premise that faith is both individ- ual and communal, as, in one of the choruses of "The Rock," Eliot had also claimed:

> What life have you if you have not life together?
> There is no life that is not in community,
> And no community not lived in praise of God.

---

6. W. H. Auden, *Collected Poems* (1991), 393.

Uncle Tom's Shantih

I

This occasion encourages me to begin with a quotation from William Empson's commentary on some excised passages from *The Waste Land*:[1] "Half the time," wrote William Empson in *Using Biography* (1984), "when the impressionable English were saying how wonderfully courageous and original he was to come out with some crashingly reactionary remark, he was just saying what any decent man would say back home in St. Louis" (196). Empson was trying to face, though not quite squarely, the bedeviling topic of Eliot's anti-Semitism, which I must leave for another time. At this time I want to address only the first eighteen lines of the first section of *The Waste Land*, the opening of "The Burial of the Dead."

> April is the cruellest month, breeding
> Lilacs out of the dead land, mixing
> Memory and desire, stirring
> Dull roots with spring rain.
> Winter kept us warm, covering
> Earth in forgetful snow, feeding
> A little life with dried tubers.
> Summer surprised us, coming over the Starnbergersee
> With a shower of rain; we stopped in the colonnade,
> And went on in sunlight, into the Hofgarten,
> And drank coffee, and talked for an hour.
> Bin gar keine Russin, stamm' aus Litauen, echt deutsch.

---

1. The occasion was the Centennial Conference on T. S. Eliot, held at Washington University in St. Louis, Missouri, in September 1988, where the remarks in section I were delivered.

And when we were children, staying at the arch-duke's,
My cousin's, he took me out on a sled,
And I was frightened. He said, Marie,
Marie, hold on tight. And down we went.
In the mountains, there you feel free.
I read, much of the night, and go south in the winter.

We have grown so familiar with and accustomed not only to *The Waste Land* itself but the diligent and learned commentaries upon it that we may be in some danger of not being able any longer to gauge the astonishment it is calculated to provoke right from the start. It is, however, a measure of the poem's greatness that it continues to surprise, in marked contrast to a lot of poetry which aims crudely at effects of shock and violence but which lies dead on the page at even a second reading. Eliot's verse is subtle, intricate, and reflexive in that it returns upon itself for the fulfilment of its significance. And this is exhibited even in its singular and compelling music. Out of the first seven lines, five end with participles—in part a musical device, providing for run-on motion and continuity. How crucial, and characteristic, it was to Eliot may be illustrated by his recurrence to it elsewhere:

Here are the years that walk between, bearing
Away the fiddles and the flutes, restoring
One who moves in time between sleep and waking, wearing

White light folded, sheathed about her, folded.
The new years walk, restoring
Through a bright cloud of tears, the years, restoring
With a new verse the ancient rhyme.

(*Ash Wednesday*)

I have trodden the winepress alone, and I know
That it is hard to be really useful, resigning
The things that men count for happiness, seeking
The good deeds that lead to obscurity, accepting
With equal face those that bring ignominy,
The applause of all or the love of none.

(Choruses from "The Rock")

This participial emphasis, besides its rhythmical "dying fall" and floating cadence, points to a curious paradox about time that is, I think, central to *The Waste Land* and slyly played out in its opening. For the participles point to "continuing action in the present," which is itself a paradox in that "the present is static, and when it ceases to be static it has become the past." "Memory and desire," which "we" were gratified to leave buried under winter snow, represent motions backwards and forwards in time, out of the present, the still point of the turning world. To exist only in the present seems to be the chief yearning of the opening lines, but the participles themselves hint at the difficulty of this. The memories and desires that are bred may have to do with the liveliness of Chaucer's characters' "longing" to go on pilgrimages, and the dirgelike grief of Whitman's belilaced elegy; after all, *The Waste Land* was first called "He Do the Police in Different Voices," and it still bears traces of being an assemblage of monologues and dialogues. But though these backwards and forwards impulses may be partly literary in this very literary poem, they also point to past and future as *history* and *destiny*, which the speaker, speaking here in the collective plural on behalf of us all, is eager not to think about. And for a reason, in part, that the verbal tenses themselves will cunningly reveal.

Christopher Ricks, in a lecture, was admirably speculative about how the first five words are to be read and how ambiguous is the copula, *is*, but rather than commit depredations on notions he may plan to publish, let me merely insist on the present tense of the verb. It encourages us to believe we are firmly situated in April. This encouragement is confirmed by the past tense of "Winter kept us warm, covering / Earth with forgetful snow," for it is in the right sequence of things to look back from April to winter. But we are in for a shock when we get to the eighth line:

Summer surprised us, . . .

All very well to look backward from April to winter, but if we can also look backward to summer, and a summer which seems very clearly to have followed winter, we are bound to be puzzled about where we are to situate ourselves.

The answer, which might dawn on us at any moment, is that we, who are the dead, can see everything as past and the only present for us consists in *not seeing*, from which we are unwillingly aroused by the engenderings of April. We are not "situated" in April but in the stasis of our death, which is the deadness of everyone in this poem, the crowds that flowed over London Bridge, the young man carbuncular, Tiresias, the drowned Phoenician Sailor.

II

These first eighteen lines of *The Waste Land* must be the most familiar opening lines of any poem in the twentieth century. I have already commented on the stasis of the participial present tense ("breeding," "mixing," "covering," "feeding," "coming"); the sad intimations of a past and a future in "memory" and "desire," both unspecified, therefore muted; and our growing sense, confirmed with Baudelairean accusation at the end of the section, that it is precisely *we* who are the cadavers of "The Burial of the Dead." But now I want to dilate on two details in these lines, ones that attract notice precisely as a consequence of the discovery and publication of the manuscript of *The Waste Land*. In the draft version, later to be revised, Eliot wrote,

> Summer surprised us, coming over the Königsee.

This lake, located at the east end of the Bavarian Alps, very near Berchtesgaden (which, at the time Eliot was writing, had not attained its later prominence), is identified in the guidebooks as "one of the most beautiful lakes in the Reich." Baedeker is unequivocal in his praise: "The gem of this district," he writes, "is the clear, dark-green Königsee, or Lake of St. Bartholomew, . . . the most beautiful lake in Germany, vying in grandeur with those of Switzerland and Italy. Some of the surrounding mountains, which rise almost perpendicularly from the water, are 6500 ft. in height above the lake." I am going to conjecture as to why Eliot chose to shift venue to the now canonical Starnbergersee, which is also located in southern Bavaria, if somewhat less touted for tourism. And I suggest that the change is connected with these lines:

> And when we were children, staying at the arch-duke's
> My cousin's, he took me out on a sled,
> And I was frightened. He said, Marie,
> Marie, hold on tight. And down we went.

Annotating these lines in her edition of the manuscript version, Valerie Eliot observes: "Writing in the *Partisan Review* (21, no. 2: 1954), Mr. G. K. L. Morris drew attention to similarities between parts of *The Waste Land* and the reminiscences of Countess Marie Larisch, *My Past* (London, 1913). The assumption was that Eliot must have read the book, but in fact he met the author (when and where is not known), and his description of the sledding, for example, was taken verbatim from a conversation he had with this niece and confidante of the Austrian Empress Elizabeth [*sic*]."

To characterize Marie Larisch as a niece and confidante of Empress Elisabeth is technically perfectly correct, though by itself it greatly and misleadingly dignifies her. She was born out of wedlock, married off to an impoverished nobleman to cover the indiscretion of her birth, and was banished from the imperial court for playing the ignoble role of pander and procuress in the last great scandal to beset the Habsburg Empire. It is not irrelevant that the nobleman she was designated to marry was impoverished. The countess had very extravagant tastes and was almost always short of cash. Because her husband could not supply her wants in this regard, she made the greatest possible use of her position and entrée at the court, and it was widely understood that she was prepared to mortify her noble pride by accepting thoughtful considerations from those who hoped for social or political advantage. She was in a position to drop names and even to arrange audiences, or *levées*. In pursuit of getting on by these methods, made so familiar to us by the members and friends of the Reagan and Clinton administrations, the countess became acquainted with the ambitions of the wealthy family of Mary Vetsera, whose mother, Hélène, was a shameless social climber. This teenage girl had fallen wildly, one might say idolatrously, in love, at a suitably devotional distance, with Archduke Rodolph, who was direct heir to the imperial throne. He was, in his way, a good-looking man, and many women of the day paled or swooned at the royal sight of him. Mary Vetsera had little to recommend her apart from her youth and good looks; and there were barriers to such a match that might have seemed insurmountable. The archduke was thirteen years her senior, married, and a father, as well as being heir to the throne. His marriage, however, was an unhappy one. His wife, Crown Princess Stephanie, was self-righteous and stupid, while he himself was intelligent, brilliantly educated, and given to liberal political views not entirely consistent with those of his father's regime. Furthermore, the marriage may have been forced upon him for dynastic reasons.

The marriage was poisoned in another way. The archduke was not only politically liberal; he was sexually liberal as well, and some three years after the birth of his only child, a daughter, he contracted gonorrhea, with which he infected his wife, rendering her sterile besides causing her continued ill health. Rodolph himself was frequently in pain because of his infection and took morphine for relief. But in no ways did he abate his life of indulgence with women or with drink. He was a handsome and troubled young aristocrat, the kind that women often find irresistible.

His troubles were not confined to his unhappy marriage, his venereal disease, or his ideological differences with an autocratic father. He was also obsessed with death and with a fear of going insane. There were reasonable grounds for the second, since his family, on both sides, was strikingly tainted. The empress's second cousin was the mad King Ludwig II of Bavaria, and by the time of Ludwig's death at the age of forty-one, both he and his brother were incurably insane. There had been, moreover, some twenty or more marriages between the Bavarian royal family of Wittelsbach and the Habsburg family; to complicate the matter still further, there was a history of mental illness in the Baden family, to which the empress's grandmother belonged. The emperor and empress were themselves first cousins whose mothers were not only sisters but also related in other ways so intricate that Rodolph had only half the normal number of grandparents. As Sarah Gainham, from whom I have derived my information, has written in *The Habsburg Twilight* (1979), "The rigid family custom as to the rank of possible marriage partners and the need for an heir to the greatest of Catholic dynasties to marry only a born Catholic, made the choices very narrow" (28).

So here was a pining seventeen-year-old beauty and an attractive, liberal, and degenerate young archduke. It was, in the words of Wodehouse, "but the work of a moment" for Marie Larisch to bring them together. And she did a great deal more than that. She arranged and facilitated the rendezvous and assignations between Mary Vetsera and Rodolph, in a liaison of which the emperor strongly disapproved and summarily ordered his son to abandon. What this peremptory command meant to Rodolph is hard to say, but it is plausible to conjecture that it strengthened his rebellious determination. Mary, in any case, became pregnant, and there followed a period of hysteria during which she threatened several times to do away with herself by (please take note) drowning herself in the Danube. Rodolph, with his fears of madness, his venereal infection, and his unhappiness and frustration as regards his political convictions (his father was healthy, in his fifties, and in no mind to resign his throne and authority to his son), embraced the thought of death as the only solution—and not, it may be added, for the first time. Hinting to the credulous Mary that the two of them would run away together in some impossibly romantic way, he contrived to smuggle her out to the imperial hunting lodge at Mayerling, where, sometime during the night and probably with her crazed consent, he shot her in the head, killing her instantly, and then later put a bullet through his own temple, using a hand mirror to assure his aim. The precise circumstances of their deaths are admittedly uncertain; imperial families are deft at covering things up, and they worked overtime in this case. It was, however, a *Liebestod* such as Rodolph had contemplated more than once in the course of his short, unhappy life; he had once proposed to a call girl named Maria Kaspar that they go to a public garden and shoot themselves together.

In any case, Marie Larisch had from the first been an aider and abettor of this final doomed and tragic romance, and for the prominent part she played in the affair she was banished from the court. When her son found out about his mother's role in the liaison, he committed suicide. Needless to say, when the countess got around to writing *My Past*, she presented a wonderfully sanitized version of these events of 1888–89.

As a consequence of Rodolph's suicide, his younger brother Ferdinand (a name that, through Shakespearean resonance with *The Tempest*, echoes inaudibly throughout *The Waste Land*) became heir to the throne of the Austro-Hungarian Empire and, on June 28, 1914, was assassinated at Sarajevo, precipitating the First World War, a conflict that furnishes one form of the rubble that fills Eliot's great poem. The war is explicitly present in the pub conversation about Lil's husband Albert, but all the images of collapsing civilization point to it, and in the years that immediately followed (the years in which Eliot's poem was written), it was viewed as a calamity from which no recovery seemed possible—as Paul Fussell has indicated in his book *The Great War and Modern Memory*.

But what of the unannotated shift from the Königsee to the Starnbergersee? The lake Eliot finally settled upon was not contemptible as regards its picturesqueness. It is the "second biggest stretch of water in Bavaria" and "much frequented as a summer resort." But Eliot's interest in it, I suggest, had rather to do with its very dramatic association with the chief of Richard Wagner's patrons. In 1864, deeply depressed and overwhelmed with debts, Wagner received out of the blue an invitation, conveyed by His Majesty's private secretary, to become the permanent and honored guest of the eighteen-year-old mad King Ludwig of Bavaria, who had fallen in love to the point of lunacy with *Lohengrin*. Wagner was invited to take up residence at the royal palace in Munich; it was for him a miraculous and totally unexpected reprieve.

Even as a teenager, Ludwig was already giving signs of being insubordinately willful and something of a psychopath. But he regarded himself as a connoisseur of the arts and had the means to become a patron; so, with a stubborn determination to make Wagner his protégé, he began by paying off most of the composer's outstanding debts. It was under Ludwig's patronage that *Tristan und Isolde* was introduced at Munich in 1865, followed, in due course, by the *Ring*. But Ludwig was not only a patron of music, he was a patron of architecture as well, and in 1876 he built a neogothic chapel for the seventeenth-century *Schloss* that belonged to his family and that was located on the Starnbergersee. In the course of time, Ludwig's behavior became so irrational that he was deposed by a council of state and placed under house arrest in the very chapel he had built. Within twenty-four hours after that arrest his corpse, and that of his physician, Dr. von Gudden, were found drowned in the lake. A plaque marks the place where the bodies were brought ashore, and a neoromanesque chapel was built there as a memorial in 1900. It was never satisfactorily determined whether Ludwig drowned in an attempt to escape from captivity or in some rash act of suicide; nor do we know whether Dr. von Gudden was his faithful and doomed accomplice or one who was trying to prevent his escape. His death, in any case, was a death by water, such as Mary Vetsera had threatened during her hysteria. So the poem is able, in covert and subtle ways, to introduce themes both personal and social or historical right in the opening lines.

A great part of the poem was worked on while the poet was being treated for nervous disorders by a doctor at Lausanne, and Eliot's first wife, Vivien, was herself seriously unstable. Her mother, Rose Haigh-Wood, was fearful that Vivien "had inherited what was then known as 'moral insanity,'"[2] and, according to Eliot's biographer, Peter Ackroyd, she may have voiced these fears to her son-in-law on the occasion of their first meeting after the marriage. The taint of insanity ("My nerves are bad tonight") that so troubled the Habsburgs, Wittelsbachs, and Badens must at this point in his life have seemed highly pertinent to Eliot. And if we consider that the poem originally began with an episode at the drunken end of a night of debauchery ("First we had a couple of feelers down at Tom's place, / There was old Tom, boiled to the eyes, blind") and then recall the profligate life of Rodolph, we recognize in that private and dynastic drama of loose behavior leading undetectably up to the collapse of western Europe a symbol of the desecration, sterility, and grief, both collective and individual, that lies at the core of *The Waste Land.*

----

2. Peter Ackroyd, *T. S. Eliot: A Life* (1984), 62.

Paralipomena to The Hidden Law

*I*n 1993 I published a book called *The Hidden Law: The Poetry of W. H. Auden.* Generally speaking, it received favorable reviews, one at least of which, by Monroe K. Spears, was better than it deserved. To compensate for that encomium, and to regulate my pride, there was a completely dismissive review, the more wounding for its brevity, in the *New York Times Book Review.* The passage of time has given me slightly greater perspective on some of the faults and merits of that book, which, it must be pointed out, did not undertake to comment on everything Auden had written but which attended, with great selectivity, to "those poems, collections, essays, plays, or fragments of Auden's recorded conversations that particularly delighted, interested, or (sometimes) provoked me, but especially those works that inspired admiration or seemed to demand comment and elucidation" (438). All by itself that declaration meant that much had been left out, and while I was not always happy with omissions, I was mindful of my publisher's anxiety that the book not be so long as to drive its price out of the reach of most readers—a consideration of which I was the more conscious because it had first been proposed to me that I write a book of about 120 pages and I delivered one of 484 instead.

There was much I left out, some of which I regretted and still regret. And there was another matter about which I still feel uncertain. At the time of writing I regarded it as my duty as a critic simply, straightforwardly, and neutrally to report Auden's ideas as they were expressed in poetry or prose, and often in both, without intruding dissenting views of my own, unless I felt such editorial liberties were truly warranted. Some of Auden's views I plainly disagreed with, though for the most part I refrained from saying so. It is, for example, of no great moment to a reader that Auden and I should disagree about the merit of Brahms. To his friend Alan Ansen, who recorded their conversations, he remarked, "Perhaps my

dislike of Brahms is extra-aesthetic. But whenever I hear a particularly ob-
noxious combination of sounds, I spot it as Brahms and I'm right every
time."[1] Now, I happen to like Brahms, and I am not alone in this; nor am
I among the musically illiterate in my views. In an essay called "Brahms
the Progressive," Arnold Schoenberg wrote, "The sense of logic and economy, and the power of development which builds melodies of such natural fluency, deserve the admiration of every music lover who expects more
than sweetness and beauty from music." What is interesting about Auden's
anti-Brahms prejudice, and which he merely hints at in his suggestion
that it may be "extra-aesthetic," is glossed and explained in Humphrey
Carpenter's biography, where it is reported of Auden and his lover,
Chester Kallman, that "he took over wholesale Chester's prejudice against
Brahms."[2] This is interesting because very often people in love, or couples
who have shared a life over long years, come to adopt one another's tastes
and views. Not uncommonly these are social or political views; but sometimes they are aesthetic tastes as well. Auden's feelings about Brahms
probably had less to do with Brahms than with his own domestic life.

Something of the same curious mechanism may be at work in his, to
my view, absurd and mistaken ideas about Shakespeare's *Henry IV.* There
are a number of essays in which, highly suspiciously, Auden claims that
there is no character development in Shakespeare's two-part play. He
writes, "Seeking for an explanation of why Falstaff affects us as he does, I
find myself compelled to see *Henry IV* as possessing, in addition to its
overt meaning, a parabolic significance. Overtly, Falstaff is a Lord of Misrule; parabolically, he is a comic symbol for the supernatural order of
Charity as contrasted with the temporal order of Justice symbolized by
Henry of Monmouth" (i.e., Prince Hal, later Henry V). It is this typo-
logical kind of thinking that allows Auden in one of his poems ("Under
Which Lyre") to refer to "the prig Prince Hal."

The real clue to Auden's views of the play may very probably be found
in his enthusiastic attitude towards Verdi's *Falstaff,* and in one of his essays on opera he flatly asserts that there is no character development in
opera. Whether or not this generalization about opera is true (and the
libretto of *The Rake's Progress* renders it doubtful), I suspect that Auden

---

1. Alan Ansen, *The Table Talk of W. H. Auden* (1989), 15.
2. Humphrey Carpenter, *W. H. Auden: A Biography* (1981), 262.

imputed to Shakespeare's play, by a sort of time-warped inference, the same kind of stasis, and one which afflicts most of his own dramatic work. The literary-critical retort to Auden is best supplied in John Dover Wilson's *The Fortunes of Falstaff* (1944), in which the maturation of Prince Hal and the concomitant corruption of Falstaff are carefully analyzed; Northrop Frye says much the same thing in *Fools of Time* (1967).[3] But such analysis would very likely have had no effect on Auden, who, by imposing upon the play his notions about the opera was again exhibiting a symbolic act of loyalty to Chester Kallman, whose devotion to opera was passionate. It might have been interesting, as well as pertinent, to have offered rebuttals to these views of Auden's about Brahms and Shakespeare, but the proportions of my text and the urgency of other matters forbade it.

Let me turn to what may be some more serious matters. Too late for mention in the book, I made what seems to me an important discovery about some lines in one of Auden's best and most celebrated poems, "In Praise of Limestone," a poem I greatly admire and wrote about at length. The discovery I made very fortunately turned out not to repudiate anything I had written, since I, perhaps lazily, slid by the lines in question without making any comment on them. They are part of a description of a south Italian landscape:

---

3. Further comment may be useful here. Verdi's opera is based, not on Shakespeare's history plays, but on *The Merry Wives of Windsor,* in which (a) "the prig Prince Hal" does not appear and which (b) is a farcical comedy requiring no character development. Which is to say that by conflating these plays Auden has made it easy for himself by some questionable splicing. The stigma of "prig" can probably only be made on the basis of Hal's rather abrupt dismissal of Falstaff at the very end of *II Henry IV:* "I know thee not, old man. Fall to thy prayers."

Dover Wilson and Frye are both quite able to construe the two halves of the play in such a way as to keep a reader (or director) from viewing Hal as some sort of "born-again" figure of pompous sanctimoniousness. But the point is not purely one of literary-critical interpretation. One of the historians of the time, Robert Fabyan, in his 1516 *Cronycle,* describes the character of Henry V (i.e., Prince Hal) in a way that may very well have served to guide Shakespeare: "Thys man before the deth of hys father applyed hym vnto all vyce and insolency and drewe vnto hym all riottours and wyldly dysposed persones. But after he was admytted to the rule of the lande, anon and sodainly he became a new man and tourned all that rage and wyldnes into sobernes and sadnes and the vyce into constant vertue. And for he would continewe the vertue and not to be reduced therevnto by the famylyarite of his olde nyce company, he therefore after rewardes to them gyuen charged them vpon payne of theyr lyues that none of them were so hardy to come wythin x myle of such place as he were lodged." Quoted in C. S. Lewis, *English Literature in the Sixteenth Century Excluding Drama* (1954), 148.

> The poet,
> Admired for his earnest habit of calling
> The sun the sun, his mind Puzzle, is made uneasy
> By these solid statues which so obviously doubt
> His antimythological myth; . . .

If I had ventured to comment on these lines at the time of writing my book, I would have assumed that the phrase "the poet" was meant generically and that it referred to the foibles of all poets, though perhaps especially to "Romantic" ones, who like to *regard* themselves as poets and who interpose nothing between the world they observe and their own "creative imaginations." Their "antimythological myth," according to this reading, would be the myth of themselves as the sole creators of everything in their poetry. Had I made this assertion I would have been only fractionally right. I discovered, to my great surprise, that Auden has something far more precise and personal in mind. In a letter written on June 7, 1947, from Cherry Grove on Fire Island to Ursula Niebuhr, the wife of theologian Reinhold Niebuhr, Auden reported, "Have been reading the latest Wallace Stevens; some of it is very good, but it provoked me to the following little short [*short* is Auden's term for a brief, epigrammatic verse comment, or obiter dictum, of his own].

> Dear oh dear, More heresy to muzzle.
> No sooner have we buried in peace
> The flighty divinities of Greece
> Than up there pops the barbarian with
> An antimythological myth,
> Calling the sun the sun, his mind *Puzzle.*

Clearly, by "antimythological myth" Auden refers to Stevens' "Supreme Fiction." You can be sure that if I had known Ursula Niebuhr's book, *Remembering Reinhold Niebuhr* (1991) (in which this letter appears on pp. 288–89) I would certainly have mentioned it, not only for the light it sheds on Auden's views of another poet but also because it exhibits his characteristic tact in concealing that what seemed like a generalized disapproval of a literary tendency had behind it a precise individual target.

Now I turn to a still more serious topic, mentioned in my book though not dwelt upon at sufficient length. In his commonplace book, *A Certain World* (1970), Auden declares, "Christmas and Easter can be subjects for poetry, but Good Friday, like Auschwitz, cannot. The reality is so horrible, it is not surprising that people should have found it a stumbling block to faith . . . Poems about Good Friday have, of course, been written, but none of them will do . . . The 'Stabat Mater,' which sentimentalizes the event, is the first poem of medieval literature which can be called vulgar and 'camp' in the pejorative sense" (168). Now, the "Stabat Mater," an anonymous thirteenth-century poem, is admittedly histrionic in its grief, but Auden's dismissal of it is very curious, coming as it does from one devoted to the campy dramas of grand opera (with their theatrical lamentations) and from one who is the author of an excellent poem about the Crucifixion called "Nones." Moreover, there are many powerful and moving poems about the Crucifixion, as Auden surely knew. Apart from many anonymous ones, including one I quote in my book, which begins

> His body is wrappèd all in wo,
> Hand and fote he may not go.
> Thy son, lady, that thou lovest so
> Naked is nailed upon a tree,

there are many others, including Jacopone da Todi's "De la diversità de contemplazione de croce" and his "Pianto de la madonna de la passione del figlio Iesù Christo," and the far more familiar poem by George Herbert, "The Sacrifice."

Why does Auden pretend to ignore all this? Perhaps because he found himself engrossed in a topical controversy surrounding Theodor Adorno's unequivocal assertion that after Auschwitz there can be no more poetry. Auden appears to have adopted Adorno's view. It is a view that has been contested by others, including Edmond Jabès, who wrote, "To Adorno's statement that 'after Auschwitz one can no longer write poetry,' inviting global questioning of our culture, I am tempted to answer: yes, one can. And furthermore, one must."[4] The American poet Mark Strand's conversational comment on Adorno's dictum was, "After Auschwitz one can no longer eat lunch, either; but one does."

---

4. Quoted in Veronique Fóti, *Heidegger and the Poets* (1992).

Were I able to, I would correct a number of outright errors, which I very much regret. I misidentify Richard Tauber as a Wagnerian tenor, when in fact his career was devoted largely to operetta by such composers as Franz Lehár, though he had begun auspiciously with the operas of Mozart. Perhaps more seriously, I declared it a "curious and inexplicable business" that Auden should have dedicated one of his poems, "Islands," to Giocondo Sacchetti (whom I identified as "an inoffensive young man who worked as a domestic in Auden's Ischian household") and then, changing his mind, rededicated it to Giovanni Maresca, who was Auden's Italian translator. I thought this withdrawal of the dedication capricious and questionable; or at least I thought so until I went back to Humphrey Carpenter's biography, where the whole thing is clearly explained. He writes, in part, about this, that "Auden himself had become involved in a public quarrel with his house-boy, Giocondo. His habit had been to send Giocondo a cheque from America each winter to cover house-keeping and wages. This was usually for 60,000 lire, but on one occasion Auden absentmindedly added an extra nought to the figure. The mistake was discovered, and Auden sent another check for the correct sum. But Giocondo kept the first cheque." At this point the two were on bad terms because the house-boy's duties were highly demanding, laborious, and perhaps unusual, so that eventually he left this employment, whereupon, Carpenter reports, "he presented the cheque for 600,000 lire to the bank, whose manager, realizing there was not enough money to cover it in the account, informed Auden."[5] Greater attention to Carpenter would have saved me from my bewilderment.

Another illuminating detail was pointed out to me by an English reader; and it is one I might have noted myself if I'd had my wits about me. In a poem called "Precious Five" Auden addresses what amounts to a prayer to the five senses: smell, hearing, touch, sight, and taste. The prayer is in fact addressed to the organs identified with these senses: the nose, the ears, the hands, the eyes, and the tongue, the last of which is ambiguously identified not merely with taste but with the power of speech. All these organs are enjoined to "behave themselves," to observe a suitable and almost reverent decorum. Each of the senses is reminded of how it can become corrupt and that it requires discipline. The tongue in particular is specifically reminded of "The old self you become / At any drink or

5. Humphrey Carpenter, *W. H. Auden: A Biography* (1981), 386.

meal, / That animal of taste / And of his twin, your brother, / Unlettered, savage, dumb, / Down there below the waist." That brother of the tongue, "Down there below the waist," is the penis. The unlettered, savage, and dumb member of this pair of brothers serves as a warning to the more articulate, civilized, and eloquent brother, the tongue, against heedless impetuosity and the carnal selfishness that takes over when the disciplines of thought and decorum are absent. The "old self" it becomes "at any drink or meal" is the crudely appetitive, infantile self, a baby's or a lust's concern only with its own immediate satisfaction.

There's another matter I wish I had pursued with more care and at greater length. As in many cases with Auden, it appears both in his poetry and in his prose. (A number of critics, by the way, have pointed out how often Auden converts some insights gained in the humble course of book reviewing into valuable details in his poems. This was true of him from the very outset of his career.) The poem I now want to address is one of the *Horae Canonicae*, specifically the one called "Sext," the canonical hour celebrated at high noon and the one that inaugurates the anguish of the Passion and anticipates the ritual hour of the Crucifixion, observed at three in the afternoon and called "Nones." The first of the three parts of "Sext" goes,

> You need not see what someone is doing
> to know if it is his vocation,
>
> you have only to watch his eyes:
> a cook mixing a sauce, a surgeon
>
> making a primary incision,
> a clerk completing a bill of lading,
>
> wear the same rapt expression,
> forgetting themselves in their function.
>
> How beautiful it is,
> that eye-on-the-object look.
>
> To ignore the appetitive goddesses,
> to desert the formidable shrines

of Rhea, Aphrodite, Demeter, Diana,
to pray instead to St. Phocas,

St. Barbara, San Saturnino,
or whoever one's patron saint is,

that one may be worthy of their mystery,
what a prodigious step to have taken.

There should be monuments, there should be odes,
to the nameless heroes who took it first,

to the first flaker of flints
who forgot his dinner,

the first collector of sea-shells
to remain celibate.

Where should we be but for them?
Feral still, un-housetrained, still

wandering through forests without
a consonant to our names,

slaves to Dame Kind, lacking
all notion of a city,

and, at this noon, for this death,
there would be no agents.

The commentary on these lines should have been much greater than
what I too hastily awarded them. It might have begun with an observation
of the ironic burden of the last lines just quoted, suggesting that mankind
had to mature, advance, and sophisticate itself before it was not only worthy of a salvific Crucifixion but also capable of the necessary act of cruci-
fying Christ. It presupposes that the devotions paid to pagan deities must
have been qualitatively different from Christian worship, the difference

being that Christian worship is putatively *disinterested*, whereas pagan worship is always concerned with personal or communal advantage. The "first flaker of flints" is made the spiritual superior of a worshipper of Demeter, to whom one would pray in hope of an abundant harvest; whereas even though the flint-flaker might be engaged in the manufacture of a weapon to be used for the practical purposes of the hunt, at the moment he is viewed in this poem he is rapt in concentration and has forgotten his dinner. We must elect not to question the claim that Christian worship is purely disinterested and that none of the saints is ever appealed to for pressing personal reasons. Having omitted all such considerations, I instead quoted some prose of Auden's as a gloss upon his lines, part of an essay called "Pride and Prayer," which appeared in the March 1974 issue of the *Episcopalian:*

> As an antidote to Pride, man has been endowed with the capacity for prayer, an activity which is not to be confined to prayer in the narrow religious sense of the word. To pray is to pay attention to, or, shall we say, to "listen" to someone or something other than oneself.
>
> Whenever a man so concentrates his attention—be it on a landscape or a poem or a geometrical problem or an idol or the True God—that he completely forgets his own ego and desires in listening to what the other has to say to him, he is praying.
>
> Choice of attention—to attend to this and ignore that—is to the inner life what choice of action is to the outer. In both cases man is responsible for his choice and must accept the consequences. As Ortega y Gasset said: "Tell me to what you pay attention, and I will tell you who you are." The primary task of the schoolteacher is to teach children, in a secular context, the technique of prayer.
>
> Petitionary prayer is a special case and, of all kinds of prayers, I believe the least important. Our wishes and our desires—to pass an exam, to marry the person we love, to sell our house at a good price— are involuntary and therefore not themselves prayers, even if it is God whom we ask to attend to them. They only become prayers in so far as we believe that God knows better than we whether we should be granted or denied what we ask.
>
> A petition does not become a prayer unless it ends with the words, spoken or unspoken, "Nevertheless, not as I will, but as thou wilt."

What both poem and prose comment present seems to me seriously muddled. And the muddles are of three kinds: historical, theological, and moral. I shall try to address these in order. First, historically, the poem invites us to move from the worship of Aphrodite, Demeter, and Diana to the act of addressing prayers to St. Phocas or San Saturnino (there seem to have been at least four of the last-named) and to remark of this change, "what a prodigious step to have taken." The taking of this step presumes an advance—religiously, to be sure, but historically as well. The pagan worship clearly predates the Christian. But when, a few lines later, the poem turns in admiration to "the first flaker of flints" and regards him as a nameless hero, we have moved backwards in time to something like *Pithecanthropus Erectus*, while still admiring that primitive as somehow superior to pagans in terms of his ability to rise through concentration into selflessness.

Theologically, in his essay Auden acknowledges that petitionary prayers cannot be called wholly disinterested, and in this sense it is only by embracing a specific Christian orthodoxy that they can be called different from, and superior to, the prayers of pagan worshippers.[6] He posits, as though it were proven, that the pagans were incapable of spiritual selflessness, a highly debatable position and one confuted by the figure of Socrates or the philosophy of the Stoics.

It is, however, the moral component of the poem that presents the chief problems. Auden is arguing that man's besetting sin is his self-concern, a species of Pride, the most fundamental and universal of the Seven Deadly

---

6. Writing of European Christianity in the thirteenth century, Jacques Le Goff declared that "the Church told the powerful and the weak that the world was growing old, was settling into a state of ruin, and that they must think of their salvation. The majority of laymen believed that the mighty had taken full advantage of the little time that remained, while the humble must pry from the earth the crumbs of pleasure within their reach. There was, of course, God and the Last Judgment. But men did not manage to discern a close link between their life and God's eventual judgment of each one of them. This God resembled the ravenous gods whom their ancestors had long adored, gods who were either natural forces such as oak trees, springs, or rocks that had either been destroyed or been baptized by the Church, or else idols that priests and monks had overturned and replaced by churches and statues. He was an entirely different God, but one whom the mass of superficially Christianized laymen sought to satisfy by the same offerings or by new gifts that resembled the old ones. The powerful and the rich gave land, money, golden objects or rents; the poor gave humbler gifts, among them some of their children as oblates of the monasteries." *Your Money or Your Life: Economy and Religion in the Middle Ages* (1988), 66–67.

Sins. (Among his very late apothegms is one that reads in its entirety: "Blessed be all metrical rules that forbid automatic responses, force us to have second thoughts, free from the fetters of Self.") This self-regard, this narcissism, whether as selfishness or self-love, is so common a human failing that any escape from it deserves to be remarked upon and applauded. Auden furthermore identified this kind of self-consciousness with the inauguration of the Romantic period, with which he had a very limited sympathy.

I find myself quite willing to assent to the claim that self-concern is a pervasive spiritual flaw, a common form of sinfulness. I would also agree that certain kinds of concentration on objects other than oneself can be wholesome and laudable. It may even be that in writing his poem Auden had in mind Simone Weil's book *Waiting for God*, in which she wrote that "training in 'attention' is the essence of prayer." There is, however, another side to the problem which neither of these authors takes into account but which is examined with great care and attention by Hannah Arendt. She wrote of it as "the banality of evil," by which she meant that bureaucracy tends to manufacture for itself a kind of moral blindness which serves as a self-protective vaccine against any consciousness of its own malfeasances. It permits the bureaucrat, at whatever level he may be stationed, the illusion of moral immunity to any dubious acts he is required to perform. By this means most of the Nazi hierarchy were able to believe that their whole labor consisted of minute attention to impersonal detail, even when this involved the extermination of millions. This seems to me a serious, valid, and important objection to Auden's poem and essay.[7]

---

7. This dehumanizing technique of self-exculpation is by no means confined merely to Nazis or Stalinists; it is, regrettably, a feature of almost all rigid hierarchies, particularly military ones, including the American variety. The *Washington Post* carried a feature article in its issue of January 30, 1993, devoted to Paul Tibbets Jr., group commander of the *Enola Gay*, the B-29 that dropped the bomb on Hiroshima. Asked by a Canadian television interviewer whether he entertained any "regrets" about "all the people you killed," Tibbets replied, "No, I've never lost a night's sleep over it, and I never will." The paper goes on to characterize him this way: "He was, in a sense, a long-haul driver, a man infected with flight line fever. His rig: a B-29 Superfortress. His mission: Deliver the cargo." In other words, Tibbets was simply a very fast and reliable truck driver.

There may be a number of factors that contributed to Commander Tibbets' untroubled sleeping habits. If he were a thoughtful man, he might claim that a case could be made, on purely statistical grounds, that in all probability more lives were saved by dropping the bomb, and thus bringing the war to an abrupt end, than would have been lost by both sides if the conflict had been protracted, entailing a costly invasion of the Japanese mainland accompanied by

Were revisions to be permitted and were all limits on the size of the book removed, I would want now to add comments on works of Auden's to which I was able to give little or no notice. Among the poems, the one beginning "Who stands, the crux left of the watershed" and another, beginning "Perhaps I always knew what they were saying," seem to me more important than most commentaries acknowledge. Were I not too badly to unbalance the proportions of my text, I'd like to examine at some length Auden's brilliant set of lectures on the Romantic spirit, *The Enchafèd Flood*. This seems to me a particularly interesting and important work because of Auden's curiously equivocal stance in regard to the Romantic period and its chief poets and authors. Opera, and his assimilated musical tastes, brought him firmly into the Romantic camp. But from the outset he was devoted to the sanity, clarity, and balance of the neoclassical poets, and in many personal ways he bore a remarkable resemblance to Dr. Johnson.

I was particularly struck by this in the course of reading *Samuel Johnson* (1975), Walter Jackson Bate's splendid biography of the great eighteenth-century poet-critic. Consider these striking parallelisms. Both Auden and Johnson had very poor eyesight; both held cleanliness in utter disregard. (About Auden, Stravinsky remarked to Edmund Wilson, "He is the dirtiest man I have ever liked.") Both Auden and Johnson were disposed, in Bate's words, to choose "the wrong side of a debate, because most ingenious, that is to say, most new things, could be said upon it" (52). Both held (again in Bate's words) a "lifelong conviction—against which another part of him was forever afterwards to protest—that indolence is an open invitation to mental distress and even disintegration, and that to pull ourselves together, through the focus of attention and the discipline of work, is within our power" (105). Both believed that "effort in daily habits—such as rising early—was necessary to 'reclaim imagination' and keep it on an even keel" (118). They shared some views of government and the dangers of tyranny. Bate described Johnson as "becoming more slovenly in dress and eating habits as he ran about London, [where he] left a train of disarray wherever he entered" (209), and Auden notoriously exhibited the same

intense conventional bombing. This is a plausible hypothesis, though one that has been hotly debated. But a "theirs not to reason why, / theirs but to do or die" attitude, while standard military procedure, is somewhat less noble, employed as it was by Nazi war criminals who claimed in self-defense that they were only following orders. It is an attitude required of all American soldiers from the moment they don uniforms.

personal habits. Auden greatly admired the kind of virtue Johnson praised in Robert Levet: "Here was a man," Bate remarked of Levet, "who, despite serious disadvantages, performed a useful and charitable function not impulsively or occasionally but with unwavering constancy. It was an example to frail human nature of what could be done" (271).

Both Johnson and Auden were, on principle, indifferent to their surroundings. In addition, Bate wrote, Johnson "was able to distinguish between 'loving' and 'being loved' and to value the first without demanding equal payment through the latter" (379), while Auden wrote, "If equal affection cannot be, / Let the more loving one be me." Both men were determined, if at all possible, "to be pleased" with their circumstances and with their fellow human beings, as a reproval of their own "impatience and quickness to irritability or despair" (434). Both men repeatedly maintained (again in Bate's words) that "the 'main of life' consists of 'little things'; that happiness or misery is to be found in the accumulation of 'petty' and 'domestic' details, not in 'large' ambitions, which are inevitably self-defeating, and turn to ashes in the mouth. 'Sands make the mountain,' [Johnson] would quote from Edward Young" (511).

Both men exhibited an uncommon courtesy and respect for others. Of Auden's considerateness I can myself attest, while Bate wrote that, much like Auden's habits in this regard, "Johnson had been making a point for some time of never beginning a conversation but of waiting until someone else spoke to him directly . . . It was part of his renewed effort to acquire 'good nature'—'easiness of approach,' grace and relaxation, and was an indication that he was not allowing himself to dominate the conversation" (557). Both firmly believed that fortitude "is not to be found primarily in meeting rare and great occasions. And this was true not only of fortitude but of all the other virtues, including 'good nature.' The real test is in what we do in our daily life, and happiness—such happiness as exists—lies primarily in what we can do with the daily texture of our lives" (593).

These resemblances might be carried one extraordinary step further: since both men were by nature disposed to admire neoclassical decorum and to exhibit it in their work, Johnson's ability to praise the pre-Romantic extravagance of Richard Savage is a precedent for Auden's "Romantic Iconography of the Sea," which is the subtitle of his Page-Barbour Lectures, *The Enchafèd Flood.*

Let me turn to a specific poem of Auden's which in my book I mentioned in passing but to which I would like to have given far more elaborate attention. It is famous, and among the more popular of his early poems: the pseudo-ballad or folksong called "As I Walked Out One Evening."

> As I walked out one evening,
> Walking down Bristol Street,
> The crowds upon the pavement
> Were fields of harvest wheat.
>
> And down by the brimming river
> I heard a lover sing
> Under the arch of the railway:
> "Love has no ending.
>
> "I'll love you, dear, I'll love you
> Till China and Africa meet
> And the river jumps over the mountain
> And the salmon sing in the street.
>
> "I'll love you till the ocean
> Is folded and hung up to dry
> And the seven stars go squawking
> Like geese about the sky.
>
> "The years shall run like rabbits
> For in my arms I hold
> The Flower of the Ages
> And the first love of the world."
>
> But all the clocks of the city
> Began to whirr and chime:
> "O let not Time deceive you,
> You cannot conquer Time.
>
> "In the burrows of the Nightmare
> Where Justice naked is,

Time watches from the shadow
And coughs when you would kiss.

"In headaches and in worry
Vaguely life leaks away,
And Time will have his fancy
To-morrow or to-day.

"Into many a green valley
Drifts the appalling snow;
Time breaks the threaded dances
And the diver's brilliant bow.

"O plunge your hands in water,
Plunge them in up to the wrist;
Stare, stare in the basin
And wonder what you missed.

"The glacier knocks in the cupboard,
The desert sighs in the bed,
And the crack in the tea-cup opens
A lane to the land of the dead.

"Where the beggars raffle the banknotes
And the Giant is enchanting to Jack,
And the Lily-white boy is a Roarer
And Jill goes down on her back.

"O look, look in the mirror,
O look in your distress;
Life remains a blessing
Although you cannot bless.

"O stand, stand at the window
As the tears scald and start;
You shall love your crooked neighbor
With your crooked heart."

It was late, late in the evening,
The lovers they had gone;
The clocks had ceased their chiming
And the deep river ran on.

The poem features three voices. The first one we may call "the speaker,"
a master of ceremonies who acts as presenter, the "I" of the poem. To him
are assigned the first seven lines, the first two lines of the sixth stanza, in
which he introduces the clocks of the city, and the final quatrain. The
other two voices are those of the lover and the clocks, to the latter of which
is given the largest, most dramatic and ominous part of the poem.

The speaker's introduction to the poem may seem innocent enough,
and the line "As I walked out one evening" might recall some opening
lines of Elizabethan poetry: Southwell's "As I in hoary winter's night,"
Richard Barnfield's lyric "As it fell upon a day," or even the American cow-
boy ballads "As I walked out in the streets of Laredo" and "As I walked out
one morning for pleasure." More apt, I think, might be the children's rid-
dle-poem that begins "As I was going to St. Ive's," for Auden's poem, as
we shall see, is laden with materials from children's folk literature and lore.
I must confess that for many years I was unable to read the third and
fourth lines about the pavement crowds as harvest wheat without thinking of Eliot's "The readers of the *Boston Evening Transcript* / Sway in the
wind like a field of ripe corn." So close was this association in my mind, so
strongly did I suspect that Eliot's lines influenced Auden, that I was long
misled as to the true significance of Auden's images. (The Eliot poem,
which is very complicated and far removed from Auden's tone and purposes, is too complex to discuss here.) The speaker goes on in the following lines, in the manner of a comparatively self-effacing emcee, to present
the lover. (I will return at the end to the imagery of the opening lines. The
river, of course, is important. It reappears at the end. It is itself a symbol
of, among other things, the passage of time. William Gass, critic, fiction
writer, professor of philosophy, who happens to live in St. Louis on the
banks of the Mississippi, wrote that "to live by a river is to live by an image of Time." And "Time," as the clocks in this poem will insist, is a central force of great significance in the poem. But in a way that I think has
not properly been noticed.)

Let's turn to the lover. What he presents is both ludicrously hyperbolic and traditional at once. It is a vaunt, a boast, a brag. His declaration of eternal love should strike us as remarkably familiar. There was an entire genre of such boasting, associated with epic heroes (in Homer as well as other authors) and appropriated by chivalric poets in the name of their knightly prowess, in praise of the virtue and beauty of their mistresses, and finally in behalf of their undying fealty to those ladies. The medieval tradition carried on well into the Renaissance, and I will offer a little smorgasbord of examples.

> Love's not Time's fool, though rosy lips and cheeks
> Within his bending sickle's compass come;
> Love alters not with his brief hours and weeks,
> But bears it out even to the edge of doom.
> (Shakespeare, Sonnet 116)

> Whatever dies, was not mixed equally;
> If our two loves be one, or thou or I
> Love so alike, that none do slacken, none can die.
> (Donne, "The Good Morrow")

And in the following lines by Petrarch, as translated by Thomas Wyatt, the phrase "my master" refers to Love personified.

> What may I do when my master feareth
> But in the field with him to live and die?
> For good is the life ending faithfully.

In his *Amoretti*, Spenser could claim that "Our love shall live, and later life renew." And when, in the fourth act of *As You Like It*, Rosalind asks Orlando how long he will be true to her, he replies, "Forever and a day." These are extravagant declarations, but the experience of love is almost by definition reckless and emphatic, so the literature of love employs hyperbole quite naturally. Orlando is no more guilty of this than Romeo, and when the lover in Auden's poem says his love will continue "Till the seven stars go squawking / Like geese about the sky," by the seven stars he means the Pleiades, a group of stars in the constellation Taurus, supposedly fixed in their astronomical positions, from which they could not be budged until the Apocalypse occurs. What the lover says is that he will be true to his love until that precise, terminal moment. Extravagant, but no more than what Othello says regarding his love for Desdemona: "Excellent wretch! Perdition catch my soul / But I do love thee! and when I love thee not, / Chaos is come again." Another instance (many more could be cited) of poetic vaunt may be found in the following "heroic brag" (not in this case associated with fidelity in love) by Thomas d'Urfey, which was set to music by Purcell.

> I'll sail upon the Dog-star,
> And then pursue the morning;
> I'll chase the moon till it be noon,
> But I'll make her leave her horning.
> I'll climb the frosty mountain,
> And there I'll coin the weather;
> I'll tear the rainbow from the sky,
> And tie both ends together;
> The stars pluck from their orbs, too,
> And crowd them in my budget;
> And whether I'm a roaring boy,
> Let all the nations judge it.

(It may be useful at this point to provide a note about the "roaring boy," not least because he turns up in Auden's poem as "a Roarer." The terms were synonymous and applied to unemployed young men who, having recently been discharged from military service, sustained themselves by terrifying and bullying the civilian population with threats of violence.)

Let me close my little case of samples with one more declaration of undying love, taken from the volume *Early English Lyrics*, edited by E. K. Chambers and F. Sidgwick (1967, 54).

> As the holly groweth green,
> And never changeth hue,
> So am I, ever hath been
> Unto my lady true;
>
> As the holly groweth green
> With ivy all alone

When flowerès can not be seen
And green wood leaves be gone.

Now unto my lady
Promise to her I make.
From all other only
To her I me betake.

Adieu, mine own lady,
Adieu, my speciàl,
Who hath my heart truly,
Be sure, and ever shall!

The point about this pledge of perfect devotion is not only that it was a literary convention and a commonplace but that it is what young men in the transports of love often genuinely feel. If your reaction to the poem is tainted with cynicism when you discover that it was written by Henry VIII, and if you go on from that discovery to the unwarranted conclusion that all men in the end are selfish and deceitful brutes who have at heart only their carnal lusts, you would do well to bear in mind what this conclusion implies about the bottomless credulity of the women to whom such verse is addressed. Modern advertisers know exactly what they are doing when they carry out a commercial campaign for a perfume manufacturer with the slogan "Promise her anything, but give her Arpège!" As for the concluding vaunt of Auden's lover regarding his beloved, and calling her "The Flower of the Ages / And the first love of the world," we may recall the claim of Yeats, in his poem "The Tower" in regard to Helen of Troy, that "Helen has all human hearts betrayed." And also recall Frost's still more marvelous assertion (in "Never Again Would Birds' Song Be the Same") that in the singing of birds is still to be heard the inflections and lilt of Eve's own voice.

Auden's lover having made his boast and had his say, it is now the turn of all the clocks to speak; and they flatly repudiate the lover. Their declaration that "you cannot conquer Time" is aimed not merely at acts of infidelity or the transience of human passion but at the universal mutability of all things mortal. It is the tolling bell of mortality, and it immediately ushers in "the burrows of the Nightmare." These burrows are the catacombs of the subconscious, and the remainder of the sermon delivered by the clocks is set in this self-accusatory, self-incriminating region. It is the region of Justice: naked, immitigable Justice of the kind Auden, in another poem, calls "The Hidden Law." And when in this poem it is said that "Time watches from the shadow / And coughs when you would kiss," the act of kissing is classed as an indelicate transgression against seemliness, a gaffe or a faux pas. This is to say that one of the most innocent gestures of love is itself condemned—condemned by Time, the grown-up, who has not only been spying and eavesdropping but who, by making its presence known (by the approved signal of a cough), will force all lovers to retire in embarrassment and confusion (like Adam and Eve at the discovery of their shameful nakedness) and thus arrest all thoughts of love.

Why is love here regarded as indiscreet? In the lines that tell us that "Time will have his fancy / To-morrow or to-day," we recognize a locution that was traditionally applied, not to Time, but to Death, especially in that medieval genre of "The Dance of Death" (written of by John Lydgate, illustrated by Hans Holbein, and the title of one of Auden's earliest works, published in 1933), in which Death is presented as inviting everyone among all the ranks of mankind to dance with him. This invitation, this fancy, whim, or choice, is always his. The phrase "to take a fancy to" someone is usually erotic in meaning. It is the theme of "Death and the Maiden." Since everyone must die, Time and Death can be recognized as equivalents, more or less, and as soon as we recognize that equation, almost everything that follows in the poem becomes, for all its hallucinatory surrealism, marvelously clarified. We grasp the meaning of the "appalling snow" that drifts (like a pall) into the green valleys of life with its deathlike chill, and the interruption of physical graces and pleasures, like the dances and the diver's "brilliant bow." The "crack in the tea-cup," that most trifling of imperfections, is a sign of some great and damning failure that leads to the grave. Self-accused and self-incriminated in this Nightmare, Mankind desperately seeks to cleanse itself—hence the plunging of hands into water. The injunction to "Stare, stare in the basin / And wonder what you've missed" refers ambiguously to what you had expected to receive but were inexplicably cheated of, as well as to how you must somehow unwittingly have taken the wrong turn, having missed some important signal. Images of inexorable fate abound. The glacier not only is cold but cannot be deflected from its course; the symbolic fruitfulness of the bed is buried under the arid sands of the desert.

The Nightmare becomes a surrealist parody of what we had hoped for, counted upon, above all been led, as children, to expect. Beggars are in control of the banks; Jack, the boy's champion against paternal tyranny, now entertains a questionable sexual interest in one he was supposed heroically to slay; Jill turns prostitute, and the "Lily-white boy" is also borrowed from the realm of children's literature. In this case it is from a Twelfth Night verse (like "The Twelve Days of Christmas") called "I'll Sing You One-O." It includes the line "Seven for the seven stars in the sky," to which Auden has already made reference, and it concludes, "Three, three, the rivals; / Two, two, the lily-white boys, / Dressèd all in green-o; / One is one and all alone, and evermore shall be so." The scholiasts have determined that the three rivals are the coequal members of the Trinity; that One is the One God and that the two lily-white boys are Jesus and John the Baptist. Which one of them becomes this nightmare's "Roarer" is uncertain, but decidedly out of character, as is everything else in this nightmare's hellish and terrifying world.

The last two stanzas given to the clocks are remarkable for their biblical and religious import, and in this they are distinct from most of the rest of the poem. The clocks assert that "Life remains a blessing / Although you cannot bless." From the clocks' point of view, Life may be blessed in its brevity, and, because it is full of misfortune, brevity is its chief merit. But from another biblical point of view, the blessedness of Life derives from its being a gift of God; and mankind's inability to confer blessing is an index of its alienation from a once blessed condition. More striking still is the warped, crippled injunction: "You shall love your crooked neighbor / With your crooked heart." This is a deliberately deformed echo of the commandment that appears first in Leviticus (19:18) and is repeated in the New Testament (Mark 12:28–31). In this nightmare world, however, imperfection has maimed everything, including the noblest acts and purposes.

The force and authority that governs all that happens in this poem, the impeachments voiced by all the clocks in the city to confound the lover and his vaunts, are the reprisals of the Justice that began with mankind's fall from grace in the Garden of Eden and have continued to torment us ever since. In Eden there was inexplicably both Time and no Time. There were days and nights, to provide variety and afford occasion for rest as for waking life; but there was no aging, nor any change of season. Milton (in Book IV of *Paradise Lost*) wrote:

> The birds their quire apply; airs, vernal airs,
> Breathing the smell of fields and groves attune
> The trembling leaves, while universal Pan,
> Knit with the Graces and the Hours in dance,
> Led on th' eternal spring.

The timeless world of which the lover sings, and which is envisioned as one in which love will last (in Orlando's words) "forever and a day," the Edenic world yearned for by children, in which the moral order is clear and Good is always triumphant, this world was ruined once and for all by mankind's act of disobedience, which, again in Milton's words, "Brought death into the world, and all our woe."

Now this interpretation may strike some as disputable when applied to the work of a poet who renounced his religious faith in 1922 and counted himself a partisan of the secular and revolutionary forces of the Communist movement. Auden himself has said that until somewhat later in his life (this poem was written in 1937) he believed he had, in his own words, "done with Christianity forever." Nevertheless, even in these years of secular preoccupations, he had written poems that were unambiguously prayers, though it was not always clear to whom they were addressed. "Sir, no man's enemy" is such a prayer, as are several others from the same period. He was, in fact, using the very language, doctrines, and symbols that he had consciously repudiated.

I think we are now in a better position to understand the imagery that opens and closes the poem and is spoken by "the speaker." The point is not to interpret the fields of harvest wheat in isolation, though harvest wheat is an apt symbol of universal mortality. Nor should we think of the "brimming river" simply as William Gass's "image of Time." The point of these images, and their effect, is determined by their conjunctions. The fields of harvest wheat are not simply that natural crop itself but also and at the same time the crowds "upon the pavement." The river in the second stanza is juxtaposed with "the arch of the railway." In both cases a residual Edenic pastoralism (the wheat and the river) is linked with urban concrete and industrial technology. The river, which in the opening "brims" and thereby calls attention entirely to its surface, in the final stanza is described as "deep," its surface ignored, its mystery and hidden character emphasized instead. Both the timeless world of the lover and the taintless world of the child are irrevocably gone. And yet we are at all times in the vicinity, not just of the signs and symbols, but of the true landscape, of early, original bliss. The fields of wheat, the river, both remind us—and we are in constant need of such reminding—that despite our offenses, despite our urbanization, our technological "improvements," paved-over grasslands, and emplaced train trestles, life is a gift of the Creator and continues to remain a blessing.

On Robert Frost's "The Wood-Pile"

Robert Frost had his first book published when he was thirty-nine. It happened in England, where, with a wife and four children and utterly unknown as a writer, he had settled with few resources in the hope of launching his career as a poet. The book, *A Boy's Will,* made its appearance around the first of April 1913, and during the first two months after publication it received only two brief and highly equivocal mentions in the press. The *Atheneum* (April 5) declared, "These poems are intended by the author to possess a certain sequence, and to depict the various stages in the evolution of a young man's outlook on life. The author is only half successful at this, possibly because many of his verses do not rise above the ordinary, though here and there a happy line or phrase lingers gratefully in the memory." The *Times Literary Supplement* (April 10) also confined itself to two sentences: "There is an agreeable individuality about these pieces; the writer is not afraid to voice the simplest of his thoughts and fancies, and these, springing from a capacity for complete absorption in the influences of nature and the open air, are often naively engaging. Sometimes, too, in a vein of reflection, he makes one stop and think, though the thought may be feebly or obscurely expressed." It should not surprise us to learn from a Frost biographer that when these slight and slighting notices appeared, "Frost's hopes melted into discouragement."[1]

Within a year he had a second book, much of it held in reserve even as he turned the first one in to David Nutt, his London publisher. This second was to become a celebrated success; but Frost had no way of knowing this in advance, whereas he had reason enough to feel apprehension. Here I want to speak briefly about the poem he chose to conclude the book,

---

1. Lawrence Thompson, *Robert Frost: The Early Years* (1966), 415.

called *North of Boston.* It is one of his most admired and popular poems, though I suspect not fully understood. It is called "The Wood-Pile."

The Wood-Pile

Out walking in the frozen swamp one gray day,
I paused and said, "I will turn back from here.
No, I will go on farther—and we shall see."
The hard snow held me, save where now and then
One foot went through. The view was all in lines
Straight up and down of tall slim trees
Too much alike to mark or name a place by
So as to say for certain I was here
Or somewhere else: I was just far from home.
A small bird flew before me. He was careful
To put a tree between us when he lighted,
And say no word to tell me who he was
Who was so foolish as to think what *he* thought.
He thought that I was after him for a feather—
The white one in his tail; like one who takes
Everything said as personal to himself.
One flight out sideways would have undeceived him.
And then there was a pile of wood for which
I forgot him and let his little fear
Carry him off the way I might have gone,
Without so much as wishing him good-night.
He went behind it to make his last stand.
It was a cord of maple, cut and split
And piled—and measured, four by four by eight.
And not another like it could I see.
No runner tracks in this year's snow looped near it.
And it was older sure than this year's cutting,
Or even last year's or the year's before.
The wood was gray and the bark warping off it
And the pile somewhat sunken. Clematis
Had wound strings round and round it like a bundle.
What held it, though, on one side was a tree

Still growing, and on one a stake and prop,
These latter about to fall. I thought that only
Someone who lived in turning to fresh tasks
Could so forget his handiwork on which
He spent himself, the labor of his ax,
And leave it there far from a useful fireplace
To warm the frozen swamp as best it could
With the slow smokeless burning of decay.

The commentary on this poem has been deservedly ample; there's a lot to be said about it, and I am going to sprint lightly past a number of topics worth careful consideration. Among these would be the Dantean setting of a solitary man who is lost in a wood; and the self-division of the speaker who not only talks to himself in both the singular and plural modes of address but is, for a while, "of two minds" about whether to proceed; the amused and amusing projection of the speaker's own paranoia—that of "one who takes / Everything said as personal to himself"—onto a small bird. All this and more I will ignore, directing your attention entirely to the final lines descriptive of the wood-pile that gives the poem its title. It is a cord of maple, piled and measured "four by four by eight," which is the proper measure of a cord. Precision in such matters is commercially significant for any transaction, even for tallying the extent of a completed task. How curious, how enigmatic, to find this perfectly stacked cord abandoned in the middle of nowhere. What does it mean? Since this wood-pile gives the poem its title, we are surely meant to give some thought to this.

One critic, whom I greatly admire and almost invariably agree with, has this to say of the poem's end: "The final line has been rightly admired, but its brilliance almost blinds us to the fact that the reflection which it concludes is in no sense stunning or profound. The thought that 'someone' who abandoned this pile of wood must be one who 'lived in turning to fresh tasks,' is certainly uncontroversial and hardly provocative of further speculation." I wish emphatically to dissent from that view. To begin with, that wood-pile, in the care and precision of its stacking, while familiar and conventional enough, is only one of a series of symbols recurrent in Frost's poetry of demanding, sometimes fatiguing, physical tasks performed with special accuracy. Consider these lines from "After Apple-Picking."

> There were ten thousand thousand fruit to touch,
> Cherish in hand, lift down, and not let fall.
> For all
> That struck the earth
> No matter if not bruised or spiked with stubble,
> Went surely to the cider-apple heap
> As of no worth.

This is a dream episode, and a frightening one. It unfolds with remorseless and precise detail.

> Magnified apples appear and disappear,
> Stem end and blossom end,
> And every fleck of russet showing clear.

If you will allow yourself to suppose that the scrupulousness, the punctiliousness, of this apple-picker—in the fastidiousness of his selections, in the scrutiny of his examinations—is a metaphor for the conscientiousness involved in the writing of a poem, the determined discard of draft after unsatisfactory draft, you will, I think, come near to understanding the hallucinatory nightmare at the center of that poem and the overwhelming sense of fatigue at its close. The same kind of metaphor appears in a later poem, "Two Tramps in Mud Time," where the poet rejoices in his prowess as a woodsman:

> Good blocks of oak it was I split,
> As large around as the chopping block;
> And every piece I squarely hit
> Fell splinterless as a cloven rock.

Now I would further argue that when, in the poem under discussion here, the poet says "I thought that only / Someone who lived by turning to fresh tasks / Could so forget his handiwork on which / He spent himself, the labor of his ax," we, as readers, are entitled to register what we may think of as either a demurral or an avowal the poet is too reserved and careful to express. For surely one easily conceivable reason that pile is there is that the man who cut and stacked it has died. This is not said; it is in fact deliberately avoided. But nothing could be more plausible, when you stop to think about it, and the more you think about it, the more it will strike you that the poet's declaration that "only someone who lived in turning to fresh tasks" could have abandoned the pile is a transparent evasion, an explanation selected precisely for its blandness, its easy evasiveness; as when with some euphemism we avoid some terrifying or unlucky topic. And if, as I urge you to consider, this "handiwork . . . on which he spent himself" were poems that had gone virtually unnoticed during the poet's lifetime, and were to be chanced upon by some stray wanderer long after the poet's death, then this wood-pile might well signify for Robert Frost the secret fears he must have entertained when, a year earlier, his first book had been greeted by such discouraging reviews; and there he was, husband and father of four—it might have been father of six, but for the early deaths of two children—in a foreign country where his work had been briefly and summarily dismissed.

Two Poems by Elizabeth Bishop

Take that brilliant early poem of Elizabeth Bishop's, "Wading at Wellfleet." It is brilliant in a whole set of ways: the scene itself is dazzling, and meant to dazzle. Its brilliant collocation of an innocent and singularly tame summer diversion, wading (and as the poem makes clear, the wading is no more than shin-deep), with military danger of an especially brutal kind is astonishing all by itself. That these two disparate matters ("The most heterogeneous ideas . . . yoked by violence together," in Dr. Johnson's definition of the "metaphysical" technique) should then be linked by a decisive allusion to a particular metaphysical poet is both brilliant and just. But finally, that this poem, which is about terror, should deal with its subject in so controlled and remote a way is its ultimate brilliance.

Wading at Wellfleet

In one of the Assyrian wars
a chariot first saw the light
that bore sharp blades around its wheels.

That chariot from Assyria
went rolling down mechanically
to take the warriors by the heels.

A thousand warriors in the sea
could not consider such a war
as that the sea itself contrives

but hasn't put in action yet.
This morning's glitterings reveal
the sea is "all a case of knives."

Lying so close, they catch the sun,
the spokes directed at the shin.
The chariot front is blue and great.

The war rests wholly with the waves:
they try revolving, but the wheels
give way, they will not bear the weight.

   Each two sets of tercets are linked by the rhymes of their final lines, and
the first two are given over to an ancient historical instrument of war. It
was, in its day, an especially hideous machine, the latest word in slaugh-
ter, and was indeed invented by the Persians or Assyrians. A single instrument, it could annihilate great hordes as it rode into their midst. It did
this, as the poet says, "mechanically," which is literally true: it was a machine and exhibited a machine's efficiency. It took "the warriors by the
heels," which is to say, it laid them low, a machine that destroyed people.
The heels, of course, are important because they will become the vulner-
able point, the Achilles' heel, of the speaker when she comes round to taking notice of herself. The next two tercets insist that, spectacular in its destructive power as that chariot was, it was as nothing compared to the
arsenal and power of the sea. This threat is the more fearful because the
grand strategies of the ocean have not been "put in action yet." The brilliance of the morning's glitterings, which one would expect to cheer a
summer vacationer, especially one engaged in as tame a pastime as wading ankle-deep, nevertheless reveals that "the sea is 'all a case of knives.'"
The direct quotation from George Herbert's "Affliction IV" is important
in more than that he happens to have been Elizabeth Bishop's favorite
poet. The original context of this phrase, from a poem with a very significant title, goes:

   My thoughts are all a case of knives,
   Wounding my heart
   With scattered smart

It is a poem of spiritual agony, an interior anguish seemingly self-inflicted, being a petitionary prayer for relief and containing the later lines,

> dissolve the knot,
> As the sun scatters by his light
> All the rebellions of the night.

Those rebellions of the night we may take to be the nightmares of doubt and the turbulence of the unconscious mind, which the light of God, like the sun's light, will scatter and disperse.

But in the Bishop poem it is not darkness that is feared but the light itself, and the power of the ocean to wield it. (As Herbert's poem is subtly knit by the echo of *scattered* as *scatters*, so Bishop cunningly repeats the words *war*, or *warriors, sea*, and *wheels*.) Not only is the sea a case of knives, its blades surround "the shin," and are pointed at it; it is the target of their hostile circle, the hub of their spokes. This is the nearest the poet comes to admitting to her own presence: not "my shin," merely "the shin." That self-effacement is characteristic, but especially so when the poet seems to fear that she is expressing undue concern about herself. It is an indirection that will be familiar to most readers of her poetry. The danger and power inherent in the sea is emphatically *not* mechanical; it is precisely ungoverned and unpredictable, and therefore more terrible than the Assyrian chariot. Its wild and ungovernable character relates it to original chaos, on the one hand, and to the personal psyche, on the other. If we glance back to that first innocent tercet, which looked like no more than historical reportage, we notice that in those ancient days the latest engine of destruction, the ultimate weapon of its day, "first saw the light," that is, both came into being and discovered its own terrible potential, awoke to the glittering idea of destruction. The light in this poem is not benign and is not the light of God. It is the gleam of weaponry and, more precisely, the self-tormenting blades of the self-assailing mind. The poem ends without destruction, but this is set down to mere chance ("The war rests wholly with the waves"). For the moment they cannot bear the weight of the huge chariot of the sea, the enormous force of which the waves are instruments. But they have brandished their blades, and we know they could defeat "a thousand warriors," so the self-effacing, solitary speaker would have no chance against them.

it isn't only the glitter around her ankles that makes him analogy limp

The poem is written in a language so simple, an idiom so colloquial, and on an occasion (wading at Wellfleet, Cape Cod) so apparently serene that a first and even a second reading may suggest only that the poet is wide-ranging in her associative gifts. And even after "mastering all its parts," in Yeats' phrase, we never cease to be astonished at recognizing that this tranquil assemblage of details is a poem of real *affliction,* and not of a sort to be banished or dismissed. The sea-chariot of the final tercets is not easily assimilable in a clear, visual way (how are the wheels attached to the "front," what is the relation of the wheels to the "spokes" around the shin, what happens to the whole contraption when "the wheels give way"?), but this is because the danger here is not something that rolls down "mechanically"; it is instead an enormous external and internal disorder. Thoughtful readers of Elizabeth Bishop's poems will know that from time to time, in other of her writings, she touches upon such terrifying matters in the same chilling and cheerful way.

"THE MAN-MOTH"*

Here, above,
cracks in the buildings are filled with battered moonlight.
The whole shadow of Man is only as big as his hat.
It lies at his feet like a circle for a doll to stand on,
and he makes an inverted pin, the point magnetized to the moon.
He does not see the moon; he observes only her vast properties,
feeling the queer light on his hands, neither warm nor cold,
of a temperature impossible to record in thermometers.

But when the Man-Moth
pays his rare, although occasional, visits to the surface,
the moon looks rather different to him. He emerges
from an opening under the edge of one of the sidewalks
and nervously begins to scale the face of the buildings.
He thinks the moon is a small hole at the top of the sky,
proving the sky quite useless for protection.
He trembles, but must investigate as high as he can climb.

*Newspaper misprint for "mammoth."

Up the façades,
his shadow dragging like a photographer's cloth behind him,
he climbs fearfully, thinking that this time he will manage
to push his small head through that round clean opening
and be forced through, as from a tube, in black scrolls on the light.
(Man, standing below him, has no such illusions.)
But what the Man-Moth fears most he must do, although
he fails, of course, and falls back scared but quite unhurt.

Then he returns
to the pale subways of cement he calls his home. He flits,
he flutters, and cannot get aboard the silent trains
fast enough to suit him. The doors close swiftly.
The Man-Moth always seats himself facing the wrong way
and the train starts at once at its full, terrible speed,
without a shift in gears or a gradation of any sort.
He cannot tell the rate at which he travels backwards.

Each night he must
be carried through artificial tunnels and dream recurrent dreams.
Just as the ties recur beneath his train, these underlie
his rushing brain. He does not dare look out the window,
for the third rail, the unbroken draught of poison,
runs there beside him. He regards it as a disease
he has inherited the susceptibility to. He has to keep
his hands in his pockets, as others must wear mufflers.

If you catch him,
hold up a flashlight to his eye. It's all dark pupil,
an entire night itself, whose haired horizon tightens
as he stares back, and closes up the eye. Then from the lids
one tear, his only possession, like the bee's sting, slips.
Slyly he palms it, and if you're not paying attention
he'll swallow it. However, if you watch, he'll hand it over,
cool as from underground springs and pure enough to drink.

The footnoted title ("Newspaper misprint for 'mammoth'") is mildly, diffidently suggestive of an etiology: the poet, innocently reading the daily papers, stumbles upon an unexpected fictive creature, the product of typographical carelessness and faulty proofreading. And taking license from this liberating premise, she goes on to indulge herself in a sort of science-fiction fantasy, not very far removed from such a comic-strip convention as Spider-Man, whose name as well as whose newspaper source seem relevant.

Good enough for a start, and not entirely wrong; though we ought immediately to add that there is in the poem a sophistication of language altogether alien to any such cartoon origins. More seriously (or at least more literarily) the poem has sources in Surrealism (and in this it is not unique among Bishop's poems; consider, for example, one called "The Monument") and also in Symbolism, if we take that last, broad movement to include Baudelaire's realms of correspondences, which, in turn, recall the parallels of allegory, though viewed through the mists of imprecision. That allegorical dimension is proposed in this poem as early as its third line ("The whole shadow of Man [with an uppercase *M*] is only as big as his hat"). It is a splendid line, and serves, incidentally, to recall

> The lengthened shadow of a man
> Is history, said Emerson
> Who had not seen the silhouette
> Of Sweeney straddled in the sun.
> (T. S. Eliot, "Sweeney Erect")

Man without a lengthened shadow (as in this poem) is historyless, without a history, a matter of great importance in the present context when he is contrasted, as in a moment he shall be, to the Man-Moth. The line suggests some other things as well: (1) Man is distinguished from other creatures by his mental endowments (the size of his hat), which make his physical qualities secondary; (2) This cerebral eminence is a precarious basis for any self-assurance; (3) Given the influence of the moon in the following lines, lunacy is a genuine threat.

Man's shadow, reduced to hat-size because the moonlight is directly overhead, anchors him to some low metropolitan rooftop or municipal vacancy, where his pointy little head is magnetized heavenward by celestial influence, which is mysterious and without sensory effects. He seems to be all alone in an urban setting completely depopulated, and even when, in the second stanza, the Man-Moth appears, the two seem to have nothing to do with each other, to be utterly unaware of the other's presence. But the same nocturnal mystery encompasses them both. Moonlight that fills the cracks in the buildings is battered because its strange, colorless light seems as tarnished and old as the buildings themselves, and is, indeed, older. The nighttime setting is central to the poem, whose six eight-line stanzas are strikingly and significantly divided into two equal halves, the first being set above ground, exposed to moonlight, *en plein air,* open to the heavens and composed of the vacant public spaces, while the second is underground in several senses, a modern catacomb, where, in the final stanza, a new character suddenly appears—an unexpected, impersonal, almost allegorical "you." But we are going too fast, and ought to return to the initial appearance, in the second stanza, of the title character.

As contrasted with allegorical Man, whose head may be drawn heavenward though he seems to entertain no confident hope of ascension or immediate salvation, the Man-Moth is drawn by the light of the moon as by a flame, towards what would certainly be self-immolation, death rather than immortal life, though "he fails, of course, and falls back scared but quite unhurt." The Man-Moth is presumably capable of flight (as Man is not), and to him the moon looks like "a hole at the top of the sky," encouraging him to dream that he could "push his small head through that round clean opening / and be forced through, as from a tube, in black scrolls on the light." This dream, or vision, has an actual pictorial analogue in a painting by Hieronymus Bosch, to be seen in the Ducal Palace in Venice.

Bosch is the sort of painter who might appeal to poets, and particularly to Elizabeth Bishop, because the mystery and symbolism of so many of his paintings—presenting apocalyptic visions and embodiments of the Temptations of St. Anthony—are terrifying and distinctly nightmarish. But the one I refer to is, at least in isolation, uncommonly benign. It is part of a set of paintings commissioned, I believe, by the Venetian Republic in behalf of the Doge. The individual paintings present (1) the descent of the damned into Hell, (2) Hell itself, (3) the Earthly Paradise, and (4) the ascent to the Heavenly Paradise, which is the one that concerns us here (see fig. 2). Charles de Tolnay, in *Hieronymus Bosch* (1965), comments: "In their ascent into the heavenly paradise the souls are leaving the dark space of the

Fig. 2 Heironymus Bosch's *Ascension to the Empireum: Visions of the Afterlife.*
Copyright Scala/Art Resource, N.Y. Palazzo Ducale, Venice, Italy.

universe and passing along a circular shaft which is already flooded with everlasting light. Intoxicated with joy, they are freeing themselves more and more from the laws of gravity and obeying the attraction of the realm of light . . . Bosch replaces the medieval Paradise and Hell, which were objective images of celestial and infernal hierarchies, with subjective visions that resemble the conceptions of the great mystics and exist only in the inner world of the soul." The tube or tunnel, which in Bishop's poem so much resembles the long telescopic cylinder of the Bosch painting that leads to a celestial brilliance at its far end, will have its analogues in this poem in the subway tunnels of the second half of the poem, and, still more, by ironic inversion, in the eye of the Man-Moth, which is "all dark pupil," as though enlarged by belladonna.

Drawn though he be to the light of the moon, the Man-Moth seems to feel profoundly ambivalent about it, since he thinks of the moon as a "small hole," "proving the sky quite useless for protection," which is tantamount to saying that he finds security only in the enclosing darkness but is nevertheless drawn to the realm of danger like any moth to a flame.

The second half of the poem returns him to his arterial underground world of the BMT or IRT, the subways "he calls his home." This system of transportation is significantly more efficient, more silent, more rapid, than anything we worldlings are familiar with. "The doors close swiftly. / The Man-Moth always seats himself facing the wrong way / and the train starts at once at its full, terrible speed, / without a shift in gears or a gradation of any sort." This seating preference is noteworthy; he is constantly moving backwards at a terrific pace. On these travels he "must be carried through artificial tunnels and dream recurrent dreams." Surely by this time we realize what world we are in: it is the world of the subconscious, the concealed world, in which the mind moves with incalculable speed to remote and hidden parts of its buried past, hence, traveling backwards. Furthermore, if the subterranean world is the subconscious, the world of the first part of the poem must be the realm of consciousness, though viewed at night, when the two realms come nearest to the possibility of contact with each other.

The ties beneath the subway set up their rhythmic pulses in the Man-Moth's brain, which (curiously, since he is now in what "he calls his home") is filled with still more terror than when, up above, he realized that the sky offered no protection. Now he is aware of "the third rail, the

unbroken draught of poison," which he regards "as a disease / he has inherited the susceptibility to." This is a second peril, analogue to the fear of
moonlight he experienced in the conscious world. In both cases he is
drawn towards a fatal danger and "has to keep / his hands in his pockets,
as others must wear mufflers" against the dangers of illness. As a figura-
tion of the subconscious, he dwells always in a state of fear, haunted by the
dangers of light, illumination, or revelation that might arise out of some
buried, unacknowledged recess. This is to say: what scares us as much as
anything else is something in ourselves too terrible to think about and
therefore carefully suppressed, and only occasionally, infrequently revealed in dreams or on the psychoanalytic couch—which, again, is as
much as to say, "when the Man-Moth / pays his rare, although occasional,
visits to the surface." These are matters of which we are not only afraid but
ashamed. Unpresentable, hence no part of the conscious world, an "unbroken draught of poison," in which the word *draught* is (1) the pull of
weight of something drawn along, (2) a mouth-filling drink, drawn from
a keg, (3) a current of air, ominous enough to prompt others to wear
mufflers. That third rail supplies both life and death, power to move the
subway at its terrible speed, a killing electricity inviting suicidal impulses.

"A disease he has inherited the susceptibility to." A genetic vulnerability, or, let us say, an ancestral guilt. If one wanted to be grandly theological about it, one might venture to call it Original Sin, which theologians
are at pains to distinguish from neurotic self-blame or self-torment. I am
unprepared to get into any theological arguments about this poem, yet it
is my impression that Bishop, while almost always skirting around such
arguments in a gingerly way, wrote too many poems with religious themes
and references for us to doubt that she had such ideas at the back, if not at
the front, of her mind. In any case, "inherited" susceptibility to danger and
death, or to the danger *of* death, is something of a biblical commonplace.

And now the second-person-singular "you" enters the poem. Is it the
author, talking to herself? She certainly does so in plenty of her poems.
Indeed, she is alone in most of them, and we often seem to be overhearing her inmost meditations, as we also do in poems by George Herbert,
whom she loved, admired, and distantly imitated. (Invited by Richard
Howard to pick one of her own poems for an anthology, and to match it
with a favorite poem of the past, Bishop chose her own "In the Waiting
Room" and paired it with Herbert's "Love Unknown," which, it may be

worth noting, is allegorical in design.) Is that second-person pronoun (*you*) masquerading as the indefinite pronoun *one*, with its potential reference to anyone? Is that "you" instead the reader, invited into this strangely alluring yet forbidding poem, the dangers of which must always remain his or her private concern (and perhaps nightmare)? The "you" is distinct not only from the Man-Moth but also from the abstract Man in the first stanza, who, in his allegorical role, is wholly impersonal and who seems to have no function but to stand quite still, bewildered by the moonlight. In any case, here, at last, for the first time in the poem, there is a genuine confrontation.

"If you catch him . . ." We "catch" moths, chiefly to dispose of them; we "catch" butterflies (also members of the Lepidoptera order) for their beauty. The purpose of "catching" the Man-Moth concerns something that can be obtained from him, but not before he has been hypnotized by a blinding light, such as attracts moths. His eye (he seems to have only one) is "all dark pupil / an entire night itself," suitable for a night-creature and for the infrared sight of the subconscious. When his eye closes, under the torment of that intense, inquisitorial flashlight, he prepares to give up his only possession, which is like the bee's sting—because it will be painful, because perhaps he will relinquish his life with the release of it. It is one solitary tear. He will try, by sleight of hand, to keep it from you, for the subconscious is fairly determined to keep its secrets, reluctant to give them up. A tear, in any case, might seem visually attractive because it is clear and crystalline. We would expect it also to be salty, but in this case, to our very considerable surprise, it is "cool as from underground springs and pure enough to drink."

Surely this poem concerns the commerce of the poet's conscious and subconscious minds in the quest for the sources of poetry. It ends with a drink, a "draught," not of poison, but of a pure and clear liquid that suggests the Pierian spring, the source of inspiration, the refreshment of the Muses themselves. It is, nevertheless, a tear, and therefore further suggests sorrow as the source of the poet's art. Such a notion would be purely a personal one for Elizabeth Bishop; much the same premise can be found in Keats' "Ode to a Nightingale," as well as in the Ovidian account of the transformation of Philomela and the lament implied by her lovely song, as well as in the funerary aria of the dying swan. But if we employ enough tact and discretion, we may not be wholly wrong in thinking that for

Bishop the sources of some of her poems were indeed anguishing ones, and that this claim, and some biographical facts that support it, account not only for the pain of some of the poems but also, paradoxically, for the conscious, determined, even gallant light-heartedness, a "whistling-in-the-dark" bravado, to be found in the words "awful but cheerful," with which she ends another poem ("The Bight") and which she directed to be inscribed on her tombstone. It is a complexity of feeling and attitude that belongs to a good number of her poems, including this one.

Let me interrupt myself at this point to invite you to notice what must have been at least subliminally evident. The poem is written entirely in the present tense. This is a matter of major importance when considering the work of Elizabeth Bishop. Of the total number of her poems in *The Complete Poems, 1927–1979,* from which I here exclude three small groups (occasional poems, poems written in youth, and translations), the tally comes to ninety-six, seventy-one of which are written in the present tense. Of the twenty-five that are not, six modulate back and forth between past and present. This is, for anyone's oeuvre, an unusually high percentage of poems in the present tense, and invites a moment's thought.

LIKE PAINTERS (and it is no accident that Bishop writes about painting, admired painters, and was herself a painter), Bishop often focuses her poems on ocular and empirical knowledge, on the actuality of the visible world. Even when painting itself is not her subject, her poems often concern themselves with the act of inspection. This is the case with her ars poetica, "The Monument," as well as with that superb poem called "Sandpiper." The sandpiper lives in what is called "a state of controlled panic," in a world that is always changing, never stable, literally shaken as by something that, given the small size of the bird, must seem nothing less than seismographic. This is, of course, because of the regular crashing of breakers. The bird is called "a student of Blake" in reference to the first line in one of Blake's poems: "To see a world in a Grain of Sand." The capacity to do this, Blake declares in his poem, is one of a number of "Auguries of Innocence" (Blake's title), and his poem goes on to enumerate and catalogue other traits that augur this innocence and the horrors that compass it about. It all begins, however, with inspection. In Bishop's poem, the bird watches his toes, or "rather, the spaces of sand between them," while beside him the whole Atlantic drains away in momentary ebb. The bird's obsession seems modest enough; he is "looking for something, something, something," always at grains of sand. But that is, first of all, the beginning of fidelity to a visible aspect of experience that, Blake assures us, could reveal a whole world. It is a fidelity to artistic practice as well, threatened by regular seismographic shocks that need deliberately to be ignored. Indeed, such conscious, active "ignoring" is nothing less than a strategy to maintain sanity in a world of constant upheaval. And if we study the work and life of Elizabeth Bishop we know that dangers threatened her from the very outset, beginning with her father's death when she was less than a year old and followed almost immediately by her mother's collapse into insanity, which required her permanent institutionalization. These facts are delicately alluded to in a few of her poems and in one of her short stories. And her own fear of instability was real and lifelong. And, whatever else it may be, acute attention to the visible world is more or less by definition a constant obsession with the *present tense,* a purposeful disregard of past and future.

Let me return to my opening sentence in this section: "The footnoted title . . . is mildly, diffidently suggestive of an etiology: the poet, innocently reading the daily papers stumbles upon an unexpected fictive creature, the product of typographical carelessness and faulty proofreading." The inadvertence is part of the charm and casual sense of discovery; but typographical carelessness and faulty proofreading are what may familiarly be called Freudian slips, which, according to *The Psychopathology of Everyday Life,* are always laden with matters of enormous consequence, revelatory of materials we have done our best to suppress. "A disease he has inherited the susceptibility to." If a parent goes mad, does this determine anything about the destiny of the child?

Richard Wilbur

An Introduction

"Encased in talent like a uniform, / The rank of every poet is well known," wrote W. H. Auden in what might seem like a moment of heedlessness. Certainly he knew how reputations alter, for better and for worse; and in a lighthearted poem addressed to Lord Byron he is sardonically amusing in his appropriation of Dow Jones quotations as a metaphor for what is currently fashionable in intellectual and artistic circles in 1936:

> The Vogue for Black Mass and the cult of devils
>   Has sunk. The Good, the Beautiful, the True
> Still fluctuate about the lower levels.
>   Joyces are firm and there there's nothing new.
>   Eliots have hardened just a point or two.
> Hopkins are brisk, thanks to some recent boosts.
> There's been some further weakening in Prousts.

The lines I first quoted, about the immediate identification of poets as ranked and recognizable by military uniforms, were taken from a sonnet in which poets, determined to catch the reader's attention and admiration in a small space, are given to ostentations of dramatic gesture and are contrasted to the more subtle, painstaking, and selfless labors of the fiction writer, who must render, not just those striking moments of revelation so sought after by poets, but the *tedium vitae* and routine boredom that attend so much of our ordinary existence. Auden knew as well as any of us the capricious nature of

---

These remarks, and the poem that concludes them, served to introduce a reading by Richard Wilbur given at the Morgan Library in New York on October 5, 1993.

celebrity and the obscurity into which artists and writers of great merit have sometimes been plunged. After being almost entirely ignored during the Victorian era, John Donne was virtually rediscovered by Herbert Grierson and T. S. Eliot. Bach was out of favor for one hundred years, and Robert Herrick's reputation underwent a shorter but equally complete eclipse.

Ah, you will say to yourselves in the comfortable surroundings of this distinguished library, some readers may be fickle or even obtuse, but the great writers are as unbudgeable as Gibraltar, as imperishable as Shakespeare claimed when he wrote "Not marble nor the gilded monuments / Of princes shall outlive this powerful rhyme." Well, my dear friends, let me beg you to hold in reserve some of your confidence. In the conference room of a certain university English department, which charity urges me to leave unidentified, it was recently proposed that Shakespeare be eliminated as a requirement; he had, in the view of an assistant professor, "very limited ideas about women." Another member of the same department asserted unequivocally that computer science was far more important to civilization than anything ever written by Herman Melville, whose works he had, in the first instance, been appointed to teach. Anyone who still cherishes a sanguine confidence in the solidity of literary reputations is in for a jolt if he addresses himself to Alvin Kernan's book *The Death of Literature.*

If Auden's metaphor, with which I began, is martial and implicitly combative, suggestive of those unmentionable feelings of rivalry, envy, and competitiveness—from which, it must fairly be acknowledged, poets are by no means free and for which evidence can be found in Yeats and Lowell and Dante himself—it is worth adding that the Dutch scholar Johan Huizinga, in a wonderful book called *Homo Ludens,* persuasively argued that the arts were like sports, or what he called, with no diminution of seriousness, "play." Robert Frost thought of poems as examples of what he called "prowess." And Richard Wilbur has written as follows: "Owing to the presence of a circular track and a tape, it is possible to judge a mile run as a work of art, to admire the runner's quick start and steady pace, his sprint and sailing at the end—and also to enjoy any variations he may make on the normal pattern of the race. But the same runner dashing limitlessly across open fields, now going full tilt, now decelerating, now hurdling a stump, is beyond one's power to appreciate because there are no terms in which to evaluate his incomparable behavior." Implicit in this observation is the sense that an athlete (and a poet) competes not alone (and

·perhaps not chiefly) with his fellows in prowess, but against the arbitrary limits set by the track or the poetic medium, and in the final analysis against himself. He is determined to demand the best of himself. And despite the indisputable presence of competitors and rivals, the finest athletes and poets can attain that sort of composure in which the player, like a Zen adept, achieves a serene indifference to anything but the perfected act, that lovely nonchalance for which Yeats borrowed the Italian word *sprezzatura,* an aristocratic freedom from anxiety in which both poet and athlete rejoice in the control of their forces within the limitations they have accepted.

I once had the occasion to try to describe the virtues of Richard Wilbur's poems in a book review, in which I wrote of them thus:

> First of all, a superb ear (unequaled, I think, in the work of any poet now writing in English) for stately measures, cadences of a slow, processional grandeur, and a rich, ceremonial orchestration. A philosophic bent and a religious temper, which are by no means the same thing, but which here consort comfortably together. Wit, polish, a formal elegance that is never haughty or condescending . . . and an unfeigned gusto, a naturally happy and grateful response to the physical beauty of life, of women, or works of art, landscapes, weather, and the perceiving, constructing mind that tries to know them. But in a way I think most characteristic of all, his is the most kinetic poetry I know: verbs are among his conspicuously important tools, and his poetry is everywhere a vision of *action,* of motion and performance. He has been from the first a poet with a gymnastic sense of bodily agility and control, a delight in the fluencies we all admire in a trained athlete . . . This nimbleness, this lively sense of coordinated and practiced skill is a clear extension of the dexterity the verse itself performs. . . . But it is more. For again and again in Wilbur's poems this admirable grace or strength of body is a sign of or a symbol for the inward motions of the mind or condition of the soul. It is remarkable that this double fluency, of style and of perception, should be so singularly Wilbur's own.

Let me now add that this agility, this stamina, this Zenlike tranquility of concentration, is summoned in poem after poem to perform a desperate and seemingly impossible task. Our experiences of life are fleeting and evanescent; even our hopes and fears and moments of untainted elation are transient and virtually irretrievable. It is the quietly heroic task of a gifted poet to recover for us the world we once knew in all its immediate glory and infinite variety. When, in a brilliant formulation of words, we are enabled to glimpse a rising flock of birds in the image of a drunken fingerprint or to assemble the blurred and brassy sensation of a red fire-truck rounding a curve, we know that a poet's genius has put itself at the humble service of salvaging from a path strewn with the leaves of sure obliteration something of the vivacity of the visible world and the activity of a lively and graceful mind. The poet's task is a labor of reclamation, a task intended to be honored in a poem called "Ballade of the Salvaged Losses."

Ballade of the Salvaged Losses

Where are they now, those tousled glories
Poets commended long ago?
Hip, thigh, and bosom inventories
Of Salome or Clara Bow?
And Master François Villon's snow?
And Villon's flair, and Villon's curses,
And all that jazz, I'd like to know?
They're all in Richard Wilbur's verses.

Where are the stately, measured forays
Of ballade, villanelle, rondeau?
Black-tie and champagne-fluted soirées
That crowned a Brian Bedford show
Of Molière's wit, or Racine's woe?
An actor studiously rehearses
Le bon—mais non—le meilleur mot;
They're all in Richard Wilbur's verses.

And where the comely allegories
Of aspen's leaf and water's flow?
The charnel house *memento mories,*

Chilling as Edgar Allan Poe?
Nightmare intent to overthrow
Daylight's conventional excursus,
Comfort's assailant, reason's foe?
They're all in Richard Wilbur's verses.

Prince, though you seek both high and low
For all Death's covetousness amerces—
The fountain's leap, the ember's glow—
They're all in Richard Wilbur's verses.

Yehuda Amichai

It took Yehuda Amichai roughly ten years to write *Open Closed Open*, a suite of poems, or more truly, a long poem divided and subdivided into sections but thematically and musically braided beautifully into something like symphonic unity and grandeur. It may be thought of as a brilliant enlargement of a major poem written earlier in the poet's career, "Travels of the Last Benjamin of Tudela"; but whereas that was a moderately long poem dealing with much of the same materials, at least as they regard the poet's biography, this new work is nothing less than a heroic achievement of the spirit, a lofty and sometimes raucous meditation on the history of his nation, his faith, and his heart. As the earlier poem was not implausibly compared to Wordsworth's *The Prelude*,[1] which is subtitled *The Growth of a Poet's Mind*, Amichai's *Open Closed Open* may be regarded as an account of the composition, the piecing together out of fragments, of the poet's soul. It is as deeply spiritual a poem as any I have read in modern times, not excluding Eliot's *Four Quartets* or anything to be found in the works of professional religionists. It is an incomparable triumph. Be immediately assured that this does not mean devoid of humor or without a rich sense of comedy. There is, in fact, an important ingredient of irreverence that plays a central part in the poet's deepest meditations.

It may be claimed that irony—even, on occasion, an irony attributed to the behavior of God—is a central element in the Old Testament; one need point only to the Books of Jonah and Job. And the sacred commentaries are almost equally ironic. There is a Jewish tradition of "religious irony" which, I think, has no true Christian parallel. To be sure, there are little moments of jest, as in the pun on Peter's name (though

1. Glenda Abramson, *The Writing of Yehuda Amichai* (1989), 18.

this jest has become a point of bitter contention between Catholics and Protestants); and Christian theology, as well as scripture, is certainly rich in paradox. The Christian irony that the most perfect of "men" should be singled out for excruciating punishment and death is somehow either veiled or mitigated by its turning out to be, in the end, a foreordained part of a redemptive plan to which the sacrificial victim assented with full knowledge of the salvational benefits his death would confer. But Jewish irony, the meditative fruit of the patriarchs and prophets, the psalmists and scribes, is often given to levity, though no less serious for all that.

In "Travels of the Last Benjamin of Tudela" (the first Benjamin was a twelfth-century traveler who wrote an account of a journey through Europe, Asia Minor, and Africa; the last is Amichai himself, who in the course of his career covered much of the globe), we encounter this passage:

> eight empty bullet-shells for a Hanukkah menorah,
> explosives of eternal flame, the cross of a crossfire,
> a submachine gun carried in phylactery straps,
> camouflage nets of thin lacy material
> from girlfriends' panties, used womens' dresses
> and ripped diapers to clean the cannon mouth,
> offensive hand-grenades in the shape of bells,
> defensive hand-grenades in the shape of a spice box
> for the close of the Sabbath, sea mines
> like prickly apples used as smelling-salts on Yom Kippur
> in case of fainting.[2]

The profanation of the sacred as described here can only have meaning if the sacred is genuinely revered; and Amichai's attitude towards the sacred is both devout and skeptical at once. It is deeply tied to his devotion to his parents, both Orthodox Jews, who brought him to Palestine from the Bavarian city of Würzburg, where he was born in 1924. The move took place in 1936, but before this he had been given Orthodox schooling, learning Hebrew prayers at the age of four or five. His filial devotion is expressed in this

---

2. *Selected Poetry of Yehuda Amichai*, trans. Chana Bloch and Stephen Mitchell (1986), 82.

new work in passages one of which begins, "My mother was a prophet and didn't know it," and another, "My father was God and didn't know it."

Speaking of the Hebrew language, Amichai has observed, "Every word we use carries in and of itself connotations from the Bible, the Siddur, the Midrash, the Talmud. Every word reverberates through the halls of Jewish history."[3] That history in its four-thousand-year totality is something the poet has immersed himself in, and it appears in every aspect of his thought and language. This is a matter for which there is no Christian equivalent. The New Testament is known in translations from the Greek original, though Jesus spoke Aramaic. There have been celebrated theologians whose expositions have been based on philological speculations regarding the density and compactness of tropes, often the most ingenious and imaginative kind, from the Latin or the Greek. In his sermons, John Donne speaks as though he took for granted that all of Holy Scripture was set down in Latin. And J. H. North, in *The Classic Preachers of the English Church*, characterizes Bishop Lancelot Andrewes, who was fascinated by words, their origins, their richness of implication, both in Latin and in Greek Scripture, thus: "He rolls his text like a sweet morsel under his tongue, until he has extracted from it not only all its nourishment but the very last vestige of its flavor."[4] But the Hebrew language in all essentials is very much the language of Moses and the prophets; and for a Jew drenched in the sacred texts, as Amichai is, all history, all sanctity, all sin and suffering resonate with holy language.

Open Closed Open is composed of twenty-two sections, each with its own title; these sections, in turn, are subdivided into varying numbers of parts. The whole is introduced by a "prelude" called "The Amen Stone" and concludes with a "postlude" about the same stone, two superimposed photographs of which appear on the front of the dust jacket. The stone is a fragment, "one survivor fragment / of the thousands upon thousands of bits of broken tombstones / in Jewish graveyards." It rested on the poet's desk and is a memorial to every fragmentation of Jewish history, to the fragment of Holocaust survivors, and even to the promise in Ezekiel of

---

3. Quoted in Abramson, *The Writing of Yehuda Amichai*, 14.
4. Quoted in Maurice F. Reidy, S. J., *Bishop Lancelot Andrewes: Jacobean Court Preacher* (1955), 62.

the reassembling of scattered bones. The stone Amichai owns bears the solitary word *Amen,* which means, "May it come to pass."

The book's title, as the valuable notes explain, derives from a rabbinic tale, or, rather, from a passage in the Babylonian Talmud, Tractate Niddah, chapter 3, folio 30a. It reads in part:

> Unto what may the fetus in its mother's womb be likened? Unto a notebook that is folded up. Its hands rest on its temples, elbows on thighs, heels against buttocks, its head lies between its knees. Its mouth is closed and its navel is open . . . When it comes forth into the air of the world, what is closed opens and what is open closes.

The twenty-two sections themselves do not make up a narrative, but rather the fragments of a narrative, or of several narratives, including the life of the poet revealed in fugitive glimpses, the history of the Jews, the lives, and still more movingly, the deaths of others. The very first section is titled "I Wasn't One of the Six Million: And What Is My Life Span? Open Closed Open." The poem proceeds in a jumble of meditations upon remembering and forgetting, a Joseph's coat of many-colored styles, from liturgy, scripture, postbiblical history, formularies, and even parodies of sacred texts. It employs passages that sound like popular lyrics, slogans, and an amusing equivalent of a college cheer: "Torah, Torah, rah, rah, rah!" as well as the following rather jazzy passage:

> King Saul never learned how to play or to sing
> nor was he taught how to be king.
> Oh he's got the blues,
> he's nothing to lose
> but the moody tune
> on his gramophone
> and David is its name-oh, David is its name,
> its name its name its name.

Throughout the poem the sacred is brought into blunt confrontation with the profane. After a particularly jubilant party that took place at the house of a friend, with much dancing, singing, and celebratory noise, the poet observes,

The last to leave
greet the first to pray at dawn—some at the synagogue,
others at the prayer houses of remembering and forgetting.

Only a little later we come upon these lines:

And from the distance, like the sound of a ping-pong game:
belief in one God and blasphemy rally with each other.

Amichai has occasion elsewhere to refer to Gods in the plural, though in
this case no blasphemy is entailed, since one of the Hebrew names of God,
Elohim, is plural in form, presumably betokening the Lord's omnipresence
and omnipotence.[5]

The personal and biographical aspects of the poem are, once again,
fragmentarily, and rather shyly, introduced. The poet's love for his parents
is richly and beautifully described, and is touched by (tainted by?) his feeling that, in renouncing Jewish Orthodoxy, he has betrayed his father's love
and perhaps rebelled against God. He was taken by his parents from his
Bavarian birthplace in 1936, when he was twelve, but not before he had
fallen in love with a girl who would come to haunt his poetry over many
years. Her name was Ruth, she suffered a severe accident that cost her a
leg, and she was subsequently annihilated with all the rest of Würzburg's
Jewish community. When Amichai was thirty-five he returned for the
first time to his birthplace to revisit the sites of his childhood, almost all
of them destroyed in the course of the war. Ruth makes a moving appearance late in *Open Closed Open*.

It may be said that Jerusalem, his not altogether happy home, elicits
amused or sardonic responses from him. It has, in these late days, become
a center for academic/religious conferences and symposia:

. . . a major conference on Job:
dermatologists on skin diseases, anthropologists
on pain and suffering, legal scholars on justice and injustice,

---

5. The two primary principles of God's dealings with nations and individuals are . . . Justice
and Mercy (which includes Love). These two attributes, according to rabbinic interpretation,
are represented respectively by the two divine names, *Elohim* ('God') and YHWH (usually
rendered 'the Lord')." Isidore Epstein, *Judaism: A Historical Presentation* (1959), 135.

God on the nature of Satan, and Satan on the notion of the divine.
Job's three friends, Bildad, Eliphaz, and Zophar, on the psychology
of suicide, the science of suicidology . . .

and ceramicists on the type of potsherd Job used
to scratch himself.

Elsewhere, of his city, he writes:

Jerusalem is a merry-go-round-and-round . . .
And instead of elephants and painted horses to ride,
there are religions that go up and down and turn on their axis
to the music of oily tunes from the houses of prayer.
. . . .
They speak with bells in their voices
and with the wailing call of the muezzin, and at their bedside, empty
    shoes
as at the entrance of a mosque. And on the doorpost of their house it says,
"Ye shall love each other with all your hearts and with all your souls."

And then there is battle. The Old Testament is full of it; postbiblical
history is full of it, as is modern history, and Amichai saw battle in Egypt
and Palestine. From earlier poems we know that, without seeming to
boast, he was able to recount the truly heroic rescue of a comrade who later
died in his arms in June 1948. He fought in the Jewish War of Independence, serving in the Palmach, commando units of the Haganah, the Israeli underground army.

I fell in battle at Ashdod
In the War of Independence. My mother said then,
He's twenty-four,
Now she says, he's fifty-four
And she lights a candle of remembrance
Like birthday candles
You blow out on a cake.
Since then my father died in pain and sorrow.
. . . .

Since then my house is my grave and my grave is my house,
For I fell in the pale sands of Ashdod.

. . . .

I carried my comrade on my back.
Since then I always feel his dead body
Like a weighted heaven upon me,
Since then he feels my arched back under him,
Like an arched segment of the earth's crust.
For I fell in the terrible sands of Ashdod
Not only him.[6]

("Me-az")

In *Open Closed Open* this occasion is only briefly and evasively alluded to:

I always have to revisit the sands of Ashdod
where I had a little bit of courage in that battle, that war,
soft hero in the soft sand. My few scraps of heroism I squandered
then.

And then, a recurrent theme, a sonorous reverberation, there is the need, the curse, the duty of remembering and forgetting:

To the confession "We have sinned, we have betrayed" I would
add
the words "We have forgotten, we have remembered"—two sins
that cannot be atoned for. They ought to cancel each other out
but instead they reinforce one another. Yes, I'm kosher.

The antepenultimate section of the poem is called "My Son Was Drafted." To one who himself served in the most terrible battles, who is now a father of two sons and a daughter, the prospect of the conscription of a son into the Israeli army of our day, when international dangers are daily threats, would provoke an understandable anxiety, and Amichai reacts with characteristic humor and irony:

---

6. Quoted by Abramson, *The Writing of Yehuda Amichai,* 28–29.

I want my son to be a soldier in the Italian army
with a crest of colorful feathers on his cap,
happily dashing around with no enemies, no camouflage.

. . . .

I want my son to be a soldier in the Vatican's Swiss Guard
with their coats of many colors, their sashes and blunt lances
glittering in the sun.

. . . . . .

I want my son to be a soldier in the British army,
guarding a palace in the rain. A tall fur hat on his head,
everyone staring at him while, without moving a muscle,
he is laughing inside.

This fine mockery of the soldierly profession as all pageantry (though, to be sure, grand pageantry in Michelangelo-motley, *bersagliere,* or busby headgear) is touching, and also impressive when it comes from someone who has seen long and dangerous duty and who had written in an earlier part of this poem:

Tova's brother, whom I carried wounded from the battle of Tel Gath,
recovered and was forgotten because he recovered, and died
in a car accident a few years later, and was forgotten
because he died.

This is part of a litany of tributes to the departed, including the great Jewish poet Paul Celan, Romanian-born, whose parents were deported and shot in 1941, who himself was incarcerated in a German forced labor camp, and who, after the war, settled in Paris and eventually drowned himself in the Seine. It is in this section that Ruth makes her appearance among the lamented dead. These encounters with the ghosts of the past in the course of a major, and, indeed, heroic poem, serve to recall those descents into the underworld we identify with the epics of Homer, Virgil, and Dante.

The sense of epic proportions and associations is certainly not based on length. As printed, the poem runs to 173 pages, which, while vastly longer than *The Waste Land,* cannot nearly match *The Cantos,* let alone

the great classics. But in its reach, in the depth of its feeling, the richness of its variety, and the dignity of its most solemn moments, it
seems to invite epic associations, as, to my mind, it does in the following
passage:

> Thus glory passes. Thus they pass, the psalms,
> crying singing cursing blessing—verses
> from the mouths of worshippers: Happy is the man,
> Like a tree planted, Happy are they that dwell
> in Thy house, All men are false, Servants of the Lord,
> My Rock and Redeemer, David and the sons of Korah, hallelujahs,
> green pastures, still waters, dark valleys of death.
> Thus they pass, like a parade when the circus comes to town
> but won't stop, won't open the big tent, elephants
> and other animals, the mea culpa band
> drumming their chests, the we-have-sinned tumblers and the we-
>   have-betrayed dancers, tightrope walkers, acrobats
> hopping Holy, Holy, Holy
> with sobs and laughter, bitter cries and sweet song.
> Thus it all passes—what was, and what never has been.
> Thus the children parade on Arbor Day
> with seedlings they won't ever plant,
> thus they pass, thus glory passes.
>
> Thus glory passes, like a long train without
> beginning or end, without cause or purpose. I always
> stand to one side at the crossing—the barrier is down—
> and I take it all in: carloads of passengers and history, carloads
> packed full of war, carloads teeming with human beings
> for extermination, windows with faces of parting
> men and women, the high spirits of travelers,
> birthdays and deathdays, pleading
> and pity and plenty of empty echoing boxcars.

Not much later, the poet ruminates upon the *deus absconditus*, the Hidden
God, the God who, having spoken to Adam and to Moses, having appeared to the prophets and debated with Abraham, became increasingly

veiled until, in Micah 3, it is declared that all prophets are now benighted, and "they shall all cover their lips: for there is no answer of God."

> When God packed up and left the country, He left the Torah
> with the Jews. They have been looking for Him ever since,
>   shouting, "Hey, you forgot something, you forgot,"
> and other people think shouting is the prayer of the Jews.
> Since then, they've been combing the Bible for hints of His
>   whereabouts,
> as it says: "Seek ye the Lord while He may be found,
> call ye upon Him while he is near." But he is far away.
>
> .   .   .   .
>
> There are days when everyone says, I was there,
> I'm ready to testify, I stood a few feet from the accident,
> from the bomb, from the crucifixion, I almost got hit, almost got
>   crucified.
> I saw the faces of the bride and groom under the wedding
>   canopy and almost
> rejoiced. When David lay with Bathsheba I was the voyeur,
> I happened to be there on the roof fixing the pipes, taking
>   down a flag.
> With my own eyes I saw the Chanukah miracle in the Temple,
> I saw General Allenby entering Jaffa Gate,
> I saw God.
> And then there are days when everything is an alibi: wasn't
>   there, didn't hear,
> heard the explosion only from a distance and ran away, saw
> smoke but was reading a newspaper, was staying in some other place.
> I didn't see God, I've got witnesses.

However skeptical, however irreverent, mocking, mischievous, and, to some readers, nearly impious this poet may seem, there can't be the least doubt that he was obsessed with the religious life in all its aspects as something lived and experienced in every waking moment of his life. And this means that if credence and credulity are held up for ironic questioning, so equally is the world of empirical and analytic experience:

People were always telling me: "You've got to live
in the real world." I heard it from parents and teachers.
To live in the real world, like a verdict. What terrible sin
could these souls have committed
that their lives in this world should begin with a verdict:
You are sentenced to reality for life.
With no possibility of parole.
The parole is death.

The two translators, Chana Bloch and Chana Kornfeld, who enjoyed
the active cooperation and assistance of Amichai himself and of his wife,
have performed more than a commendable job. Though I do not know the
poem in its original, we have the poet's oversight as certification for its accuracy (and Amichai spoke fluent English). The English version of the
poem is vivid with living idiom and is so astonishingly varied in tone, so
multileveled in implication, so full of puns and verbal exuberance that it
brilliantly conveys great depths of feeling, a wide and generous knowledge
of scripture, of ancient and modern history, of all the poet's countless resources. It succeeds as a poem in English, and does so in ways that persuade us that it must be those very ways in which the Hebrew succeeds: in
making the reader feel that the total sum of these assembled fragments co-
heres in spirit and in art, leaving the reader awed, delighted, and profoundly grateful.[7]

The poet's work is gently, modestly, amusedly heroic, and in its assembled totality it is nothing less than majestic. It is, moreover, unlike any
poem from the past or present that I can think of. It does honor not only
to the poet, and what he made of feeling, thought, cerebral cortex, cardiac
chambers, his knowledge, and his life, but also to his people, celebrated
here in loving, equivocal terms and in the poet's very name, *Ami-chai,*
which in Hebrew means "my people's lives."

---

7. I found one small error, which may well be the fault of an editor. The note on the section
named "Conferences, Conferences . . . ," no. 11, page 151, applies instead to an eleventh fragment on page 159. This, with its important echo of the closing verses of Ecclesiastes, needs to
be corrected in later editions.

Charles Simic

*I*n our bicentennial year, Charles Simic and Mark Strand, two poets of kindred excellences and temperaments, published an anthology entitled *Another Republic* and devoted to seventeen European and Latin American poets whose work was (and still largely remains) outside the orbit and canon of this nation's taste and habit of mind. The seventeen included Vasko Popa, Yannis Ritsos, Fernando Pessoa, Miroslav Holub, Zbigniew Herbert, Paul Celan, and Johannes Bobrowski, along with a few more familiar Nobel laureates–to–be. The editors lumped their poets into two general batches, the "mythological," a group that included Henri Michaux, Francis Ponge, Julio Cortázar, Italo Calvino, and Octavio Paz, and another group, the "historical," devoted to Yehudah Amichai, Paul Celan, Zbigniew Herbert, Czesław Miłosz, and Yannis Ritsos, while acknowledging that some of the poets fall between the two stools or partake of both categories while resisting identification with either one. They furthermore define the "mythological" strain by deriving it from sources in Surrealism.

Surrealism has never really enjoyed much favor in North America, a fact Octavio Paz has explained this way:

> The French tradition and the English tradition in this epoch are at opposite poles to each other. French poetry is more radical, more total. In an absolute and exemplary way it has assumed the heritage of European Romanticism, a romanticism which begins with William Blake and the German romantics like Novalis, and via Baudelaire and the Symbolists culminates in twentieth-century French poetry, notably Surrealism. It is a poetry where the world becomes writing and language becomes the double of the world.[1]

---

1. Quoted by Paul Auster in the introduction to his *Random House Book of Twentieth-Century French Poetry* (1982), xxxi.

Furthermore, our sense of Surrealism, at least when it figures in poetry, is of something facile, lazy, and aimless except in its ambition to surprise by a violation of logic, taste, and rigor. Bad Surrealism can grow tiresome very easily, and one does not feel encouraged to continue reading a poem such as Charles Henri Ford's "He Cut His Finger on Eternity," which begins:

> What grouchy war-tanks intend to shred
> or crouch the road's middle to stop my copy?
> I'll ride roughshod as an anniversary
> down the great coiled gap of your ear.

If we have no good native Surrealists, we can at least boast of a few fine imported ones, of which Charles Simic is certainly one of the best. "Imported," however, is the wrong term for someone who was a refugee, a DP (Displaced Person) who was born in Belgrade in 1938 and left when he was fifteen. The poetry Simic writes is not simply better than bad Surrealism; it is what we instantly recognize as a responsible mode of writing, a poetry that, for all its unexpected turns, startling juxtapositions, dream sequences, mysteries, will be found, upon careful consideration, to make a deep and striking kind of sense. It is utterly without Dali pretensions or Dada postures. It makes no appeal to the unconscious for the liberty to write nonsense. In Simic's art especially we must attune our ear to a voice usually soft-spoken, often tender, not infrequently jolly, the sort of lover of food who has been instructed in starvation. No single poem of his can be said to represent the whole range of his gifts or the variety of his comedic sense, so often tinged with grief or laced with that special brand of the sardonic, ironic humor characteristic of Corbière or Laforgue. Yet I think that in a poem of his called "Views from a Train" something essential of his poetic intelligence makes itself beautifully audible:

> Then there's aesthetic paradox
> Which notes that someone else's tragedy
> Often strikes the casual viewer
> With the feeling of happiness.
>
> There was the sight of squatters' shacks,
> Naked children and lean dogs running

On what looked like a town dump,
The smallest one hopping after them on crutches.

All of a sudden we were in a tunnel.
The wheels ground our thoughts,
Back and forth as if they were gravel.
Before long we found ourselves on a beach,
The water blue, the sky cloudless.

Seaside villas, palm trees, white sand;
A woman in a red bikini waved to us
As if she knew each one of us
Individually and was sorry to see us
Heading so quickly into another tunnel.

This is neither simple allegory nor dream, but a fused vision embracing both. The first four lines initially seem to recall La Rochefoucauld's bitter acknowledgement, "In the misfortunes of our best friends we often find something that is not displeasing." But the poet gives depth to what passes in the *Maxims* for ruthless candor and lacerating exposure. The "aesthetic paradox" connects the brutal pleasure in another's pain with Aristotle's *Poetics* and the classic demonstration of how an audience, by a double act of identification and distancing, can find artistic and poetic pleasure in viewing deep torment and agony.

The next four lines seem to be offered as illustration to the generalization of the opening. They served to remind me precisely of a photograph by Henri Cartier-Bresson in which a group of boys, viewed through a hole in a wall undoubtedly made by a bomb, appear to be taunting and attacking one of their number who is on crutches. The picture is titled simply *Seville, 1933*. It may well be quite unknown to the poet, but he is the survivor of bombings by the American Air Force, occupation by the Nazis, and further occupation by the Communists, in a war-ravaged and desperately poor country, so he knew, both from close up as well as distanced by time and travel, the situation depicted in the photograph.

"All of a sudden we were in a tunnel." The lines that immediately follow blot out all the external world for a brief interval, as we return to our inwardness, not only as we slip in and out of sleep but as our very thoughts negotiate between external and internal experience. The woman waves to us from a privileged setting of seaside villas with palms and white sand. Our view of her is as fleeting as was the view of the naked children and lean dogs. Tragedy, we are being reminded, is not a presentation of pure agony but of the change of state from good fortune to misfortune. The poem presents both in what seems like the wrong order. But the order doesn't matter, since we are "heading so quickly into another tunnel." It may be we ourselves who are the tragic figures in this poem, for we do nothing, we are simply passive viewers, while the children, the dogs, and the woman lead lives of which we catch only a glimpse. In the manner of other Simic poems, there are no neat and easy conclusions to be drawn, yet the poem is full of strange revelation, darkness and brilliance, sadness and luxury.

The luxury is, for the most part, a rare ingredient in Simic's poetry, where it is more than likely to appear as some simple but satisfying food. What this poet is particularly gifted at revealing is the derivation of joys and pleasures from the most unlikely, and even forbidding, sources, as here in a poem called "Unmade Beds":

> They like shady rooms,
> Peeling wallpaper,
> Cracks on the ceiling,
> Flies on the pillow.
>
> If you are tempted to lie down,
> Don't be surprised,
> You won't mind the dirty sheets,
> The rasp of rusty springs
> As you make yourself comfy.
> The room is a darkened movie theater
> Where a grainy,
> Black-and-white film is being shown.
>
> A blur of disrobed bodies
> In the moment of sweet indolence
> That follows lovemaking,

When the meanest of hearts
Comes to believe
Happiness can last forever.

The last six lines compose a "sentence" without a main verb. It is purely descriptive, a blurred, grainy vision of a movie, itself a vision, of something fleeting that is nevertheless both wonderful and durable. Of course, being an old black-and-white film, this can be pure delusion, and not very persuasive at that. Is all our happiness mere delusion? Is that film like the shadow-play on the walls of Plato's cave? And if it is no more, isn't it still to be cherished, being all we have? If we find ourselves in a fleabag hotel room, is this an adequate symbol for our normal existence? Is it folly or heroism to be able to rise above the sordors of this world? The elements of Simic's remarkable life, to which I will turn shortly, may suggest what answers he might give to such questions. Certainly that hotel room, soiled as it is, nevertheless is much to be preferred to Sartre's in *Huis Clos*. Another poem, "Firecracker Time," starts off with some of the same mixed ingredients:

I was drumming on my bald head with a pencil,
Making a list of my sins. Well, not exactly.
I was in bed smoking a cigar and studying
The news photo of a Jesus lookalike
Who won a pie-eating contest in Texas.

Is there some unsuspected dignity to this foolishness?
I inquired of the newly painted ceiling.

There are sixty-eight poems in *Night Picnic*, none of them long, most of them fitting on a single page. But it's not easy to convey the fine variety this collection so generously presents. Here, for example, is a poem that itself revels in variety:

The Altar

The plastic statue of the Virgin
On top of a bedroom dresser

With a blackened mirror
From a bad-dream grooming salon.

Two pebbles from the grave of a rock star,
A small, grinning windup monkey,
A bronze Egyptian coin
And a red movie-ticket stub.

A splotch of sunlight on the framed
Communion photograph of a boy
With the eyes of someone
Who will drown in a lake real soon.

An altar dignifying the god of chance.
What is beautiful, it cautions,
Is found accidentally and not sought after.
What is beautiful is easily lost.

The heterogeneous simplicity of these assembled items brings to mind certain photographic interiors by Eugène Atget or Walker Evans, pictures full of deep feeling, eloquent of frugal and damaged lives that nevertheless cling to small tokens of hope. And I can think of no poem that so powerfully conveys the raging, frenzied lusting of pubescent boys as does "The Cemetery":

Dark nights, there were lovers
To stake out among the tombstones.
If the moon slid out of the clouds,
We saw more while ducking out of sight,

A mound of dirt beside a dug grave.
Oh God! the mound cried out.
There were ghosts about
And rats feasting on the white cake
Someone had brought that day,

With flies unzipped we lay close,

Straining to hear the hot, muffled words
That came quicker and quicker,
Back then when we still could
Bite our tongues and draw blood.

Such a poem cannot fairly be labeled "Surrealist," and yet it has about it a pungency of pain, fear, sex, and death blended into an extraordinary brew of life that is far from the literal world of commonplace experience. The distinct miscellaneousness that crops up in so many Simic poems does not lend itself to the confident summing-up that Emerson so cheerfully posits in "The American Scholar":

What would we really know the meaning of? The meal in the firkin; the milk in the pan; the ballad in the street; the news of the boat; the glance of the eye; the form and the gait of the body;—show me the ultimate reason of these matters;—show me the sublime presence of the highest spiritual cause lurking, as always it does lurk, in these suburbs and extremities of nature; let me see every trifle bristling with the polarity that ranges it instantly on an eternal law; and the shop, the plough, and the ledger, referred to the like cause by which light undulates and poets sing;—and the world lies no longer a dull miscellany and lumber room, but has form and order; there is no trifle; there is no puzzle; but one design unites and animates the farthest pinnacle and the lowest trench.

While it is true that Simic lives, writes, and teaches in New Hampshire, he does not share the New England Transcendentalist's serene assurance of ultimate coherence. It may be that the determining difference between the two poets is to be found in the fact that Simic's childhood was spent in a war zone, a condition that tends to discourage an easy credence in universal laws. When Simic resorts to poetic apostrophe, which he permits himself to do only rarely, it is with abundant irony, as in "Book Lice," which begins,

Dust-covered Gideon Bibles
In musty drawers of slummy motels,

Is what they love to dine on.
O eternities, moments divine!
Munching on pages edged in gold

—and which continues towards an anguished, grotesque, and altogether
unforeseen ending. Simic's hard-bitten distrust of the facile reconciliation
of disparities is finely expressed in "Bible Lesson":

There's another, better world
Of divine love and benevolence,
A mere breath away
From this grubby vacant lot
With its exposed sewer pipe,
Rats hatching plots in broad daylight,
Young boys in leather jackets
Showing each other their knives.

"A necessary evil, my dear child,"
The old woman told me with a sigh,
Taking another sip of her sherry.
For birds warbling back and forth
In their gold cage in the parlor,
She had a teary-eyed reverence.
"Angelic," she called them,
May she roast in a trash fire
The homeless warm their hands over,

While beyond the flimsiest partition
The blessed ones stroll in a garden,
Their voices tuned to a whisper
As they dab their eyes
With the hems of their white robes
And opine in their tactful way
On the news of long freight trains
Hauling men and women
Deeper into the century's darkness.

And yet it strikes a reader with considerable force that the word *happiness* figures in Simic's poems with uncommon and notable frequency—sometimes humbly, to be sure, as when he writes of "That mutt with ribs showing / . . . His tail on the verge of happiness"—but by my estimate more often and more unselfconsciously than in the work of any other poet I can think of. It is clearly a feeling about which he has much to say.

It has been a matter of some importance for a number of writers deliberately to deflect the public's interest in their personal lives and to insist that it is only their work that really counts. They may claim that their work, carefully read, becomes self-portraiture; or that they have extinguished their personalities through their art, which has its own aesthetic interest wholly distinct from their personalities. Eliot forbade any biography to be written about him (a bidding that has been frequently disregarded); Auden requested that all his letters be burned (a wish that has not been widely honored).

This distinctive shyness is in part a way of pointing to, and affirming the significance of, the finished oeuvres, as contrasted, perhaps, with their as yet unfinished, and possibly disorderly, lives. For art can be polished to a fare-thee-well, while life is not always shapely or subject to complete control. To an intermediary who sought to arrange a newspaper interview with A. E. Housman, the poet responded,

> Tell him that the wish to include a glimpse of my personality in a literary article is low, unworthy, and American. Tell him that some men are more interesting than their books but my book is more interesting than its man. Tell him that Frank Harris found me rude and Wilfrid Blunt found me dull. Tell him anything else that you think will put him off.

There have indeed been men whose lives eclipse the public's interest in their works (Dylan Thomas, Byron, Wilde, Pound, Cellini), while there have indisputably also been those, like Wallace Stevens, whose lives have been comparatively colorless, or who, like Eliot and Auden, feel that their private lives are none of the public's damn business.

Charles Simic is unusual in that the events of his life, both large and small, continue to interest him enormously without for a moment seeming to compete with the no less interesting but altogether different and distinctive realm of his poems. He has previously published a number of memoirs under the titles *Wonderful Words, Silent Truth* (1990), *The Unemployed Fortune-Teller* (1994), and *Orphan Factory* (1997), all published by the University of Michigan Press. He has made use of details from these accounts, sometimes revising them slightly, in the course of composing *A Fly in the Soup*, an eloquent, candid, and touching account of the life he shared, off and on, with his parents in Yugoslavia and America, an account that is, by turns, deeply moving and hilarious.

There is very little posturing in these pages. Simic avoids all bids for sympathy, and is able, with remarkable courage, to present himself in moments of childhood heedlessness, in a critical and unfavorable light. Even before he got to the United States he acquired lifelong American tastes for jazz, films, and food, about which he can be enthusiastic:

> Some years back I found myself in Genoa at an elegant reception in Palazzo Doria talking with the Communist mayor. "I love American food," he blurted out to me after I mentioned enjoying the local cuisine. I asked him what he had in mind. "I love potato chips," he told me. I had to agree, potato chips were pretty good.

As an apt epigraph for this book, Simic quotes Raymond Chandler: "Don't tell me the plot . . . I'm just a bit-player." And given the violent international dimension of the tale he has to tell his choice of this quotation is self-effacing, witty, and characteristic of this book throughout, not least in its distinctive Americanness. It recalls not only *noir* fiction and film, but that special American film idiom in which the grandeurs of Shakespearean vision, with all the world a stage, with one man in his time playing many parts, "his acts being seven ages," are set aside and we have instead the Hollywood caste and cast system, with superstars and walk-ons, and with a high likelihood of a something less than conclusive plot.

When Charles Simic was three years old, in April 1941, the building across the street from where he lived was hit by a bomb at five in the morning:

> The number of dead for that day in April in what was called by the Germans "Operation Punishment" ranges between five thousand and seventeen thousand, the largest number of civilian deaths in a single

day in the first twenty months of war. The city was attacked by four hundred bombers and over two hundred fighter planes on a Palm Sunday when visitors from the countryside swelled the capital's population.

Three years later, on Easter Sunday, April 16, 1944, "The British and the Americans started bombing Belgrade . . . , heavy bombers 'conducting strikes against Luftwaffe and aviation targets' with 'approximately 397 tons of bombs.'"

By this time he was all of six. He recalls that

Belgrade was a city of the wounded. One saw people on crutches on every corner . . .

Once, chased by a friend, I rounded the corner of my street at top speed and collided with one of these invalids, spilling his soup on the sidewalk. I won't forget the look he gave me. "Oh child," he said softly. I was too stunned to speak. I didn't even have the sense to pick up his crutch. I watched him do it himself with great difficulty . . .

Here's another early memory: a baby carriage pushed by a hump-backed old woman, her son sitting in it, both legs amputated.

She was haggling with the greengrocer when the carriage got away from her. The street was steep, so it rolled downhill with the cripple waving his crutch as if urging it on faster and faster; his mother screaming for help, and everyone else was laughing as if they were watching a funny movie . . . Keystone cops about to go over a cliff . . .

They laughed because they knew it would end well in the movies. They were surprised when it didn't in life.

What deeply impresses a reader of Simic's memoirs is his strong hold on humanity, which is completely divorced from any taint of sentimentality. Even as a child he had acquired an uncommon fortitude, humor, and balance. In the midst of chaos and calamity he is poised and good-natured and is able to find a redeeming comedy in the most unlikely places:

When my grandfather was dying from diabetes, when he had already one leg cut off at the knee and they were threatening to do the same to the other, his old buddy Savo Lozanic used to pay him a visit every morning to keep him company. The two would reminisce about this and that and even have a few laughs.

One morning my grandmother had to leave him alone in the house, as she had to attend the funeral of a relative. That's what gave him the idea. He hopped out of bed and into the kitchen, where he found candles and matches. He got back into the bed, somehow placed one candle above his head and the other at his feet, and lit them. Finally, he pulled the sheet over his face and began to wait.

When his friend knocked, there was no answer. The door being unlocked, he went in, calling out from time to time. The kitchen was empty. A fat gray cat slept on the dining room table. When he entered the bedroom and saw the bed with the sheet and lit candles, he let out a wail and then broke into sobs as he groped for a chair to sit down.

"Shut up, Savo," my grandfather said sternly from under his sheet. "Can't you see I'm just practicing."

Simic writes well of his parents, though he shows a clear preference for his father. Both parents were cultivated, his mother having done graduate work in music in Paris, his father having become an engineer, and young Charles discovering serious reading—Dickens, Dostoevsky, Mann, Serbian ballads and folk poems—in their library when he was ten. His mother tended to look down upon her husband's family as somewhat coarser and inferior to her own, and this, together with the fact that she was not a good cook, may have swayed her older son in his partiality. For young Simic, then and still, seemed to favor the more disreputable members of his family. Of one of his mother's aunts, he writes,

> Nana was the black sheep in the family. It was whispered that she cheated on her old husband, was spending his money recklessly, and used bad language. That's what I loved about her. This elegant, good-looking woman would swear often and shamelessly.

He feels the same affection for a blacksmith great-grandfather:

> I liked the stories about this great-grandfather of mine, one of them

especially! How he had not been paying taxes for some time and how one day the cops came in force to arrest him. He pleaded with them not to take him away and make his children orphans. He even had a suggestion. What if they were to give him a part-time job at the police station, make him a deputy or something, so he could earn some extra money and pay his taxes?

Well, the cops, being local fellows and knowing [this great-grandfather], took pity on him. At the police station the arrangements were made. He was issued a rifle and was even given a small advance on his pay for other purchases related to his new duties. There were tears of gratitude on his part, everyone was moved, and after many handshakes [he] left. He made his way straight to the tavern, where he stayed for three days raising hell. When he was thoroughly out of his mind, he made the waiters carry four tables outside at gunpoint. Then he ordered that the tables should be stacked one on top of the other, with a chair and a bottle of booze at the very top. There he climbed, drunk as he was. A crowd had gathered by then. There were Gypsies, too, fiddling and banging on their tambourines. When he started shooting his rifle and shouting that no Simic was ever going to be a stupid cop, the police showed up. They beat the daylights out of him and threw him in jail.

Like other kids his age, young Simic trafficked in gunpowder. This was obtained from unexploded shells, bullets lying about in the streets. The nose of the bullet was inserted into a kitchen spigot and pried away from the shell casing. The gunpowder was traded for valuables like comic books, toys, above all cans of food. Extraction of the gunpowder was obviously a delicate operation. "One day a kid on our block lost both his hands." Yet in the midst of all this, the poet assures us, "I was happy," and we believe him, even though we learn that his father was arrested by the Gestapo, released, and after making his way to Italy, rearrested by the German army, which accused him of being a spy. They put him in a prison in Milan, from which he was released by American forces. He subsequently made his way to the United States, his wife and two children following by graduated stages, stopping in Paris for about a year, where they lived frugally and were rarely able to eat at a restaurant. "We didn't have much money," observes Charles, now about fifteen, "and my mother was a type of person who didn't care what she ate."

It was a gloomy, damp, and lonely interval, during which he befriended a few boys his own age:

> These French boys I hung around with were very nice. They came from poor families. Now that they were doing badly in school, they knew their lives would be hard. They had absolutely no illusions about that. In the meantime, they had the street smarts, the humor and appetite for adventure, that reminded me of the friends I had left behind in Belgrade

—and that remind the reader of the author himself. Although he has become a highly sophisticated and well-educated man, it is still these non- or anti-academic virtues that most please him, and please us in him.

What is important in this book is not its narrative thrust or chronological development. It reads like a child's box of jumbled treasures, made the more wonderful by the oddness of their assortment. But since what is most important about Charles Simic is his poetry, I will home in now on what he has to say on this topic:

> The book that made all the difference to my idea of poetry was an anthology of contemporary Latin American verse that I bought on Eighth Street. Published by New Directions in 1942 and long out of print by the time I bought my copy, it introduced me to the poems of Jorge Luis Borges, Pablo Neruda, Jorge Carrera Andrade, Drummond de Andrade, Nicholas Guillen, Vincente Huidobro, Jorge de Lima, César Vallejo, Octavio Paz, and so many others. After that anthology, the poetry I read in literary magazines struck me as pretty timid. Nowhere in the *Sewanee Review* or the *Hudson Review* could I find poems like "Biography for the Use of the Birds" or "Liturgy of My Legs" or this one by the Haitian poet Emile Roumer, "The Peasant Declares His Love":

> > High-yellow of my heart, with breasts like tangerines,
> > you taste better to me than eggplant stuffed with crabs,
> > you are the tripe in my pepper pot,
> > the dumpling in my peas, my tea of aromatic herbs.
> > You're the corned beef whose customhouse is my heart,

my mush with syrup that trickles down the throat.
You're a steaming dish, mushroom cooked with rice,
crisp potato fried, and little fresh fish fried brown . . .
My hankering for love follows wherever you go.
Your bum is a gorgeous basket brimming with fruits and meats.

It is perfectly understandable that this poem should have met with sympathy and delight in Simic. He will later tell us, "If I were to write about the happiest days of my life, many of them would have to do with food and wine and a table full of friends." Lest anyone think this a trifling matter, Simic will note, on the same page, "I have to admit, I remember better what I've eaten than what I've thought. My memory is especially vivid about those far-off days from 1944 to 1949 in Yugoslavia, when we were mostly starving."

Neither should we be surprised to find, in *Night Picnic*, this fine poem:

Sweet Tooth

Take her to the pastry shop on Lexington.
Let her sample cream puffs at the counter,
The peach tarts on the street.
If topping or filling spurts down her chin,
Or even better, down her cleavage,

Lick it off before it dribbles down her dress.
With people going by, some pretending
Not to see you, while others stall,
Blinking as if the sun was in their eyes
Or they've left their glasses at home.

The uniformed schoolgirls, holding hands
In pairs, on their way to the park,
Are turning their heads, too, and so are
The red-faced men humping sides of beef
Out a freezer truck into a fancy butcher shop

While she continues to choke on an éclair,
Stopping momentarily with a mouthful
To wince at a brand-new stain on her skirt,
Which you've had no time to attend to,
Giving all your devotion to the one higher up.

"When I started writing poetry in 1955," Simic tells us in *The Unemployed Fortune-Teller,* "all the girls I wanted to show my poems to were American. I was stuck. It was never possible for me to write in my native language." And his beginnings as a poet were not always met with sympathy and understanding:

"Your poems are just crazy images strung arbitrarily together," my pals complained, and I'd argue back: "Haven't you heard about surrealism and free association?" Bob Burleigh, my best friend, had a degree in English from the University of Chicago and possessed all the critical tools to do a close analysis of any poem. His verdict was: "Your poems don't mean anything."

"Another time," he recalls,

I was drinking red wine, chain-smoking, and writing, long past midnight. Suddenly the poem took off, the words just flowing, in my head a merry-go-round of the most brilliant similes and metaphors. This is it! I was convinced there had never been such a moment of inspiration in the whole history of literature. I reread what I'd written and had to quit my desk and walk around the room, I got so excited. No sooner was I finished with one poem than I started another even more incredible one. Toward daybreak, paying no attention to my neighbor's furious banging on the wall, I typed them out with my two fingers and finally passed out exhausted on the bed. In the morning I dragged myself to work, dead tired but happy.

When evening came, I sat down to savor what I wrote the night before, a glass of wine in my hand. The poems were terrible! Incoherent babble, surrealist drivel! How could I have written such crap? I was stunned, depressed, and totally confused.

He learns a lesson about his art while listening to the jazz saxophonist Sonny Rollins:

> It was great. The lesson I learned was: cultivate controlled anarchy. I found Rollins, Charlie Parker, and Thelonious Monk far better models of what an artist could be than most poets. The same was true of the painters. Going to jazz clubs and galleries made me realize that there was a lot more poetry in America than one could find in the quarterlies.

And near the end of this lively and heartening book of memoirs, Simic is able to articulate his own artistic credo or *ars poetica:*

> The task of poetry, perhaps, is to salvage a trace of the authentic from the wreckage of religious, philosophical, and political systems.
>
> Next, one wants to write a poem so well crafted that it would do honor to the tradition of Emily Dickinson, Ezra Pound, and Wallace Stevens, to name only a few masters.
>
> At the same time, one hopes to rewrite that tradition, subvert it, turn it upside down, and make some living space for oneself.
>
> At the same time, one wants to entertain the reader with outrageous metaphors, flights of imagination, and heartbreaking pronounce-ments.
>
> At the same time, one has, for the most part, no idea of what one is doing. Words make love on the page like flies in the summer heat, and the poem is as much the result of chance as it is of intention. Probably more so.

"The god of chance" of whom he has written—see "The Altar," above—has looked with a very special favor upon Charles Simic, and he is fully aware of this, and manifestly grateful.

Seamus Heaney's Prose

De la musique avant toute chose.
—PAUL VERLAINE

The just man justices . . .
—GERARD MANLEY HOPKINS

It is gratifying, as well as convenient, to have this generous assemblage of Seamus Heaney's essays (a good number of which appeared in various earlier collections) now brought together in one volume. Some have been slightly abridged, but all retain a lucid and incontestable coherence and display a mind of delightful agility: delicate, robust, discriminating in its love for every topic it addresses. Heaney's title is half of the old, familiar playground taunt that in this country concludes, "losers weepers." It rejoices not only in possession but in the appropriating of what had once belonged to another. But Heaney has rendered the first half innocent by applying it solely to the work of authors he so deeply admires and so thoroughly understands that they have become possessions that chime with and quicken his sensibility. In fact, he makes the same claim regarding Osip Mandelstam's feeling for and knowledge of Dante's *Divine Comedy:* "He possesses the poem as a musician possesses the score, both as a whole structure and as a sequence of delicious sounds."

This acoustical sensitivity and musical faculty Heaney exhibits everywhere as he addresses poetry, and he delights to find others who share what Eliot called "the auditory imagination." To one essay he affixes Joseph Brodsky's statement:

Poets' real biographies are like those of birds . . . their real data are in the way they sound. A poet's biography is in his vowels and sibilants, in his meters, rhymes and metaphors . . . With poets, the choice of words is invariably more telling than the story they tell.

He quotes, with relish, some lines of his countryman W. R. Rodgers:

> I am Ulster, my people an abrupt people
> Who like the spiky consonants in speech
> And think the soft ones cissy.

Of Robert Lowell's style in his early book *Lord Weary's Castle,* Heaney comments:

The percussion and brass sections of the language orchestra are driven hard and, in a great set piece like "The Quaker Graveyard in Nantucket," the string section hardly gets a look-in. Distraught woodwinds surge across the soundscape; untamed and inconsolable discords ride the blast.

And in regard to a lovely passage in *Macbeth:*

The poetry . . . is to a large extent in the phonetics, in the way the English words waft and disseminate their associations, the flitting of the swallow being airily present in phrases like "they most breed and haunt" and "The air is delicate," while the looming stone architecture is conjured by the minatory solidity of terms like "masonry" and "buttress."

Of Ted Hughes's *Wodwo:* "His diction is consonantal, and it snicks through the air like an efficient blade." And of Geoffrey Hill: "There is in Hill something of Stephen Dedalus's hyperconsciousness of words as physical sensations, as sounds, to be plumbed, as weights on the tongue." More generally, he remarks,

In a poem, words, phrases, cadences and images are linked into systems of affect and signification which elude the précis maker. These under-ear activities, as they might be termed, may well constitute the most important business which the poem is up to and are a matter more of the erotics of language than of the politics and polemics of the moment.

This puts more tersely what Cleanth Brooks elaborated into an essay called "The Heresy of Paraphrase." But I can think of no one, critic or poet, whose ear is as perfectly pitched to the plain song as well as the full operatic pomps of poetic discourse. So we should not be surprised to find him writing, "I am sure that Coleridge's excitement on first hearing Wordsworth read was as much a matter of how the poem sounded as of what it intended."

James Joyce begins his autobiographical novel *A Portrait of the Artist as a Young Man* this way: "Once upon a time and a very good time it was there was a moocow coming down along the road and this moocow that was coming down along the road met a nicens little boy named baby tuckoo." And Heaney reminds us of this by beginning his book with a section, chiefly autobiographical and topical, titled "Mossbawn" (the name of the farm on which he was born), which begins:

> I would begin with the Greek word *omphalos,* meaning the navel, and hence the stone that marked the centre of the world, and repeat it, *omphalos, omphalos, omphalos,* until its blunt and falling music becomes the music of somebody pumping water at the pump outside our back door. It is County Derry in the early 1940s.

And like in Joyce, it is not long before considerations of locality take a political turn and coloration. Ireland is, alas, a riven nation, and Heaney was so placed by birth, as a Catholic born into the Protestant segment of the land, as to feel as keenly as anyone the cleft of cultures that became his inheritance. It can trace itself back to the twelfth century, and the incursion into Ireland by Henry II—he whose impatient exclamation "Who will rid me of this priest?" (muttered under his breath, but loud enough to be heard by some loyal and dutiful barons) led to the murder of Thomas à Becket. Then came Essex at the behest of Elizabeth, and Cromwell and King William. Heaney tallies the losses at Derry, Aughrim, and the Boyne. The Troubles, as they are called, date far back, to be sure, but are kept alive by, among other forces, the Reverend Ian Paisley's sectarian rancor, which somehow resembles the Ayatollah Khomeini's. Politics have consequences for poetry, especially for a poet subject to the snubs and persecutions that are heaped upon minorities; and Heaney is marvelously alive to how this works in such poets as Zbigniew Herbert, Czesław Miłosz, and Joseph Brodsky, for example. He tells us that Brodsky

> decried the yoking together of politics and poetry ("The only thing they have in common are the letters p and o") not because he had no belief in the transformative power of poetry per se but because the political requirement changed the criteria of excellence and was likely to lead to a debasement of the language and hence a lowering of "the plane and regard" (a favorite phrase) from which human beings viewed themselves and established their values.

Henry Adams observed, "Politics, as a practice, whatever its professions, has always been the systematic organization of hatreds." But Heaney interests himself in it, as did Yeats and Joyce, because it has such important historical consequences: for language, as well as other things.

What began with the sound of a Greek-speaking pump was to lead him into poetry: "I was getting my first sense of crafting words, and for one reason or another words as bearers of history and mystery began to invite me." As regards words as bearers of history, he would find in due course:

> We have learned how the values and language of the conqueror demolish and marginalize native values and institutions, rendering them barbarous, subhuman and altogether beyond the pale of cultivated sympathy or regard. But even so, it still seems an abdication of literary responsibility to be swayed by these desperately overdue correctives to the point where imaginative literature is read simply and solely as a function of an oppressive discourse, or as a reprehensible masking.

These paired sentences express deep sensitivity and sound critical sense. And as regards words as bearers of mystery, he writes of becoming enchanted by the gorgeous and inane phraseology of the catechism; or by the litany of the Blessed Virgin that was part of the enforced poetry of our household: Tower of Gold, Ark of the Covenant, Gate of Heaven, Morning Star, Health of the Sick, Refuge of Sinners, Comforter of the Afflicted. None of these things was consciously savored at the time, but I think the fact that I still recall them with ease, and can delight in them as verbal music, means that they were bedding the ear with a kind of linguistic hardcore that could be built on some day.

At one point, in the course of explaining how "an exuberant rhythm, a display of metrical virtuosity, some rising intellectual ground successfully surmounted . . . gratifies and furthers the range of the mind's and the body's pleasures and helps the reader to obey the old command: *Nosce teipsum.* Know thyself," he quotes a splendid stanza of his own:

> This is how poems help us live.
> They match the meshes in the sieve
> Life puts us through; they take and give
>   Our proper measure
> And prove themselves most transitive
>   When they give pleasure.

Coming upon this stanza in an essay on Christopher Marlowe, we may instinctively recall Robert Burns, who famously employed the same form in a good number of his poems, like "Holy Willie's Prayer," "The Vision," and "To a Mouse." We have come to think of it as Burns's stanza, though it is no more his than the Shakespearean sonnet in Shakespeare's creation. But in his essay on Burns Heaney identifies the stanzaic form as "Standard Habbie metre."[1]

His characteristic mode of approach is by indirection. He begins with a poem by the Czech Miroslav Holub which describes two characters as a means of representing the different poetical postures of W. B. Yeats and Philip Larkin. He begins writing about Sylvia Plath through the prism of some marvelous lines by Wordsworth. Normally, one would think of

---

1. The stanzaic form dates at least as far back as the early-seventeenth-century poem by Robert Sempill of Beltrees called "The Life and Death of Habbie Simson, the Piper of Kilbarchan."

Plath as being Wordsworth's polar opposite; and in some ways indeed she is. But the Wordsworth lines are used allegorically, as is the Holub poem, and in both cases the illumination provided by those surprising juxtapositions is richly rewarding.

The main body of *Finders Keepers,* following upon the autobiographical prelude, is devoted to an examination of the work of those poets Heaney especially prizes and has made his own by admiring appropriation. They are: Ted Hughes, Geoffrey Hill, Philip Larkin, Yeats, Lowell, Derek Mahon, Paul Muldoon, Michael Longley, Patrick Kavanagh, Zbigniew Herbert, Dante and Eliot, Elizabeth Bishop, Sylvia Plath, Thomas Kinsella, Edwin Muir, Christopher Marlowe, John Clare, Hugh MacDiarmid, Dylan Thomas, Robert Burns, W. R. Rodgers, John Hewitt, Stevie Smith, Norman MacCraig, Italo Calvino, Joseph Brodsky, and Czesław Miłosz.

The list is impressive enough in its diversity, but lurking behind the appreciative considerations of these poets lie a number of other writers so thoroughly appropriated by Heaney as to have become melodiously woven into his own sensibility, and hence to flavor his thought almost everywhere. Of these the chief one is Shakespeare, whose language flows in and out of the of the author's thought so unobtrusively as not to call for quotation marks but simply to lend a noble music to what is going forward. Others include Keats, Gerard Manley Hopkins, Frost, Wordsworth, Osip and Nadezhda Mandelstam, the Sir Philip Sidney of the *Defence of Poesy,* and the Robert Graves of *The White Goddess.*

Heaney's vivid enjoyment of poetry that he loves is always persuasive in its own right, but the more so when he acknowledges some occasional reservations. Of Hugh MacDiarmid, he is frank about the poet's bluster and rant, saying, "He was more devoted to opening salvos than to finishing touches . . . His polemical writings had all the troublemaking tactics of a dangerman in a bar, stripped to his shirt-sleeves and squaring up to anyone and everyone." Of Stevie Smith, after quoting a quite Dickinsonian poem of hers, he observes that "her vision [is] almost tragic . . . Yet finally the voice, the style, the literary resources are not adequate to the somber recognitions, the wounded *joie de vivre,* the marooned spirit we sense they were destined to express."

Such gentle demurrals serve to validate unqualified enthusiasms when we encounter them, and this is most evident in the case of T. S. Eliot. Heaney first encountered this formidable figure at the age of fifteen, and was balked and daunted by the celebrated obscurities. He admits, "I was never caught up by Eliot, never taken over and shown to myself by his work, my ear never pulled outside in by what it heard in him." But he was to discover

> that what is to be learned from Eliot is the double-edged nature of poetic reality: first encountered as a strange fact of culture, poetry is internalized over the years until it becomes, as they say, second nature. Poetry that was originally beyond you, generating the need to understand and overcome its strangeness, becomes in the end a familiar path within you, a grain along which your imagination opens pleasurably backwards towards an origin and a seclusion. Your last state is therefore a thousand times better than your first, for the experience of poetry is one which truly deepens and fortifies itself with reenactment.

On Elizabeth Bishop:

> Wit confronts hurt and holds a balance that deserves to be called wisdom ... Like [George] Herbert, Bishop finds and enforces a correspondence between the procedures of verse and the predicaments of the spirit ... Losses of all sorts have caused the mind's scales to tilt drastically, and so they desperately need to be evened out by a redistribution of the mind's burdens—and the act of writing is depended upon to bring that redistribution about.

On the divisions and allegiances in W. R. Rodgers and his poems:

> In the triangulation of Rodgers's understanding of himself between London, Loughgall and the Lowlands, in that three-sided map of his inner being that he provided with its three cardinal points, in all of that there is something analogous to the triple heritage of Irish, Scottish and English traditions that compound and complicate the cultural and political life of contemporary Ulster.

Such rifts and cleavages remind us of Derek Walcott's "A Far Cry from Africa," and the bitter cry of another of his poems, "Ah, brave third world!"

Of Marlowe's "Hero and Leander," Heaney comments,

> Marlowe is involved here with a show-off performance, operating with real spontaneity and affection. . . . The intonation of "Hero and Leander" is not as ominous or stricken as the great scenes of *Doctor Faustus,* yet it does issue from a kind of seasoned knowledge that is almost unshockable, certainly undupable but still not altogether disenchanted.

I can't help observing that Heaney's account here fails to register any sense of the absurd comedy of the first two sestiads of the poem.[2] He quotes some lines about Hero's very peculiar footwear, but omits those that immediately precede them:

> Her kirtle blue, whereon was many a stain
> Made with the blood of wretched lovers slain.
> Upon her head she ware a myrtle wreath,
> From whence her veil reached to the ground beneath.

That is, she never changes her bloody garments because they testify to the suicides of her previous conquests; and she is clothed from head to toe, though when in due course Leander is described, he is buck-naked.

After quoting a poem by Patrick Kavanagh, he observes,

> When I read those lines in 1963, I took to their rhythm and was grateful for their skilful way with an octosyllabic metre. But I was too much in love with poetry that painted the world with a thick linguistic pigment to relish fully the line-drawing that was inscribing itself so lightly and freely here. I was still more susceptible to the heavy tarpaulin verse of *The Great Hunger* than to the rinsed streamers that fly in the clear subjective breeze of "Prelude."

On Eliot:

> This hankering for a purely delineated realm of wisdom and beauty sometimes asks literature to climb the stair of transcendence and give

---

2. The remaining four sestiads were composed with humorless solemnity by George Chapman.

us images free from the rag-and-bone-shop reek of time and place . . . Eliot's achievement in his Dantean stanzas is to create just such an illusion of oracular authority by the hypnotic deployment of a vocabulary that is highly Latinate.

This observation somewhat covertly sets Eliot in opposition to Yeats (who embraced the foul rag-and-bone shop of the heart). But the curious fact is that in the Dantean stanzas of "Little Gidding," composed in a variant form of terza rima, Eliot first wrote of encountering Brunetto Latini in bomb-scarred London, just as Dante met his old teacher in the *Inferno;* but decided to replace him with "a familiar compound ghost." When asked about the change by John Hayward, Eliot replied that

> The visionary figure has now become somewhat more definite and will no doubt be identified by some readers with Yeats, though I do not mean anything so precise as that. However, I do not wish to take the responsibility of putting Yeats or anybody else into Hell and I do not want to impute to him the particular vice which took Brunetto there.[3]

AT ONE POINT in the midsection of this book, Heaney quotes a long passage from Wordsworth's 1802 preface to *Lyrical Ballads,* and follows that quotation with a gloss or paraphrase of his own:

> Essentially, Wordsworth declares that what counts is the quality, intensity and breadth of the poet's concerns between the moments of writing, the gravity and purity of the mind's appetites and applications between moments of inspiration. This is what determines the ultimate human value of the act of poetry. That act remains free, self-governing, self-seeking, but the worth of the booty it brings back from its raid upon the inarticulate will depend upon the emotional capacity, intellectual resource and general civilization which the articulate poet maintains between the raids.

Wordsworth in his statement is not quite as straightforward and clear as Heaney in his gloss, and though I dare not claim that Heaney's version is

---

3. Helen Gardner, *The Composition of Four Quartets* (1978), 176.

very different from Wordsworth's, I think it is fair to say that Heaney brings to the topic of where poems come from a moral tone and ethical dignity that has about it a nobility and sense of vocation that are not far from religious. We feel this pressure often in Wordsworth's poems more powerfully, perhaps, than in his preface. But the side-by-side statements of the two poets appear in Heaney's essay on Sylvia Plath, and its presence there invites some disturbing considerations. When we are asked to consider "the gravity and purity of the mind's appetites and applications *between moments of inspiration*," we must sooner or later find ourselves facing Plath's *Journals* and Larkin's *Letters*. And these volumes do not testify to the gravity and purity of their respective authors' minds.

Plath's *Journals* are rancorous, scornful, envious, and at times quite vicious; Larkin's *Letters* are occasionally petty and often ungenerous. And yet I find myself disposed to think Heaney's instinct is right in affirming the importance of a poet's mind and spirit as it manifests itself in what Wordsworth elsewhere called "that best portion of a good man's life, / His little nameless, unremembered, acts / Of kindness and of love." Heaney is inviting us to see a spiritual comportment that informs a poet's work, brought to that work by something like disinterested devotion. If I understand him correctly, Heaney is putting in positive terms what Ruskin once put negatively, though with great force:

> The emotions of indignation, grief, controversial anxiety and vanity, or hopeless, and therefore, uncontending, scorn, are all of them as deadly to the body as poisonous air or polluted water; and when I reflect how much of the active part of my past life has been spent in these states— and that what may remain to me of life can never more be in any other,—I begin to ask myself, with somewhat pressing arithmetic, how much time is likely to be left me, at the age of fifty-six, to complete the various designs for which, until past fifty, I was merely collecting material.[4]

There are dangers in positing too neat a correspondence between the moral character of an artist and the work he produces; we know of too many cases where such correspondence is nearly impossible to find. But

---

4. John Ruskin, The Introduction to *Deucalion*, vol. 7 (Wiley, 1886), pp. 1–2.

elsewhere in this book, in connection with Larkin and approaching the topic more indirectly, Heaney is able to find in the poet's very *technique* something akin to the devotion he feels belongs to poetry. After quoting Larkin's "Aubade," a bitter, almost resentful meditation on his solitary, mortal condition, a muttered litany of whining complaint, Heaney goes on to reflect:

> Still, when a poem rhymes, when a form generates itself, when a metre provokes consciousness into new postures, it is already on the side of life. When a rhyme surprises and extends the fixed relations between words, that in itself protests against necessity. When language does more than enough, as it does in all achieved poetry, it opts for the condition of overlife and rebels at limit. In this fundamental artistic way, then, Larkin's "Aubade" does not go over to the side of the adversary.

In the course of time a number of young poets have asked me what I would recommend that they read—apart from poems themselves—to help them understand their craft, not in a handbook way, but as informal discourse. And I have proposed a number of texts that provoke long and lively thought, most often among them the letters of Keats. I get asked that question less frequently these days, but if a young writer were to come up with the same question I would now happily and gratefully add *Finders Keepers*.

PART III

Moby-Dick

On a note of modesty not altogether serious, Melville concluded his celebrated chapter "Cetology," which is given to the classification of whales by species, with these words: "It was stated at the outset, that this system would not be here, and at once, perfected. You cannot but plainly see that I have kept my word. But I now leave my cetological System standing thus unfinished, even as the great Cathedral of Cologne was left, with the crane still standing upon the top of the uncompleted tower. For small erections may be completed by their first architects; grand ones, true ones, ever leave the copestone to posterity. God keep me from ever completing anything. This whole book is but a draught—nay, but the draught of a draught. Oh, Time, Strength, Cash, and Patience!" (127–28).[1]

How suitable, then, that Herman Melville should be memorialized in the Poets' Corner of the Cathedral of St. John the Divine, which in its vast incompletion not only corresponds to Cologne's Cathedral and the author's description of his masterwork but may also be imagined as participating, through its clergy, in the same prayerful and concluding sigh—for "Time, Strength, Cash, and Patience." Yet Melville's pose of modesty here is guileful, or deceitful, as is much of his great book. For example, this chapter appears to compare whales taxonomically as they vary in kind and size to the varying sizes of books, beginning with folios, or the largest whales, and diminishing in measured gradations by way of octavos and duodecimos. Yet while the book-maker's metaphor is being used, the whales throughout are in fact consistently being compared, more covertly

---

This essay grew from remarks given at the Cathedral of St. John the Divine on the occasion of the dedication of a plaque to Melville.

1. Quotations from *Moby-Dick* are all from the Norton Critical Edition, ed. Harrison Hayford and Hershel Parker (1967).

but no less consistently, to men. "The Fin-Back is not gregarious . . . very shy; always going solitary . . . this leviathan seems the banished and un-conquerable Cain of his race" (122). The Hump Back "is the most game-some and light-hearted of all the whales" (123). The Razor Back is "of a retiring nature," while the Sulpher Bottom is "another retiring gentleman" (123). The Mealy-mouthed Porpoise "is of a quite neat and gentleman-like figure" (127) with "sentimental Indian eyes of hazel hue" (127). But most tellingly of all, the Killer whale resembles us, "For we are all killers, on land and on sea; Bonapartes and Sharks included" (125).

This sinister note, one of many omens and portents, is only partly con-cealed behind a prose that at the beginning, and throughout a large part of the book, is genial, playful, and full of deceptive levity. Ishmael's tone in the opening chapter is that of a cheerful and jesting misanthrope (not unlike Shakespeare's Jaques). This cynical frame of mind is dramatically altered by the bond Ishmael forms with Queequeg, a bond strong enough to be called marriage and so deep as to justify Ishmael's making Queequeg the beneficiary of his will. A number of well-known critics have pointed, snickeringly or otherwise, at what they deem the homosexual component in this intimacy. That is not a view I can authoritatively contradict, but it is one that seems to me of minor, if any, consequence. The fact is that to Ishmael, Queequeg is initially repellent, and no pains are spared to make this point clear: "Good heavens! what a sight! Such a face! It was of a dark, purplish, yellow color, here and there stuck over with large, blackish look-ing squares" (28). "His bald purplish head now looked for all the world like a mildewed skull" (29). Ishmael's ability to overcome his early revulsion, fear, and distrust and to become Queequeg's friend and equal (a conde-scension on both sides, since in his native land Queequeg is a Prince of the Blood) is a topic taken up and dismissed quite early in the novel, though both characters continue to the very end of the book. This is one of many puzzles that have been excused as due to Melville's faulty methods of con-struction; it's claimed that the friendship is made much of, and then, through negligence, never pursued. I reject this argument, and instead suggest that the bond between Ishmael and Queequeg is the first step in Ishmael's repudiation of his misanthropy, the beginning of his pilgrim's progress, a spiritual advance that reaches its lyric and beatific climax in Chapter 94, titled "A Squeeze of the Hand."

In this chapter (although the second half seems savagely to contradict the first with Melville's most brutal and characteristic irony) Ishmael experiences an almost ecstatic sense of union with all those in his immediate vicinity as they are engaged in squeezing spermaceti with their bare hands, and during which process Ishmael declares, "while bathing in that bath, I felt divinely free from all ill-will, or petulance, or malice, of any sort whatever" (344). He was continually looking about him, "as much as to say,—Oh! my dear fellow beings, why should we longer cherish any social acerbities, or know the slightest ill-humor or envy! Come; let us squeeze hands all round; nay, let us squeeze ourselves into each other; let us squeeze ourselves universally into the very milk and sperm of kindness." This sanctifying and redemptive experience has been purchased at the cost of a sacrificed whale.

Though I am unable to prove that one thing was the result of the other, the beatific vision here described bears a remarkable comparison with one of Melville's most famous letters to Hawthorne, and to this particular passage: "Whence come you, Hawthorne? By what right do you drink from my flagon of life? And when I put it to my lips—lo, they are yours and not mine. I feel like the Godhead is broken up like the bread at the Supper, and that we are the pieces. Hence this infinite fraternity of feeling" (566). This fraternity is expressed, in what seems inarguably pious terms, in the language of the Eucharist. But Melville's employment of that metaphor is cunningly ambiguous and may even undermine and subvert its superficially religious impression. For the notion that the Godhead is broken up and that we are its pieces may mean that there is no God except as manifested in individual human beings. This is a topic to which I must return.

In any case, in express contrast to Ishmael's experience of being cleansed, baptized, and fraternally bound to all the members of mankind, and in which he is vouchsafed a vision of "angels in paradise" (349), Ahab specifically rejects such kinship, first by his lofty isolation, but more dramatically and decisively when he refuses to extend any help or compassion to the bereaved captain of the *Rachel*, whose ten-year-old son was left adrift in a whaleboat and lost upon the vast ocean waters. And as if this were not enough, Ahab confirms his resolute hardness of heart in rejecting, as though it were an impermissible weakness, his own sense of pity for Pip.

The note of levity in the opening chapters makes up one tone of a richly orchestrated and polyphonic blend, and it may be said that *Moby-Dick* resembles Joyce's *Ulysses* in its stylistic variety and inventiveness, as in its promiscuous use of many forms, including dramatic script, stage directions, soliloquy, tall tales and other narratives, expository prose, minstrel-show dialogue, homily, parable, instruction manual, catechism, biblical exegesis, allegory and parody, as well as the larger forms of the epic, and of comedy and tragedy.

Not only this, the book bristles with exotic and recondite learning, exhibiting more than casual acquaintance with records of whaling and shipping, accounts of exploration, Byzantine chronicles, mythology and legend, Renaissance painting, comparative anthropology, history both ancient and modern, as well as a valuable indebtedness to Cervantes, Burton, Rabelais, Bunyan, Sir Thomas Browne, Darwin, Plato, Homer, Shakespeare, the Bible in general and the Book of Job in particular, as well as Charles Dickens. The following, for example, echoes Dickens at his coziest and most domestic: "And like a sister of charity did this charitable Aunt Charity bustle about hither and thither, ready to turn her hand to anything that promised to yield safety, comfort, and consolation to all on board a ship in which her beloved brother Bildad was concerned, and in which she herself owned a score or two of well-saved dollars" (90). There is an encyclopedic embrace to Melville's reach of references that lends, all by itself, a weighty universality to this book; and that reach is the more impressive when we consider that both Melville and his narrator, Ishmael, were autodidacts. They "have swum through libraries" (118) in the creation of this work, and the painstaking travails of a "sub-sub librarian" (2) are in evidence even in Melville's most facetious moments.

There is something ungainly in the monumental scale of the book that may in part be justified by its pretensions to and echoes of the epic. Writing of the ambiguous lure of the sea for certain men such as the blacksmith, whose life and career have been a pathetic failure, Melville said that "from the hearts of infinite Pacifics, the thousand mermaids sing to them—'Come hither, broken-hearted; here is another life without the guilt of immediate death; here are wonders supernatural, without dying for them. Come hither! bury thyself in a life which, to your now equally abhorred and abhorring, landed world, is more obvious than death. Come hither! put up *thy* gravestone, too, within the churchyard, and come hither, till we marry thee!'" (402). We have here a witty version or paraphrase of the Siren's Song in *The Odyssey*. And much earlier there appeared a celebrated and much debated chapter which concludes, "Take heart, take heart, O Bulkington! Bear thee grimly, demigod! Up from the spray of thy ocean-perishing—straight up, leaps thy apotheosis!" (98). Since Bulkington was only scantily described before his sudden and total disappearance early in the novel, critics have pretty well concluded that this again is one of Melville's many errors of construction; that Bulkington was originally supposed to play some important part in the book but that Melville changed his plans and never troubled to smooth out his discrepancies. I think it worth pointing out, however, that when he disappears Bulkington is the helmsman; and his early departure from this epic is like the loss of Elpenor in *The Odyssey* and of Palinurus, the helmsman who, having fallen asleep, falls overboard, in the fifth book of *The Aeneid.*

Epic, indeed Miltonic, is the contest between Ahab and his fated, numinous, and monumental antagonist, the whale. And this contention also echoes those contests with God that figure so prominently in the Old Testament, conducted with heroic endeavor by the likes of Abraham in behalf of the innocent minority of inhabitants of Sodom and Gomorrah, of Jacob wrestling with the angel, of Jonah in his dispute with God about the fate of the citizens of Nineveh, of Job in his bewilderment about the ways of God, of Moses in his negotiations with God in the matter of Korah, of Jeremiah when he complains: "Righteous art thou, O Lord, when I plead with thee: yet let me talk with thee of thy judgments: Wherefore doth the way of the wicked prosper? Wherefore are all they happy that deal very treacherously?" (Jer. 12:1). Such inquiries, such seeking for reasons about the manifest inequities in human experience, the misfortunes of the innocent, the triumphs of the unworthy, have been a part of religious and philosophic speculation at all times and have been a theme of tragedy. A passion for intelligible justice from on high plagued Lear and Gloucester, but while Shakespeare's characters are humbled, Melville's Ahab is not.

Contentions about Justice and the forces of Destiny are a central theme to Melville as well as to Milton, and Ahab's lonely and intransigent confrontation with the faceless, unintelligible Disposer of life and death, good fortune and bad, may remind us of Shelley's description, in *The Defense of Poetry,* of Milton's Satan:

Milton's devil as a moral being is as far superior to his God, as one who perseveres in some purpose which he has conceived to be excellent in

spite of adversity and torture, is to one who in the cold security of un-
doubted triumph inflicts the most horrible revenge upon his enemy,
not from any mistaken notion of inducing him to repent of a persever-
ance in enmity, but with the alleged design of exasperating him to deserve new torments.

Construed, if you like, with the libertarian bias of Shelley, Ahab may be
seen as Prometheanly heroic, even to the point of blasphemy, which is just
the term Starbuck uses about his fixed and inflexible purpose.

We should consider for a moment the fixity of that purpose, which
Melville frequently and firmly calls *monomania*. Among Ahab's most majestic, Brunonian soliloquies we find passages that express his determination with defiant extravagance: "The path of my fixed purpose is laid with
iron rails, whereon my soul is grooved to run. Over unsounded gorges,
through the rifled hearts of mountains, under torrents' beds, unerringly I
rush! Naught's an obstacle, naught's an angle to the iron way!" (147). Ut-
tered in the name of freedom and independence, these words of Ahab, in
their absolute resolve, bear a meaning that seems almost *predestinate*, another word that receives great emphasis and attention in this book. It is a
theological term, and we must attend to it, but for the present I want to
point out that Ahab has drawn his metaphor in this passage from the field
of civil engineering, and more specifically, the laying of railroad tracks.
And railroads played a major part in what was called America's Manifest
Destiny, its ravenous and acquisitive expansion westward, at the fatal expense of all Indian populations who offered any resistance to this national
impulse.

"*Pequod*, you will no doubt remember," says Ishmael, "was the name
of a celebrated tribe of Massachusetts Indians, now extinct as the ancient
Medes" (67). Their extinction was not due, of course, to a change of cli-
mate, as may have been the case with dinosaurs: they were openly and
brutally exterminated. To this day the Smithsonian Institution owns the
bones of an estimated 18,000 American Indians, which the powerless
descendants of those slaughtered multitudes are now endeavoring to
reacquire for decent burial, but without much help from our courts. It
was an American general of the Civil War, Philip Henry Sheridan, who
fully twenty years after Melville's novel was written was still able to proclaim, "The only good Indian is a dead Indian," a sentiment which for a

long time expressed the general American view and became a part of our heritage.

Melville makes much of the exploitation and extermination of others by the white settlers in this country, remarking that "it is the same with the American whale fishery as with the American army and military and merchant navies, and the engineering forces employed in the construction of American Canals and Railroads . . . in all these cases the native American [by which is meant the white settler] liberally provides the brains, the rest of the world generously supplying the muscles" (108), a proposition born out in large part by the constituency and rank of the *Pequod*'s crew. It is furthermore to be remembered that Melville's first readers lived in a society that tolerated slavery of the black race; and though Melville's home state of New York had abolished slavery in 1827, it lagged well behind Britain, which ceased its toleration in 1772, but did so well before our nation as a whole, which had to go through the costly Civil War before the slaves were freed.

Since throughout this book whales are identified with men, the killing of whales is, by this metaphor, tantamount to *murder*, a word Melville explicitly uses more than once. Ishmael describes entering the Spouter Inn and seeing a display of whaling instruments: "You shuddered as you gazed," he says, "and wondered what monstrous cannibal and savage could ever have gone a death-harvesting with such a hacking, horrifying implement" (21). It is not long before, with decided pride, the same Ishmael is able to declare that "our vocation amounts to a butchering sort of business; . . . when actively engaged therein, we are surrounded by all manner of defilements. Butchers we are, that is true. But butchers, also, and butchers of the bloodiest badge have been all Martial Commanders whom the world invariably delights to honor" (98). Men are likened to ravenous sharks in their savagery and rapacity, and Ishmael candidly admits, "I myself am a savage, owning no allegiance but to the King of the Cannibals; and ready at any moment to rebel against him" (232). That streak of barbarity is borne out when Ishmael unblushingly describes his dissection of a cub, or baby whale, and shortly thereafter goes so far as to speculate, like modern conservationists, on the possibility of the total extermination of the genus.

The brutality of the whaling enterprise—not merely the initial killing, but the dismemberment and technological processing of the whale—is rendered in horrifying, in nothing less than stomach-turning, detail, and Melville was surely trying to shock us into a sense of our own savagery. In this he succeeds all the more for his capacity to make whales, upon occasion, positively endearing. The description of the murder of a whale ends: "At last, gush after gush of clotted red gore, as if it had been the purple lees of red wine, shot into the frighted air; and falling back again, ran dripping down his motionless flank into the sea. His heart had burst!" (245). Later we encounter, in the midst of the grand Armada of whales, the females and young of the company: the camp-followers, as it were: "Keeping at the center of the lake, we were occasionally visited by the small tame cows and calves; the women and children of this routed host" (324). These are described with so much tenderness and respect that when Ishmael finds himself telling us how he dissected a baby whale the effect is genuinely appalling. The point is brought home with special force when, late in the novel, in a chapter called "The Symphony," which begins with a description of a day of celestial beauty, the sea and sky seemingly wedded in a bridal bond of tranquility, Ahab says, "Oh, Starbuck! it is a mild, mild wind, and a mild looking sky. On such a day . . . I struck my first whale" (443).

This novel is gleefully or sardonically subversive on a number of topics, and religion is one of these; but another is unrestrained American capitalism and the ideas and sanctions (some of these religious ones) that support it. Whaling is a commercial enterprise, and though it would be fully seventy-five years before President Coolidge would proclaim that "the business of America is business," this was already an article of faith at the time Melville was writing. Even earlier Tocqueville had written: "I know no country, indeed, where the love of money has taken stronger hold upon the affections of men." He also wrote, "The especial taste that men of democratic ages entertain for physical enjoyments [by which he means opulence and luxury] is not naturally opposed to the principles of public order . . . It may even be frequently combined with a species of religious morality: men wish to be as well off as they can be in this world, without forgoing their chance of another."[2] This prudential attitude is analyzed in Max Weber's *The Protestant Ethic* with many citations from Ben Franklin to the general effect that God helps them that help themselves, especially if the helping is to a generously large share of the pie. "The summum

2. Alexis de Tocqueville, *Democracy in America,* ed. Henry Steele Commager (1947), 43, 342.

bonum of this ethic," Weber wrote, "the earning of more and more money, combined with strict avoidance of all spontaneous enjoyment of life, is above all completely devoid of any eudamonistic, not to say hedonistic, admixture."[3] He mentioned the Calvinists, and how they delighted to cite the text of Proverbs 22:29, "Seest thou a diligent man in his business? He shall stand before kings."

This characteristically American form of rapacity is liberally represented here. Urging on the crew of his whale-boat, Stubb shouts to them, "There goes three thousand dollars, men!—a whole bank! The Bank of England!" (297). Commercial prudence also characterizes Captain Bildad, who is a familiar type of New England tightwad. The whole expedition of the *Pequod,* expected to last for years, departs punctually on Christmas Day, either in flat defiance of conventional domestic ritual and established religion or else with implied Christian sanction of the business ethic, to say nothing of various types of killing. Great specificity is offered with regard to the sorts of profit that may be looked for in the whaling industry: "How comes it that we whalemen of America now outnumber all the rest of the banded whalemen of the world; sail a navy of upwards of seven hundred vessels; manned by eighteen thousand men; yearly consuming 4,000,000 of dollars; the ship's worth, at the time of sailing, $20,000,000; and every year importing into our harbors a well-reaped harvest of $7,000,000[?]" (99). If, in the bloated economy of our own day, with the dizzying cost estimates of the Stealth Bomber and the holdings of corporate giants, these sums do not seem especially impressive, recall that the gold doubloon, with which Ahab lures the entire crew to his maniacal purposes and keeps them eagerly alert for sighting Moby-Dick, is declared to be worth sixteen dollars and is welcomed with unanimous enthusiasm. This notion of Big Business (mid-nineteenth-century style), suitably embellished with metaphors of piracy and plunder, colors much of the book and most of the crew, but apart from the cabin-boy, Pip, three characters are clearly untainted by it: Ishmael, Ahab, and the Parsee, Fedallah.

The Parsee, of course, is not a Christian, but this alone is not enough to explain his exemption from Christian vices. His role in the novel is akin

---

3. Max Weber, "The Spirit of Capitalism," in *The Protestant Ethic,* quoted by C. F. Calverton, *The Making of Society* (1937), 511.

to that of the Weird Sisters in *Macbeth:* he is a seer, a clairvoyant with divinatory powers, whose disinterested objectivity can in part be certified by his having no common interest with any other character in the tale. He stands apart and remote, a commentator upon Fate, a forecaster of improbabilities, of what seem, indeed, impossibilities. For just as the witches provided Macbeth with three uncanny warnings and reassurances (that he must fear Macduff, that none of woman born can harm him, and that he shall never be vanquished till Birnam Wood come to Dunsinane), so does Fedallah make Ahab three promises: "that ere thou couldst die on this voyage, two hearses must verily be seen by thee on the sea; the first not made by mortal hands; and the visible wood of the last one must be grown in America" (410); second, that Ahab will survive the Parsee, who will nevertheless return to the world to be his guide; and third, that only hemp (which Ahab interprets to be the hangman's rope) can kill him, which convinces him that he will not die at sea.

Fedallah is the voice of the uncanny, as the whale is its image. He speaks in riddles, the equivalent of the hieroglyphics that Melville mentions frequently throughout his book, as he also mentions Champollion, the finder of the Rosetta stone. Ishmael is exempted from this curse of money because he is a greenhorn, so inexperienced in the skills and technology of whaling that he is offered only the 777th lay, or share, of the profits when he signs on. Moreover, he makes it plain from the first that money is not his motive in going to sea, and though he is guilty of the same atrocities as the other members of the crew, he survives because, after all, Melville needed a survivor to tell the tale and because Ishmael is, possibly as a consequence of his momentary love for all mankind (like that moment in which the Ancient Mariner is able to bless the sea-creatures), the one nearest to salvation.

As for Ahab, his purpose is not monetary but metaphysical, and it is only because he depends upon the crew for his monomaniacal ambitions that he allows them at first to go about the regular course of harvesting whales, their loyalty being indispensable to his designs. Ahab is positively Marlovian in his defiance, his Faustian ambition, his pride, egotism, independence, and isolation. When Stubb tells Flask that he takes Fedallah "to be the devil in disguise," and Flask then asks, "what's the old man have so much to do with him for?" Stubb replies, "Striking up a swap or a bargain, I suppose" (275). His proud independence, it could be argued, is the incarnation of America's dream of its own Manifest Destiny. Ahab fanta-sizes about commissioning the manufacture of an Ideal Man, made to his own specifications, as follows: "Imprimus, fifty feet high in his socks; then, chest modelled after the Thames Tunnel; then, legs with roots to 'em, to stay in one place; then, arms three feet through the wrist; no heart at all, brass forehead, and about a quarter of an acre of fine brains; and let me see—shall I order eyes to see outwards? No, but put a skylight on top of his head to illuminate inwards" (390).

Such total dependence upon one's own faculties, such distrust of out-side authority or tradition, was once described in these terms:

> I have shown how it is that in ages of equality every man seeks for his own opinion within himself: I am now about to show how it is that, in the same ages, all of his feelings are turned towards himself alone. Ego-tism is a passionate and exaggerated love of self, which leads a man to connect everything with his own person, and to prefer himself to ev-erything in the world . . . Egotism blights the germ of all virtue; indi-vidualism, at first, only saps the virtue of public life; but, in the long run, it attacks and destroys all others, and at length is absorbed in downright egotism.[4]

That was Tocqueville; this is from Father Mapple's sermon:

> Delight is to him—a far, far upward, and inward delight—who against the proud gods and commodores of this earth, ever stands forth his own inexorable self . . . Delight is to him, who gives no quarter in the truth, and kills, burns, and destroys all sin though he pluck it out from under the robes of Senators and Judges. Delight—top-gallant delight is to him, who acknowledges no law or lord, but the Lord his God, and is only a patriot to heaven. (57)

Yet the man who repudiates all worldly authority may acquire a taste for the repudiation of authority of any kind, save for his own solipsistic in-ward voice. And Father Mapple illustrates and personifies his doctrine of spiritual independence and isolation by mounting to his pulpit by

---

4. Tocqueville, *Democracy in America*, 310, 51.

means of a rope ladder, which he hauls in after him, leaving him high and solitary.

We encounter a good deal of irony at the expense of religion, as well as of the sort of optimistic, Emersonian Pantheism and Transcendentalism that was much admired at the time. In an essay on Goethe, Emerson had written, "The air is full of sounds; the sky, of tokens; the ground is all memoranda and signatures, and every object covered over with hints which speak to the intelligent." The cheery confidence of such utterances is constantly contravened and undermined in Melville. He presents us with countless numbers of indecipherable hieroglyphics, of which one prominent example is the gold doubloon. As in Plato's *Symposium,* where the various speakers in turn address the topic of Love and in each case reveal, not what may be called the truth, but some aspect of themselves (Socrates excepted, because he presents no view of his own, but those of Diotima), so here in the chapter "The Doubloon" Melville parades all his major characters past the gold coin, allowing each an interpretation of its enigmatic symbols. Ahab, Starbuck, Stubb, Flask, the Manx Sailor, Queequeg, Fedallah, and Pip all pass by and offer their singular conjectures as to the meaning of those signs; and each in turn presents us, not with an "objective" reading, but with a "subjective" elucidation that is profoundly self-referential.

The doubloon, however, is a mere instance of the ambiguities, paradoxes, oxymorons, and contradictions with which this book abounds. Let me offer a selective list. The gentleness of Queequeg, who is an acknowledged cannibal. His tomahawk, which turns out to be a peace-pipe. His coffin, which turns out to be a life-raft. The whiteness of the whale, signifying qualities both malign and benign. And here are a few representative quotations: "Some of these same Quakers are the most sanguinary of all sailors and whale-hunters. They are fighting Quakers; they are Quakers with a vengeance" (71). To paraphrase *Hamlet,* this was sometime a paradox, but Richard Nixon has given it proof.

> The port would fain give succor; the port is pitiful; in the port is safety, comfort, hearthstone, supper, warm blankets, friends, all that's kind to our mortalities. But in that gale, the port, the land, is that ship's direst jeopardy; she must fly all hospitality; one touch of land, though it but graze the keel, would make her shudder through and through. She

crowds all sail off shore . . . for refuge's sake forlornly rushing into peril; her only friend her bitterest foe! (97)

Oh, man! admire and model thyself after the whale! Do thou, too, remain warm among ice. Do thou, too, live in this world without being of it. Be cool at the equator; keep thy blood fluid at the Pole. Like the great dome of St. Peter's, and like the great whale, retain, O man! in all seasons a temperature of thine own. (261)

Finally, the penultimate sentence of the Epilogue reads: "The unharming sharks, they glided by as if with padlocks on their mouths; the savage seahawks sailed with sheathed beaks."

Queequeg is explicitly called a *noble savage,* a term that goes back beyond Rousseau to John Dryden, and we learn that in his native country, "far away to the West and South" (56), he is of royal blood; but he has ventured into our regions "actuated by a profound desire to learn among the Christians, the arts whereby to make his people still happier than they were; and more than that, still better than they were. But, alas!" sighs Ishmael, "the practices of whalemen soon convinced him that even Christians could be both miserable and wicked; infinitely more so, than all his father's heathens" (57).

This natural superiority of the unbaptized races might remind us not only of Montaigne's essay *Of Cannibals,* and of its importance to Shakespeare, especially in relation to *The Tempest,* but also of a rebuttal to Thomas Hobbes's *Leviathan* written by Bishop Bramhall, who, in *Catching the Leviathan* (1685), denied that there had ever been any place "where mankind was altogether without laws or governors," even "among the most barbarous Americans [by which he meant the Indians] who . . . have more principles of natural piety than are readily to be found in [Hobbes's] writings."[5]

Moby-Dick is a book in which the words *Christian* and *Christianity* reappear with thundering frequency, and this is all the more notable in a book in which the person of Christ himself is referred to only twice. Once it occurs near the end of the novel, when Starbuck prays, "In Jesus' name no more of this" and in which he characterizes the pursuit of Moby-Dick

---

5. Bishop Bramhall quote from Hugh Honour, *The Golden Land* (1975), 118–19.

as "devil's madness" (459). There is a second reference in a curious meditation on aesthetics, which is worth extended quotation:

> Real strength never impairs beauty or harmony, but often bestows it; and in everything imposingly beautiful, strength has much to do with the magic . . . When Angelo paints even God the Father in human form, mark what robustness is there. And whatever they may reveal of the divine love of the Son, the soft, curled, hermaphroditical Italian pictures, in which his idea has been most successfully embodied; these pictures, so destitute as they are of all brawniness, hint nothing of any power, but the mere negative, feminine one of submission and endurance, which on all hands it is conceded, form the peculiar practical virtues of his teachings. (315)

But it is Ahab's disregard of or contempt for the figure of the Son that is most conspicuous and dramatic. His defiance throughout is always of God the Father, in all His faceless, enigmatic mystery and power. Ahab cries, "In the midst of the personified impersonal, a personality stands here," and he continues, with an acknowledgment that the Godhead has more than one Person, "Come in thy lowest form of love, and I will kneel and kiss thee; but at thy highest, come as mere supernal power; and though thou launchest navies of full-freighted worlds, there's that in here that still remains indifferent. O, thou clear spirit, of thy fire thou madest me, and like a true child of fire, I breathe it back to thee" (417).

Nowhere is Ahab's repudiation of the Son made more emphatic than by conspicuous omission in the blasphemous inversion of the Catholic baptismal formula employed when he solemnizes the completion of the manufacture of his own harpoon, anointing it in the blood of his three heathen harpooners, and declaring, "Ego non baptizo te in nomine patris, sed in nomine diaboli" (404). These words may remind us that under the influence of his wife, Jezebel, the original, biblical Ahab restored Baalism, enforcing its lewd Tyrian form and its human sacrifices. We may also remember that Melville once called this Latin formula "the book's secret motto" (562).

Finally, we ought to remember that this disregard of the Son consorts with the strict Puritan desire for the individual to confront God directly in his own person, without any humanized intermediary. It is this hunger for unimpeded intercourse with God, who has no "likeness" and has forbidden the making of "graven images," that accounts for the severity of those New England churches that, though Christian, exhibit not even so much as a crucifix and are models of architectural purity and simplicity. The ardent desire for personal confrontation with God is Lutheran or Calvinist in character, and probably also has its origin in the Old Testament confrontations I mentioned earlier. In any case, such buildings perfectly represent that type of Christian worship from which the presence and person of Christ have largely been eliminated.

Christianity takes a drubbing at Melville's hands, but only as one species of religion, the whole practice and impulse of which fills him with the deepest suspicions. And it may be, indeed, that these suspicions, and the voice he gives to them here, explain his declaration to Hawthorne that, in his words, "I have written a wicked book, and feel spotless as the lamb" (566). His distrust is not for one strain or variety of religion; it is positively ecumenical in its embrace. And this may be one reason why he was so partial to the writings of Sir Thomas Browne, who has been described by Jonathan Post, one of Browne's latest and most probing commentators, as "a connoisseur of doubt";[6] though, of course, Browne's humor, his majestic, syntactical rhythms, Latinate diction, and arcane learning were also much to Melville's taste.

Melville undertakes his subversive campaign against Christianity with a good deal of cunning, initially enlisting the reader's unsuspecting sympathy under the banner of tolerance and good will. On such a basis religions are made to seem pretty much like one another. Queequeg attends chapel service, and Ishmael, using as a pretext the Golden Rule of doing for Queequeg what he would have Queequeg do for him, joins Queequeg in the worship of his wooden idol, Yojo. This notion is repeated with some frequency and in different ways, but perhaps most explicitly when Ishmael observes: "I say we good Presbyterian Christians should be charitable in these things, and not fancy ourselves so vastly superior to other mortals, pagan and what not, because of their half-crazed conceits on these subjects . . . Heaven have mercy on us all—Presbyterians and Pagans alike— for we are all somehow dreadfully cracked about the head, and sadly need mending" (78).

---

6. Jonathan F. S. Post, *Sir Thomas Browne* (1947), 63.

In a benevolent mood, the liberal and well-disposed reader will assent to such sentiments; and if he is as generous in this regard as Bishop Bramhall or Montaigne, he will even acknowledge the moral values of so-called heathens as equivalent or superior to the ways Christians sometimes conduct their lives. He will not, in any case, immediately be aware of what Melville is up to, which is not, as it first seems, to propose a moral equation between all religions, but rather to suggest that all of them, without exception, are based on a willing and supine credulity that on the face of it he finds ludicrous. Gazing out upon a calm and beautiful seascape of paradisal tranquility, Starbuck muses: "Loveliness unfathomable, as ever lover saw in his young bride's eye!—Tell me not of thy teeth-tiered sharks, and thy kidnapping cannibal ways. Let faith oust fact; let fancy oust memory; I look down deep and do believe" (406).

It is Ishmael who, though he describes himself as "born and bred in the bosom of the infallible Presbyterian Church" (54), with barely disguised irony reports on the credulity of others, beginning with Queequeg's outlandish religion. He also recounts curiosities derived from such sources as Pliny's *Natural History,* which offers itself as sound empirical science, even when Pliny, among other wonders, claims to have seen the ashes of the phoenix. Ishmael pretends to chide those who doubt the literal truth of the account of Jonah and the whale, and says of such a person, with obvious irony, "I say it only shows his foolish, impious pride, and abominable, devilish rebellion against the clergy" (308). Hearing the plaintive cry of seals, described as "wild and unearthly—like the half-articulated wailings of the ghosts of all Herod's murdered Innocents" (428), but unaware at first of the source of the sound, Ishmael reports "the Christian or civilized part of the crew said it was mermaids" (429).

But Melville's critique of religion is not confined to credulity. There are a number of wanton insults that are very probably intended to shock. Of these perhaps the most obvious is the manifestly obscene chapter titled "The Cassock," in which the skin of the genitals of the male whale are tailored into religious vestments. This is the more striking since no one in the entire novel, though its cast is made up largely of uncouth and irreverent sailors, ever says anything, irrespective of provocation, that would bring a blush to the cheeks of Edith Wharton. Only slightly more concealed is an elaborate and complicated joke based on a biblical text. Queequeg tells Ishmael early in the novel that in his native country the rump is called the face.

We are expected to be mildly amused and to smile tolerantly at this quaint inversion of terms, and to feel indulgent towards a representative of a primitive culture. But later in the novel, having come close to exhaustiveness in his accounts of all the features of the whale's anatomy, its behavior, habits, color, and character, Ishmael finally devotes an entire chapter to its tail. And here he says, after having told us that even this appendage of the creature is enigmatic, "But if I know not even the tail of this whale, how understand his head? much more, how comprehend his face, when face he has none? Thou shalt see my back parts, my tail, he seems to say, but my face shall not be seen . . . I say again he has no face" (318).

This is undoubtedly an insolent parody of a passage (33:18–23) in Exodus in which Moses, in colloquy with God, says, "I beseech thee, shew me thy glory," and God replies,

I will make all my goodness pass before thee, and I will proclaim the name of the Lord before thee; and will be gracious to whom I will be gracious, and will show mercy on whom I will show mercy.

And he said, Thou canst not see my face: for there shall no man see me and live.

And the Lord said, Behold there is a place by me, and thou shalt stand upon a rock:

And it shall come to pass while my glory passeth by, that I will put thee in a clift of the rock, and will cover thee with my hand while I pass by:

And I will take away mine hand, and thou shalt see my back parts: but my face shall not be seen.

I maintain that Melville's joke (if that's what it is) is more than boyish naughtiness, for it bears precisely on the degree and kind of intimacy that a human may aspire to in his confrontation with God. When Melville characterized his book as "wicked," he did not intend simple insolence but had something more serious and subversive in mind. And by way of suggesting what this may be, I want to quote from a letter written by Flaubert in 1861 to Mme. Roger des Genettes.

You are right: Lucretius must be spoken of with respect. I see only Byron as comparable with him, and Byron has neither his seriousness nor his sincerity in sorrow. The melancholy of the antique world seems to me more profound than that of the moderns, all of whom more or less imply that beyond the dark void lies immortality. But for the ancients that "black hole" was infinity itself; their dreams loom and vanish against a background of immutable ebony. No crying out, no convulsions—nothing but the fixity of a pensive gaze. With the gods gone, and Christ not yet come, there was a unique moment, from Cicero to Marcus Aurelius, when man stood alone. Nowhere else do I find that particular grandeur.[7]

This is a sentiment to which Edward Gibbon might have given cheerful assent, but is there any reason to suppose that Melville, too, would have done so? I think there is, and offer in evidence the first and last stanzas of a three-stanza poem of his called "The Age of the Antonines."

> While faith forecasts millennial years
> Spite Europe's embattled lines,
> Back to the Past one glance be cast—
>   The Age of the Antonines!
> O summit of fate, O zenith of time
> When a pagan gentleman reigned,
> And the olive was nailed to the inn of the world
> Nor the peace of the just was feigned.
>   A halcyon Age, afar it shines,
> Solstice of Man and the Antonines.
>
> . . . .
>
> Orders and ranks they kept degree,
> Few felt how the parvenu pines,
> No law-maker took the lawless one's fee
>   In the Age of the Antonines!
> Under law made will the world reposed
> And the ruler's right confessed,
> For the heavens elected the Emperor then,
> The foremost of men the best.
>   Ah, might we read in America's signs
> The Age restored of the Antonines.

---

7. *The Letters of Gustave Flaubert, 1857–1888,* ed. and trans. Francis Steegmuller (1982), 20.

Ahab is no Marcus Aurelius or Antoninus Pius, and he is not much given
to the "pensive gaze." It has instead been his fate to bear the burden of a
Puritan theology, to demand justice from an intractible, predestinate order, to defy the unfathomable, invisible powers that haunt the life of modern man and that seem to consign him, with a savage mockery, to a tragic
end. The dark serenity of the ancient Romans is a luxury (however hol-
low) that we can no longer enjoy, Melville seems to assert. For Christianity and American history have come to pass; and have done so with a
vengeance.

St. Paul's Epistle to the Galatians

I

In the first chapter of *The Structure of Complex Words* (1951), William Empson sets out some of the ground rules he means to observe and some of the problems he intends to face. Among these problems is one he calls "Range," which concerns the breadth of meaning a word may afford and the overlaps from vaguely synonymous words.

> One can . . . drag the idea of Range into the puzzle about "thrifty" and "miserly"; it is clear that the behavior thought proper for a farm labourer might be given a different name when adopted by the squire. But it would only be useful to put this into the definition if you were dealing with a simple and clear-cut society. And then again, there might be much odder uses of the Range idea about misers. Some people think they can recognise misers by their manner or their smell or something, so that any sign of thriftiness in one of these men will then be called Miserly. (35)

Empson was an unusually liberal as well as liberated man, without, as far as I know, the least taint of racial prejudice or bigotry about him. But this passage of his contains an enthymeme, or a suppressed premise, of which he may himself have been unaware, so much is it a part of received, or folk, tradition of, alas, great antiquity. No mention is made in this passage (or in the surrounding context) of Jews; but Jews were commonly associated with miserliness (most critics mistakenly call Shylock a miser, though there is no evidence for this in the play), and from the Jew to the medieval *foetor Judaicus* (Jewish stench)[1] is the corollary association putatively ex-

---

1. The topic is also dealt with by Sir Thomas Browne in *Pseudodoxia eridemica.*

plaining why misers might be recognized by their "smell or something." Luther makes casual mention of this even in the period around 1523, when he was best disposed towards the Jews and acknowledged that Jesus Christ was born as one. He remarks:

> I would advise and beg everybody to deal kindly with the Jews and to instruct them in the Scriptures; in such a case we could expect them to come over to us. If, however, we use brute force and slander them, saying that they need the blood of Christians to get rid of their stench and I know not what other nonsense of that kind, and treat them like dogs, what good can we expect from them?[2]

Brutality, be it noted, is rejected on purely pragmatic grounds; and by 1543 Luther had grown far less charitable as regards the Jews, urging that their homes and synagogues be set on fire, that they be deprived of their prayer books and the Talmud, that rabbis be prohibited under threat of death from teaching, that passports and traveling privileges of all Jews be abrogated, their rights to lend money rescinded, and concluding, "Let us apply the same cleverness as other nations," namely, expulsion (ibid., 167).

All this bears upon St. Paul's Epistle to the Galatians, first because Luther, starting at the age of thirty, delivered a great trilogy of lectures on the Psalms, Romans, and Galatians between 1513 and 1516. More important, shortly after the birth in 1526 of his son Hans, "Luther again developed severe anxiety, this time protracted and bordering on deep melancholia," as Erik Erikson reports. In this condition his "conscience" expressed itself as an inner voice that mocked him.

> "You alone know everything? But what if you were wrong, and if you should lead all these people into error and into eternal damnation?" [jeered the voice] . . . He was able to overcome this voice sometimes [Erikson says] only by a kind of cosmic grandiosity putting his teaching above the judgment of even the angels on the ground that, since he so deeply knew it was right, it must be God's teaching and not his own. In his own support he quoted Galatians 1:8—"But though

---

2. *The Jews in the Medieval World—A Source Book: 315–1791*, ed. Jacob R. Marcus (1981), 166.

we, or an angel from heaven, preach any other gospel unto you, let him be accursed."[3]

One of the problems of Paul's Epistles, especially of Romans and Galatians, is the curious authority they seem to furnish for the Reformation—curious because, while the Christian church had dealt with many varieties of heresy in the course of its history, a very long time had to elapse before this seemingly irreconcilable split began to show itself. Galatians, a text not easily accessible, is, if anything, made more obscure in the King James Version. For example, as regards 2:6–10, Raymond Stamm says of Paul's original formulation:

> This sentence of ninety-five Greek words, strung together with relative pronouns and tumbling participles, is typical of Paul's headlong style. What he started to say was that James and Peter and John had found nothing lacking in his conception of the gospel and recognized the equality of his apostleship by shaking hands with him. But having dictated the first six words, he interrupted with a reminder that God plays no favorites; then after a fresh start he broke the sentence again to give the reason why these pillar apostles recognized him; and finally he wrote an appendix to it to give the details of the agreement to divide the mission field [James, Peter, and John to be apostles to the Jews, "the circumcised," and Paul to the Gentiles, "the uncircumcised"] and remember the poor.[4]

This "stylistic" observation could be extended to other parts of the epistle, which presents many puzzles as regards its tone, which, according to one commentator, is by turns "haughty, aggressive, defensive, abusive, sarcastic and self-justifying."[5] But leaving aside such personal and idiosyncratic matters for the moment, the account above offers no comment on the possibility that the meeting between Paul and the pillar apostles may be the one mentioned in Acts 15, or that Acts 15 presents a large assortment of

---

3. Erik H. Erikson, *Young Man Luther* (1958), 241–42.
4. Raymond T. Stamm, *The Interpreter's Bible* (1953), 10:473.
5. Michael Goulder, "The Pauline Epistles," in *The Literary Guide to the Bible*, ed. Robert Alter and Frank Kermode (1987), 488.

problems that may in turn reverberate in Galatians. The council at Jerusalem described in Acts concerns a controversy about how much, if any, of the Mosaic Law was to be enjoined upon Gentile converts to the new faith. Since for the Jews circumcision was a religious essential, could it be dispensed with? And if the answer was yes, did it follow that the entire Mosaic Law could likewise be set aside? Acts 15 in fact begins, "And certain men which came down from Judea taught the brethren, and said, Except ye be circumcised after the manner of Moses, ye cannot be saved." This appears flatly to contradict Galatians 5:2–4, which declares, "Behold, I Paul say unto you, that if ye be circumcised, Christ shall profit you nothing. For I testify again to every man that is circumcised, that he is a debtor to do the whole law. Christ is become of no effect unto you, whosoever of you are justified by the law; ye are fallen from grace." Peter speaks first at the council, declaring the universal embrace of Christian salvation, extending it to Gentiles as well as Jews. James speaks next, and seems to offer a kind of regulatory compromise: "Wherefore my sentence is, that we trouble not them, which from among the Gentiles are turned to God: But that we write unto them, that they abstain from pollutions of idols, and from fornication, and from things strangled, and from blood" (Acts 15:19–20).

This looks very much like a selective list of items of the Law that must continue to be observed even by Gentile converts, and it brings up, awkwardly and pertinently, the whole complex and insoluble problem involved in any attempt, Jewish or Christian, to codify and make doctrinal the expression and experience of the love of God, the "minimal requirements" for salvation, and the grounds for orthodoxy and religious authority. The chapter of Acts ends on a very divisive and disturbing note. "And the contention was so sharp between them [Paul and Barnabas, who was to accompany Paul on his mission to the Gentiles], that they departed asunder one from the other" (15:39). There is a lot of speculation about what brought on this dissension, and one view is that Paul's position regarding the liberty from Mosaic Law that was conferred by the crucifixion of Jesus differed profoundly from Peter's attitude, and that Barnabas, caught in the middle, or else largely disposed to agree with Peter, was summarily dismissed by Paul. If this were the case, it would simply confirm the view of his irascible personality that his Epistles evidence.

As contrasted with "the Twelve," who were "called" by Jesus in his lifetime, Paul, a Hellenized Jew, first became a fanatical Pharisee, during which time he energetically persecuted Christians, and then, after a strange and much-debated "vision" on the road to Damascus, became not only a convert to the Christian faith but one who came to regard himself as divinely appointed by Christ to be the apostle to the Gentiles. He is evidently touchy about the validation of his claim to apostleship and vigorous in asserting it. That claim is based, of course, on his private and unverifiable "vision," and this is entirely consistent with his insistence on the doctrine of justification (i.e., acquittal from sin) by faith alone. Joseph Klausner, whose views I generally share, writes thus of the man:

> Paul fought all his life against the idea of his "inferiority," if it is possible to speak thus, as an apostle. The disciples and brethren of Jesus who were intimate with the crucified Messiah during his lifetime and had received instructions, parables, and promises from his own lips, would reproach Paul in this effect: You are not a true apostle, and in vain do you on your own authority set aside the ceremonial laws; for you did not attend the Messiah, you were not intimate with him, and you cannot know his teaching firsthand. To this Paul would reply, that the important thing is not corporeal knowledge ("after the flesh") but spiritual knowledge—the revelation by vision whereby Jesus revealed himself to him. The *heavenly* Jesus is more significant than the *earthly* Jesus. For the earthly Jesus is important only because of his sufferings and death, which were propitiatory sufferings and a ransoming death.[6]

What Paul does, quite brilliantly, by this kind of rebuttal is at once to turn what appears to be in his initial disadvantage in never having known Jesus of Nazareth during his lifetime into a distinction denied the other apostles, and at the same time to adopt the position most likely to appeal not only to those of his contemporaries who likewise had never met Jesus but, by implication, to all posterity as well—an immeasurable advantage in terms of plain numbers. In fact, he makes his own inward experience the equivalent of Peter's recognition (Matt. 16:13–18) of Jesus' messiahship at the moment of the Transfiguration, thereby effectually silencing any opposition. He even has the temerity publicly to rebuke Peter (Gal. 2) for hypocrisy in his fear of offending those Jewish converts who believed that

6. Joseph Klausner, *From Jesus to Paul* (1943), 314.

Gentiles must accept the Jewish Law, including circumcision, before achieving salvation through Christ. If the doctrine of justification by faith alone, so central to Galatians, gave solace and ammunition to Luther in his revolt from Catholic orthodoxy, the doctrine of predestination, based on God's election of Jacob over Esau, is strongly implied in Romans 9:6–13. So the grounds for doctrinal rebellion seem to have been sown by a man Klausner characterizes this way: "Saul-Paul was lacking in humility, and boastfully condescending. But he knew his shortcomings, fought against them, and sometimes conquered them."[7] In view of Paul's arrogance, are we to notice any connection between 2:6 and 6:3 of Galatians, which appear to be another slur aimed at Peter, though without naming him?

So curious is the personality exhibited by Paul that it invites us to puzzle over even his most famous pronouncements. His vituperations are almost as celebrated as his benedictions: in Galatians 1:8–9 he offers curses against any deviation from his theology, and in 1 Corinthians 16:22 he declares, "If any man love not the Lord Jesus Christ, let him be Anathema Maranatha," the final term being equivalent to "perdition at the coming of Christ the Lord." It is a tone of voice I recognize from news accounts of the desecraters of graveyards, synagogues, and even of churches; it is the tone of the fanatic. Yet perhaps of all Paul's utterances none is more ringing than 1 Corinthians 13:1: "Though I speak with the tongues of men and of angels, and have not charity, I am become as sounding brass, or a tinkling cymbal." Many a heart has melted at this thought and cherished Paul for that exaltation of loving-kindness, which is what we have taken the verse to intend. But we must remember that Paul was a celebrated evangelist and preacher, and this verse sounds very much like ostentatious self-abasement, as if the golden-tongued hierophant were saying, "Not by my skills or merit am I made persuasive, but by the grace of God," and we are expected to be struck by this exemplary modesty. Doubtless we would be more struck by it if it were not so frequently in abeyance. Again, in Galatians 5:6, which puts observers of the Jewish Law and nonobserving Gentiles on an equal footing, Paul declares, "For in Jesus Christ neither circumcision availeth any thing, nor uncircumcision; but faith which worketh by love." And who could find fault with so admirable an impulse, save those for whom orthodoxy and authority were themselves matters of reverence? Is not *love,* after all, the

---

7. Ibid., 424.

generous solution in which all factions dissolve? Yet it doesn't need much reflection to see how easily love in its finer throes can become zeal, and zeal in its fiercest devotion can become fanaticism, and demand persecution.

It has been the troubling and virtually impossible task of many sects, Jewish and Christian, to furnish a codification of love and a doctrine to define it. There is no more mistaken and self-serving Christian commonplace than the one that makes the New Testament the gospel of love and the Old Testament the book of law, a distinction almost universally maintained, in bland contradiction to Mark 12:28–31:

> And one of the scribes came, and having heard them reasoning together ["certain of the Pharisees and of the Herodians" had been attempting "to catch Jesus in his words"], and perceiving that he had answered them well, asked him, Which is the first commandment of all?
>
> And Jesus answered him, The first of all the commandments is, Hear, O Israel; The Lord our God is one Lord:
>
> And thou shalt love the Lord thy God with all thy heart, and with all thy soul, and with all thy mind, and with all thy strength: this is the first commandment.
>
> And the second is like, namely this, Thou shalt love thy neighbour as thyself. There is none other commandment greater than these.

In these verses Jesus is quoting Leviticus (19:18) though this point seems always to be forgotten or suppressed; but the arrogation to the New Testament of the primacy of love is a curious act of piracy.[8]

A good deal of puzzling has gone into the question of just what it means to love one's neighbor. In *The Genesis of Secrecy* Frank Kermode pre-

---

8. "In the end, however, what are we to expect of the aftereffects of a religion that enacted during the centuries of its foundation that unheard-of philological farce about the Old Testament? I refer to the attempt to pull away the Old Testament from under the feet of the Jews—with the claim that it contains nothing but Christian doctrines and *belongs* to the Christians as the *true* Israel, while the Jews merely usurped it. And now the Christians yielded to a rage of interpretation and interpolation, which could not possibly have been accompanied by a good conscience. However much the Jewish scholars protested, everywhere in the Old Testament there were supposed to be references to Christ and only to Christ, and particularly to his cross. Whenever any piece of wood, a switch, a ladder, a twig, a tree, a willow, or a staff is mentioned, this was supposed to indicate a prophecy of the wood of the cross . . . Has anyone who claimed this ever *believed* it?" Friedrich Nietzsche, *The Dawn* (1887), 84.

sented a set of illuminating and irreconcilable interpretations of the parable of the Good Samaritan, some of which are eschatological (e.g., Saint Augustine's) and have nothing to do with the normal ethics of human behavior. Some have wondered long and thoughtfully about just who one's neighbor actually *is,* a problem complicated by translation: "'Thou shalt love thy fellow as thyself' . . . is expressly stated to include the non-Israelite stranger," writes Rabbi Isidore Epstein, in commentary on Leviticus, and adds, "This is the precise meaning of the Hebrew term *rea;* the usual rendering 'neighbor' is misleading."[9]

If "neighbor" has led to puzzles, "love" has led to disagreement, bewilderment, rancor, and violence. Most commonly it has been Christians who have set up the opposition between Law and Love, an opposition of the most unsound and perilous kind.[10] It may in fact be that the Pharisees of the sixties were the hard-line hawks who maintained that since America was at war, even an undeclared war, and conscription was in effect, no citizen had the right to resist military service on the grounds of personal moral repugnance, because this was simply choosing which laws one cared to observe and which ones to flout. And the law is not to be subject to the caprices of personal taste. Any tendency to rely on one's instincts, on the dim standards of solipsism, on the evasions of the private psyche, the warp of individual feelings, leaves us hopelessly adrift, and not merely in secular matters. "Certainly, anyone who is wholly sincere and pure in heart may seek for guidance from the Holy Spirit," writes T. S. Eliot in *Thoughts after Lambeth,* "but who of us is always wholly sincere, especially where the most imperative of instincts may be strong enough to simulate to perfection the voice of the Holy Spirit?"[11] Such thoughtful scruples seem not to have troubled Paul. Eliot was concerned here with the question of whether communicants of the Church of England should be required to consult ecclesiastical opinion and advice regarding birth control

---

9. In Luke 10:29ff Christ tells the parable of the Good Samaritan by way of answering "a certain lawyer" who has asked, "What is written in the law" regarding the injunction to love one's neighbor, and asking specifically, "And who is my neighbor?"

10. "Christ does not call his benefactors loving or charitable. He calls them just. The Gospel makes no distinction between the love of our neighbor and justice. In the eyes of the Greeks also a respect for . . . the suppliant was the first duty of justice. We have invented the distinction between justice and charity." Simone Weil, *Waiting for God* (1951), 139.

11. T.S. Eliot, *Selected Essays* (1932), 320.

at all times or only when they are "perplexed." This may to some seem a minuscule or trifling consideration, but for sound reasons *de minimis non curat lex* does not apply to matters of reverence.

It is not always easy or possible, and arguably not desirable, to distinguish between laws that are purely ceremonial and others that are purely ethical. The love of God may be expressed, among other ways, ceremonially; and the love of one's fellow human being is shown, in what Jesus declares to be a part of the First Commandment, to be itself an expression of the love of God. "The meat of animals killed by strangling," writes G. H. C. MacGregor, "considered a delicacy in pagan society, would contain blood which, in accordance with the principle that 'the life is in the blood,' was strictly prohibited to the Jews (cf. Gen. 9:5; Lev. 3:17; Deut. 12:16, 23–25)" (*Interpreter's Bible*, vol. 9, p. 203). This is not merely a ceremonial consideration, since it reflects upon the sanctity of life itself. And Rabbi Epstein reminds that according to the Talmud "it is . . . sinful to give someone an address without being sure that it is the correct one. It is likewise sinful to go into a shop and ask the price of an article when there is no intention of buying it." These adumbrations of the Law might seem fussy in their detail and in the slenderness of their moral import; but they are based upon the importance of respect for human feelings and are therefore regarded by pious Jews as graver than a wrong caused to fellow men in respect to material values.

The retreat to private instincts of morality need not have any bearing upon either reverence for God or even a real respect for fellow human beings, and it can end at best with the cloying sentimentality of comfortable Dickensian piety, which was able to find ample room for two varieties of anti-Semitism: it is a hard choice between the wicked passivity (and complicity) of Mr. Riah and the active villainy of Fagin. Dickens himself saw no implied slur to Jews in either portrait, which all by itself suggests that his is not a vision of love that could be sustained as doctrine; and some of his best-known commentators have seen no more in the matter than Dickens.

II

Paul begins his Epistle to the Galatians by reproving them for being in danger of backsliding and relapsing into Jewish orthodoxy and dependence on the Law; and the chief burden of the entire text is that the Law has been abrogated, and bondage under the Law has been ended by the emancipation of Christ's sacrifice. The metaphors that weave throughout the Epistle are drawn from the realms of law and of slavery, and the two themes are related and intertwined. To try to fulfill the Law is to be "in bondage under the elements of the world" (4:3), but Christ came "to redeem them that were under the law, that we might receive the adoption of sons . . . wherefore thou art no more a servant but a son; and if a son, then an heir of God through Christ" (4:5, 7). In place of the King James Version's "servant," other versions have "slave."[12] This is perhaps why Raymond Stamm calls Galatians the Magna Charta of the Christian faith, though he may have had sectarian reasons as well. It may also be why commentators as different as Hyam Maccoby and Paul Johnson have been at one in calling Paul the "founder" of Christianity.[13] In any case, Galatians tells us that Christ frees us from the bondage of the Law, and once freed we are no longer slaves or children but sons and heirs. The "slavery" metaphor must have meant a great deal to Paul, a sometime Pharisee well acquainted with the history of enslavement and emancipation, which was annually and ceremonially recalled at the Passover.

By one of the painful and characteristic ironies of history, Paul's metaphor of slavery, applied to those who, by failing to adopt the Christian faith, were not freed from the bondage of the Law, was changed from

---

12. "Protectiveness toward children manifested itself during wartime in a paradoxical way. A child was a precious commodity, as precious as a woman, and as such was part of the spoils of war. Whenever a city was captured, the victors slaughtered 'everyone who could piss against the wall.' In other words, they led away into slavery all the women and nursing children, including boys under the age of three; the older boys were killed along with their fathers. This practice gave rise to the custom of referring to the child as 'slave' (*puer* in Latin)." Michel Rouche, *A History of Private Life* (1987), 1:462. See also I Kings 14:10; I Kings 21:21; II Kings 9:8; I Samuel 25:34.

13. "*The first Christian.* All the world still believes in the authorship of the 'Holy Spirit' or is at least still affected by this belief: when one opens the Bible one does so for 'edification.' . . . That it also tells the story of one of the most ambitious and obtrusive of souls, of a head as superstitious as it was crafty, the story of the apostle Paul—who knows this, except a few scholars? . . . That the ship of Christianity threw overboard a good deal of its Jewish ballast, that it went, and was able to go among the pagans—that was due to this one man, a very tortured, very pitiful, very unpleasant man, unpleasant even to himself . . . he found that—hot-headed, sensual, melancholy, malignant in his hatred as he was—he was himself unable to fulfill the law." Nietzsche, *The Dawn,* 68. Such a portrait of Paul is not far-fetched and would go a long way to explaining how Paul came to find the "law" superfluous and irrelevant to salvation.

metaphor to literal truth by the Dominican Pope Paul IV (1555–59), "acting in everything with a bitterness agreeable to the virulency of his nature," according to one of his contemporaries. He enclosed the Roman Jews within the walls of the Ghetto and commanded the men never to set foot outside it unless they wore distinguishing hats, which, according to Rodolpho Lanciani, the eminent archeologist and historian, were conical caps "not unlike in shape to the one characteristic of our popular mask, Pulcinella"[14]—that is, a dunce cap. These hats had to be yellow; and women who came beyond the Ghetto walls had to wear yellow veils, because, as the papal bull *Cum nimis* declared, "It is most absurd and unsuitable that the Jews, whose own crime has plunged them into everlasting slavery, under the plea that Christian magnanimity allows them, should presume to dwell and mix with Christians, not bearing any mark of distinction, and should have Christian servants, yea, even buy houses." Under Gregory XIII (1572–85) the Jews were forced to hear a sermon every week in a church appointed specifically for them, and on every Sabbath police agents were sent to the Ghetto to drive men, women, and children into churches with scourges and to lash them if they appeared inattentive. To this barbarity had come the plea of Jesus, "Suffer the little children to come unto me, and forbid them not." Robert Browning remembers this behavior in a poem called "Holy Cross Day." So Paul's metaphor had terrific consequences which he himself might not have foreseen, confident though he was of the illumination and eternal truth vouchsafed to him. It is that confidence of his that may in the end be most alarming and that may serve as a warning against my replacing his fixed convictions with fixed convictions of my own.

III

As a Jew living in a society essentially secular but nominally Christian, I have felt a need to learn the ways and something of the faith of the majority, for a Gentile is no longer, as in the Hebrew liturgy, "the stranger dwelling in our midst." It is impossible to be a Jew of my generation without being keenly aware of anti-Semitism, and sensitivity on this point alone has invited a study of Christian doctrine. My training in my own faith was of the most rudimentary and desultory kind, but over the years

14. Rodolfo Lanciani, *New Tales of Old Rome* (1901), 258.

I not only grew to know it better but became increasingly acquainted with the convictions of my Christian neighbors. Many of these were good people whom I admired and from whom I learned goodness itself, among other things. And there was much in Christian doctrine that seemed appealing as well. But few things struck me with more force than the profound and unappeasable hostility of Protestants and Catholics towards one another. The blood hatred of the Old World was brought over, with pike and Bible, to the New, undiluted but never so finely focused that there was none left over for the Jews. I heard an Easter Sunday sermon in a Catholic church on Lexington Avenue in New York in the middle 1950s (before the Second Vatican Council) in which, on this day of unique Christian rejoicing and gratitude, the preacher devoted the whole of his discourse to proclaiming Jews the murderers of Christ and all living Jews of our time as guilty of the crime by inheritance. The fierceness of such hatred is the more pronounced in direct ratio, it would seem, to the fervor of religious piety and conviction. Klaus Scholder's book *The Churches and the Third Reich*, vol. 1, 1918–1934, plainly details the enthusiasm with which both Catholics and Protestants rose to embrace Nazism, including its most hideous racial policies. Karl Adam, a Roman Catholic theologian, declared that the "purity and freshness" of German blood was not only a "requirement of German self-expression" but "in line with God's revelation in the Old Testament." And, as Harvey Cox reported in a review of Scholder's book, Emanuel Hirsch, in a five-volume history of Protestant thought, wrote in 1933, "If the Protestant Church . . . wishes really to proclaim the Gospel, then it must take as its natural standpoint the circle of destiny of the National Socialist movement."

Even as I write, the bishops of the Anglican church have irresolutely concluded their conference at Lambeth Palace. Most Americans who interested themselves in these deliberations were concerned with the question of the consecration of women as bishops. But a far more serious matter presented itself to the council and was, perhaps understandably, left unsettled. It has to do with the "justifiable use of force" to eliminate manifest and intolerable social wrongs. As I understand it, Archbishop Desmond Tutu was eloquent in arguing that the huge black majority in South Africa must not be categorically denied the last resort to such violent force. He seems to have been met with almost universal sympathy. But the bishops were understandably troubled that the same argument, based on the same principles, could be advanced in behalf of the IRA.

IV

I can remember being assigned in grade school to read *The Merchant of Venice.* It was mortifying, and in complicated ways. I was being asked to admire the work of the greatest master of the English language, and one universally revered, who was slandering all those of my race and religion. I was not even allowed to do this in private, but under the scrutiny and supervision of public instruction. And it took many class periods to get through the whole text. I can also remember the unseemly pleasure of my teacher in relishing all the slanders against the Jews in general and Shylock in particular. It was a wounding experience and the beginning of a kind of education for which I received no grades. And it has continued for the rest of my life. Despite that early anguish I went on to find myself increasingly devoted to Shakespeare, and to literature in general, always tensely alerted to the possibility of being wounded, nearly always surprised by genuine kindness and understanding in matters that touched upon race and religion. And increasingly I found that it was nearly impossible to read the canon of English and American literature without becoming mired or entangled in questions of doctrine. There have been those who have tried to exempt Shakespeare from these controversies, by claiming that they were matters of indifference to him. In any case, my profession as teacher has required of me, in pursuance of an understanding of the works I teach, that I understand the parti pris that may color or define them, and these are often religious positions and doctrinal stances. It is impossible to read authors as different as Kafka and Hawthorne, Bunyan and Joyce, or any major poets, from Chaucer and Milton through Donne and Herbert to Hopkins and Lowell, without an acquaintance with their doctrinal and spiritual preoccupations.

I have given some thought to these matters over the years and have read a good deal, though in a disorderly way. And it has occurred to me that the best and most telling answer to the solipsism and contemptuous repudiation of the Law of Moses by Paul is made by Jesus himself in words reported in Luke 16:19–31:

There was a certain rich man, which was clothed in purple and fine linen, and fared sumptuously every day:

And there was a certain beggar named Lazarus, which was laid at his gate, full of sores,

And desiring to be fed with the crumbs which fell from the rich man's table: moreover the dogs came and licked his sores.

And it came to pass, that the beggar died, and was carried by the angels into Abraham's bosom: the rich man also died, and was buried;

And in hell he lifted up his eyes, being in torments, and seeth Abraham afar off, and Lazarus in his bosom.

And he cried and said, Father Abraham, have mercy on me, and send Lazarus, that he may dip the tip of his finger in water, and cool my tongue; for I am tormented in this flame.

But Abraham said, Son, remember that thou in thy lifetime received st thy good things, and likewise Lazarus evil things: but now he is comforted, and thou art tormented.

And beside all this, between us and you there is a great gulf fixed: so that they which would pass from hence to you cannot; neither can they pass to us, that would come from thence.

Then he said, I pray thee therefore, father, that thou wouldest send him to my father's house:

For I have five brethren; that he may testify unto them, lest they also come into this place of torment.

Abraham saith unto him, They have Moses and the prophets; let them hear them.

And he said, Nay, father Abraham; but if one went unto them from the dead, they will repent.

And he said unto him, If they hear not Moses and the Prophets, neither will they be persuaded, though one rose from the dead.

On Rhyme

Because there's no hope of treating the subject of rhyme exhaustively, what follows is no more than an assemblage of disorderly ideas about a topic that defies taxonomic treatment, the materials of which are essentially acoustic and phonic: not only unsusceptible to demonstrations of incontrovertible proof but also subject to views that alter from region to region and period to period, as well as, idiosyncratically, ear to ear. In *Beppo*, composed in 1818, Byron was able unexceptionably to rhyme *Giorgione* with *balcony*, a word that still paid reverence to its derivation from the Italian *balcone*, accented on the second of its three syllables, a pronunciation that lasted until 1825, when our modern version of the word (which the poet Samuel Rogers declared "makes me sick") became orthodox. Similarly, many rhymes that to the modern ear are sight-rhymes (*wind / mind*) were true rhymes in Shakespeare's day (as were *goats* and *Goths*) and are sometimes wistfully employed by modern poets in a spirit of nostalgia:

> Their strokes and counters whistled in the wind
> I wish he had delivered half his blows
> But where she should have made off like a hind
> The bitch bit off his arms at the elbows.
> (John Crowe Ransom, "Captain Carpenter")

It is sometimes heedlessly supposed that verbal consonance is a matter so elementary and self-evident as not to require discussion, but few "self-evident" issues prove indisputable, and this is not one. In his *Essay on French Verse*, Jacques Barzun discriminates five kinds of rhyme: *feeble, sufficient, rich, Norman,* and *licentious.* Of the *rich* rhyme he observes, "The consonants preceding the vowels must be alike: *sommeil* and *vermeil, ar-*

mant and *charmant*. The rhyme is still richer when the two words sound exactly alike: *bois* (wood) and (je) *bois* (drink). In English, this total sameness would make no rhyme at all; in French, it is felt as agreeably surprising in its juxtaposition of remote ideas—which is what Victor Hugo implies in calling it a 'jumped-up pun.'"[1] Such perfect identity of sound, as distinct from meaning, is precisely what Théodore de Banville recommends in stating: "Vous ferez rimer ensemble, autant qu'il se pourra, des mots très-semblable entre eux comme SON, et très-different entre eux comme SENS." But in English, too close an identity of sound (*weight / wait; some / sum*) strikes the ear as banal, obvious, and flat, unless employed in a sestina, where the remorseless repetition of terminal words is charitably relieved by such homophones.

In his introduction to *The Selected Poems of Marianne Moore* (1935), T. S. Eliot has some characteristically shrewd things to say about rhyme. I want to quote a single paragraph of his, interrupting him at certain points to illustrate his comments.

> In the conventional forms of rhyme the stress given by the rhyme tends to fall in the same place as the stress given by the sense. The extreme case, at its best, is the pentameter couplets of Pope. Poets before and after Pope have given variety, sometimes at the expense of smoothness, by deliberately separating the stresses, from time to time; but this separation—often effected simply by longer periods or more involved syntax—can hardly be considered as more than a deviation from the norm for the purpose of avoiding monotony. (xii)

Here, in a pre-Pope example, are some lines from Christopher Marlowe's *Hero and Leander,* with enjambment and subordinate clause to lighten, however slightly, the weight of the rhymed couplets:

> Here wide sleeves greene, and bordered with a grove,
> Where *Venus* in her naked glory strove,
> To please the careless and disdainfull eies
> Of proud *Adonis* that before her lies.

---

1. Jacques Barzun, *An Essay on French Verse* (1991), 26–27.

A post-Pope example may be supplied by Robert Browning's "My Last Duchess," with its own enjambments, to be sure, but also with the effects of a brilliantly discontinuous catalogue, the very randomness of which enforces the Duke's point and mutes, or perhaps voids, the resolutions usually provided by mating rhymes:

> Sir, 'twas all one! My favor at her breast,
> The dropping of the daylight in the West,
> The bough of cherries some officious fool
> Broke in the orchard for her, the white mule
> She rode with round the terrace—all and each
> Would draw from her alike the approving speech.

"The tendency of some of the best contemporary poetry," Eliot continues, "is of course to dispense with rhyme altogether; but some of those who do use it have used it here and there to make a pattern directly in contrast with the sense and the rhythm patterns, to give a greater intricacy. Some of the internal rhyming of Hopkins is to the point."

What Eliot is leading towards are those less and less obtrusive rhymes, not only buried "internally" but slighter by their transitory modesty, confined on occasion—in Marianne Moore, for instance—to an article, a mere schwa. They rejoice in lying unnoticed unless by the most patient and discerning reader. An example may be found in Brad Leithauser's "In Minako Wada's House," of which the first four stanzas are quoted here:

> In old Minako Wada's house
> Everything has its place,
> And mostly out of sight:
>   Bedding folded away
> All day, brought down
> From the shelf at night,
>
>   Tea things underneath
> Low tea table and tablecloth—
> And sliding screen doors,

Landscape painted, that hide
Her clothes inside a wash
Of mountains. Here, the floors

Are a clean-fitting mosaic,
Mats of a texture like
A broom's; and in a niche
In the tearoom wall
Is a shrine to all her
Ancestors, before which

She sets each day
A doll-sized cup of tea,
A doll-sized bowl of rice,
She keeps a glass jar
Of crickets that are fed fish
Shavings, an eggplant slice.

A casual reading of the first stanza would recognize the rhyming of the third and sixth lines and would plausibly assume that the "internal" rhyme of *away* and *day* in the fourth and fifth lines was simple inadvertence, the sort of thing that happens commonly in everyday speech. Indeed, the phrase "folded away all day" doesn't call much attention to itself as a musical chiming. But we go on to observe that in each ensuing stanza the terminal word of the fourth line rhymes with some word in the interior of the fifth, some of these fleetingly: for example, "crickets that are fed fish," where the auxiliary verb, a slight thing, rhymes with *jar*. This slightness of rhyme consorts gracefully with the miniature elements of which the poem speaks. Such rhymes are often unnoticed and thus are not felt as "constraints," which is the way rhyme is sometimes regarded; and this is partly due, though only partly, to the freedom of position allowed the rhyming word in the fifth line. I must add that only when I moved to Washington, D.C., did I encounter anyone, in this case a building contractor, who pronounced *niche* as though it rhymed with *MacLeish*, a pronunciation that would have thrown a monkey wrench into Leithauser's poem. Few poets have resorted to such furtive, concealed rhymes as W. H.

Auden, whose disconcerting pleasure it was to rhyme an unaccented with an accented syllable, as Ransom did in the quatrain cited above:

> On Sunday walks
> Past the shut gates of works
> The conquerers come
> And are handsome
>
> (Poems, XXI)

> Sir, no man's enemy, forgiving all
> But will his negative inversion, be prodigal:
> (Poems, XXX)

Robert Graves claims that the rhyming of accented with unaccented syllables gives "the effect of uncertainty, incompleteness, suspense,"[2] and it seems to bear something like the audible effect of some slant rhyming, a deliberate dissonance; though in the hands of some poets, it confers the effect of a tin ear. Auden for his part was, in the course of time, to become still more cunning. Poems like "Pleasure Island," "Music Is International," and "The Duet" rhyme the penultimate syllable of one line with the final syllable of the next, a technique that yields *friendship* / *weekend* as rhymes. In "The Managers" he simply reverses the order, rhyming the final syllable of the odd-numbered lines with the penultimate syllable of the even-numbered ones, which affords, among other curiosities, *vows* / *flowers* and *sees* / *policemen*. But it is time to return to Eliot.

"(Genuine or auditory internal rhyme must not be confused with false or visual internal rhyme. If a poem reads just as well when cut up so that all the rhymes fall at the end of lines, then the internal rhyme is false and only a typographical caprice, as in Oscar Wilde's *Sphinx*.)"[3]

Oscar Wilde's poem appears to the eye to be composed in unrhymed octameter distichs:

> False Sphinx! False Sphinx! By reedy Styx old Charon, leaning on his oar,
> Waits for my coin. Go thou before, and leave me to my crucifix,

---

2. Robert Graves, *The Common Asphodel* (1949), 5.

3. Eliot, *The Selected Poems of Marianne Moore*, xii–xii.

Whose pallid burden, sick with pain, watches the world with weary eyes,
And weeps for every soul that dies, and weeps for every soul in vain.

It takes no great shrewdness (the last line quoted is a dead giveaway, with its caesura falling so neatly in the middle, between two drearily parallel phrases) to determine that each of these octameter distichs can easily be recast as tetrameter quatrains, rhyming *abba:*

> False Sphinx! False Sphinx! By reedy Styx
> Old Charon, leaning on his oar,
> Waits for my coin. Go thou before,
> And leave me to my crucifix.

Eliot is right in calling this "typographical caprice," though many of e. e. cummings's effects come to much the same thing. What we dislike about the lines by Wilde derives from our sense that he may believe his music is achieved by mysterious subtlety, when in fact it is too nakedly apparent, unredeemed by any real linguistic interest. But Eliot's point about typographical setting raises some interesting puzzles. Arthur Golding's 1567 translation of Ovid's *Metamorphoses* is framed in English fourteener rhymed couplets, though every once in a while he extends his rhyme to cover three consecutive lines:

> Then all both men and women feared Latona's open ire,
> And far with greater sumptuousness and earnester desire
> Did worship the great majesty of this their goddess who
> Did bear at once both Phoebus and his sister Phoebe too,
> And through occasion of this chance, as men are wont to do.

Though laid out differently on the page, the last three lines are identical in meter and rhyme pattern with "The Walrus and the Carpenter." Continuing his discussion of internal rhyme, Eliot declares, "This rhyme, which forms a pattern *against* the metric and sense pattern of the poem, may either be heavy or light—that is to say, either *heavier* or *lighter* than the other pattern. The two kinds, heavy and light, have doubtless different uses which remain to be explored. Of the *light* rhyme, Miss Moore is the greatest living master; and indeed she is the first, so far as I know, who has investigated its possibilities." He goes on to instance rhymes produced by hyphenation, and thus extremely transitory:

> al-
> ways has been—at the antipodes from the init-
>   ial great truths. "Part of it was crawling, part of it
> was about to crawl, the rest
>   was torpid in its lair." In the short-legged fit-
> ful advance . . .

I leave off quoting both Miss Moore and Eliot, who has brought me to what, adapting a term from Gerard Manley Hopkins, may be called rove-over rhyme. The thirty-first stanza of Hopkins' great and deeply serious poem "The Wreck of the *Deutschland*" rhymes *unconfessed of them* with *the breast of the* and borrows the needed *m* sound that would complete the rhyme from the word at the beginning of the following line, *Maiden*. More daringly still, and in the same stanza, he rhymes *Providence* with *it, and,* borrowing the *s* of *Startled* from the beginning of the following line. Clearly this liberty, this vocal athleticism and audacity, can be justified by an impetuosity and rapidity of movement, both narrative and meditative, that urges the poem headlong through enjambments, accelerated by heightened devotion and sprung rhythm. The stanza deserves quotation, but it may be useful in advance to gloss its stanzaic form. It occurs in the second part of a two-part poem, the two parts differing ever so slightly in formal detail. Part One concerns the poet's conversion from the Anglican to the Roman Catholic faith. Part Two is about the shipwreck. The stanza form of both parts is identical, except that the first lines of Part Two are longer by one foot than those of Part One. The rhyme scheme throughout is *ababcbca,* and the respective line-lengths (always allowing for the discrepancies permitted by sprung rhythm) run 3, 3, 4, 3, 5, 5, 4, 6.

31

> Well, she has thee for the pain, for the
> Patience; but pity of the rest of them!
> Heart, go bleed at a bitterer vein for the

Comfortless unconfessed of them—
No not uncomforted: lovely felicitous Providence
Finger of a tender of, O of a feathery delicacy, the breast of the
    Maiden could obey so, be a bell to, ring of it, and
Startle the poor sheep back! is the shipwrack then a harvest, does
    tempest carry the grain for thee?

It should be noted that, since lines 1, 3, and 8 rhyme (a pattern maintained throughout this thirty-five-stanza poem), Hopkins has linked *pain, for the* with *vein for the* and *grain for thee*, thus mating the muted, inconspicuous article with the elevated, hieratical pronoun. This is startling, and resembles, I think, some of the light rhyming of Marianne Moore.

The exoticisms of such rhyming practices could legitimately lead to considerations of light verse, where virtuosity parades itself with ostentations of ingenuity. The field is too vast to compass, reaching as it must from Swinburne's limerick "There was a young girl from Aberystwyth," backward to Winthrop Praed and Thomas Hood, onward through Charles Calverley, Lewis Carroll, W. S. Gilbert, James Kenneth Stephen, and Owen Seaman, to American song lyricists, Cole Porter being only one of these, and then spreading in every direction. But, abandoning any such ambitions, we may consider the narrower domain of deliberate and of naïve incompetence. Both furnish pleasures, though of different kinds, and although incompetence is common enough, it rarely achieves the distinction of the ludicrous so carefully culled in *The Stuffed Owl* and its sequel, *Pegasus Descending*. From the first of these, we may savor some crudités from the poetry of Julia Moore, the Sweet Singer of Michigan.

> Swiftly passed the engine's call,
>   Hastening souls on to death,
> Warning not one of them all;
>   It brought despair right and left
>   (Chorus from "The Ashtabula Disaster")

> "Lord Byron" was an Englishman
>   A poet I believe,

His first works in old England
Was poorly received.
Perhaps it was "Lord Byron's" fault
And perhaps it was not.
His life was full of misfortunes,
Ah, strange was his lot.
(from "Byron: A Critical Study")

Ineptitudes here only partially concern rhyme, but in their aggregate they so much amused the public of her day (she died in 1920), including Mark Twain, who commended her work in the press, that her book ran to three editions. That she was an untutored farmer's wife who was not only deficient of ear and without skill as a poet but who took at face value the critical approval, often conferred by commentators convulsed by efforts to smother their giggles, adds a note of pathos and a flavor of shame to our pleasure in her work. (In this she resembles the singer Florence Foster Jenkins, who enjoyed the same sort of barely concealed ridicule in the world of music.)

But there is also a poetry of mock-incompetence, whose chief modern exemplar is Ogden Nash. Though a superbly deft artificer of complex verse forms, Nash most commonly adopted the composition of poems in rhymed couplets in which the first line tends to be long and the second incomparably longer, as though the poet, desperate to find some rhyming mate, is obliged to push on, awkwardly tottering towards his distant goal through barricades of necessary exposition and grammatical necessity, like the insomniac in the following lines:

You all know the story of the insomniac who got into such a state
Because the man upstairs dropped one shoe on the floor at eleven
o'clock and the unhappy insomniac sat up until breakfast time
waiting for him to drop the mate.

So much has this kind of rhyming (feigned incompetence) become Nash's trademark that its distinguished genealogy is usually forgotten.

Our village, that's to say not Miss Mitford's village, but our village
of Bullock Smithy,

Is come into by an avenue of trees, three oak pollards, two elders,
    and a withy;
And in the middle, there's a green of about not exceeding an acre
    and a half;
It's common to all, and is fed off by nineteen cows, six ponies,
    three horses, five asses, two foals, seven pigs, and a calf!
                    (Thomas Hood, "Our Village")

There are still earlier examples, provided by Jonathan Swift. Shakespeare, a supremely accomplished maker of verse, was therefore capable of foisting the authorship of wonderfully incompetent doggerel upon his buffoons, most famously in the "tedious brief scene of young Pyramus / And his love Thisby: very tragical mirth." Perhaps less well known are the lines spoken by Holofernes about Moth, a boy who, in mute charade, represents one of the Nine Worthies in his infancy, in *Love's Labour's Lost*.

Great Hercules is presented by his imp,
Whose club killed Cerberus, that three-headed canus;
And when he was a babe, a child, a shrimp,
Thus did he strangle serpents in his manus.
Quoniam he seemeth in minority,
Ergo I come with this apology.

John Dover Wilson called the rhymed couplets spoken by the Player King and Queen in *Hamlet* "deliberately commonplace . . . so as to provide a rest for the audience after the excitement connected with the dumb-show and the prologue."

From these varieties of inferior poetry we must turn in another direction and consider the fact that partly, perhaps, because much poetry secures its rich and powerful effects without rhyme—Homer, Virgil, *Paradise Lost*, William Wordsworth, Walt Whitman, and many others—rhyme is relegated to the province of decorative adornment, an inessential luxury that may be regarded as effete (coinciding with its identification with light verse) or dated, a throwback to medieval preoccupations with arbitrary impediments, self-imposed constraints, spiritual and imaginative submission to rigorous laws and self-mortifying discipline; or else with the tinkling verse of troubadours and minnesingers. Such a view of rhyme as fundamentally ornamental fails to do justice to its versatility, for when properly integrated into a poem of serious character, it becomes an operational part, a functional instrument of the work. A poem may usefully be thought of as a gestalt or congeries of elements assembled in delicate balance; and although any given poem may dispense with some of these elements, the ones employed ought to cooperate smoothly enough to give the effect of a happily conceived ensemble. Of the single element of rhyme, Robert Graves observed, "it must come unexpectedly yet inevitably, like presents at Christmas, and convey the comforting sense of free will within predestination."[4] However lightheartedly Graves may resort to this theological language (a slightness indicated by "presents at Christmas"), what he is saying is not mistaken or trifling. It is put analogously, with regard to ornamental elements in architecture, by John Ruskin. "Observe," he writes in *The Stones of Venice,*

> that the value of this type does not consist in the mere shutting of the ornament into a certain space, but in the acknowledgement *by* the ornament of the fitness of the limitation;—of its own perfect willingness to submit to it; nay, of a predisposition in itself to fall into the ordained form, without any direct expression of the command to do so; an anticipation of the authority, and an instant and willing submission to it, in every fibre and spray; not merely *willing* but *happy* submission, as being pleased rather than vexed to have so beautiful a law suggested to it, and one which to follow is so justly in accordance with its own nature. You must not cut out a branch of hawthorn as it grows, and rule a triangle round it, and suppose that it is then submitted to a law. Not a bit of it. It is only put in a cage, and will look as if it must get out, for its life, or wither in the confinement. But the spirit of triangle must be put into the hawthorn. It must suck in isoscelesism with its sap. Thorn and blossom, leaf and spray must grow with an awful sense of triangular necessity upon them, for the guidance of which they are to be thankful, and to grow all the stronger and more gloriously. And although there may be a transgression here and there, and an adaptation to some other need, or a reaching forth to some other end, greater even than triangle, yet this liberty is to be always accepted

---

4. Graves, *The Common Asphodel,* 5.

under the solemn sense of special permission, and when the full form is reached and the entire submission expressed and every blossom has a thrilling sense of its responsibility down to its tiniest stamen, you may take your terminal line away if you will. No need of it any more. The commandment is written in the heart of the thing.

Tony Tanner, who cited this remarkable passage in his fine book *Venice Desired* (1992), remarked that it accommodates architectural elements to "laws at once natural and religious" (85), both of these domains having been of great concern to Ruskin. One detects somewhere lurking behind his paragraph the medieval dictum that perfect freedom is perfect obedience to perfect order. There are those who will find this attitude, and the way it is stated, mystical, fuzzy-minded, and silly. Among other things, while nominally writing about carved stone, Ruskin makes free with pathetic fallacies, permitting ornamental details to "acknowledge" the "fitness" of limitations, express a "predisposition" to submit to "ordained forms," a submission not only "willing but happy," and so on. Ruskin himself, in his earlier *Modern Painters,* had been highly suspicious and condemnatory of the pathetic fallacy, and it clearly has something to do with capacities for empathy and with the imagination itself. "Art, being a thing of the mind, it follows that any scientific study of art will be psychology. It may be other things as well, but psychology it will always be," declares Max Friedländer, and the question such an assertion raises concerns whose psychology is involved. That is to say—with specific regard to rhyme—are these elements to be regarded as "constraints," limiting the freedom of the poet? Or are they useful devices that, astutely linked with metrical patterns, can provide the raising of expectations (as regards an anticipated rhyme), the calculated delay or even disappointment of such expectations (as, for example, George Herbert provides in "Denial"), surprise at the fulfillment of the rhyming sound, either by the use of an exotic, unexpected word (often a feature of light verse) or because the chiming lines are so widely spaced that the suspended sound, awaiting concordance and resolution, has all but been forgotten by the mind's ear?

Further still, are they—continuing to regard rhymes as psychological devices—simply a way of preoccupying some part of the poet's mind, liberating it to unconscious fluencies or filling it with unforeseen suggestions? Can *Christians* and *resistance* taken together propose some line of

thought? Further still, and nearer to Ruskin's paragraph, does the match-
ing of rhymes satisfy some curious but deeply human craving for a formal
order that is meant in homage to some universal order we need to posit, if
not out of reverence, then out of dread of its possible absence? Or is there
something in the human psyche that delights in order "for its own sake,"
wherever it may be found, in symmetries, harmonies, repetitions, and resolutions? And can an answer to these questions be found that would apply equally well to nursery rhymes, Alexander Pope's couplets, and a
Stephen Sondheim song? We should not be surprised if, among the poets
themselves, we find a few who make light of the matter:

> But to my story.—'Twas some years ago,
>   It may be thirty, forty, more or less,
> The Carnival was at its height, and so
>   Were all kinds of buffoonery and dress;
> A certain lady went to see the show,
>   Her real name I know not, nor can guess,
> And so we'll call her Laura, if you please,
> Because it fits into my verse with ease.

This is the twenty-first stanza of Byron's *Beppo,* a poem of ninety-nine
such stanzas that from time to time indulge in acrobatic, virtually contor-
tionist rhyming. Here we meet the heroine, and given the libertine nature
of the tale to be unfolded, already hinted at in one of the poem's epigraphs,
we may take it that her pseudonymity is emphasized for several reasons:
(1) gentlemanly discretion, linked by literary tradition to the practice of
the Latin poets and their Renaissance heirs, who bestowed fictive names
on their loved ones to protect them from scandal or from the jealous
reprisals of their husbands; (2) a masquerade appropriate to the spirit of
Carnival, during which the events of the poem take place; (3) a slightly
provocative gesture by the poet ("Her real name I know not"), whose very
protestations of ignorance invite us to suspect that he knows more than
he will be telling and raise the whole question of how fact and fiction are
to be played with; (4) the proposed name *Laura* may have been chosen to
contrast ironically with Petrarch's Laura, an icon of purity; and (5) the final couplet suggests that the name, from the poet's point of view, is a mere
poetic convenience, chosen possibly because at some future point he will

find it expedient to rhyme it with *Flora, aura, begorra,* or *Gomorrah* (some rhymes, like *fedora* or *Floradora,* were not available in 1818). He would, of course, have been quite willing to use any of these. As it happens, he didn't use any of them, so we may surmise that when he was composing his twenty-first stanza he may have been keeping open his rhyming options, or that when he says he has chosen the name "because it fits into my verse" he means only, and lamely, that it doesn't violate his meter; though we know perfectly well that if meter is his only consideration, *Polly, Gerty,* or *Suky* would have worked just as well. The topic invites our attention because it deliberately raises the issue of how formal considerations may require the poet to reorganize the literal world to make it conform to artistic goals.

Just as lightly, here is a stanza from Part One of Auden's *Letter to Lord Byron,* in which the poet pretends to anxiety about whether his publishers will be irked or angered by his frequent Byronic digressions.

> But now I've got uncomfortable suspicions,
>   I'm going to put their noses out of joint.
> Though it's in keeping with the best traditions
>   For travel books to wander from the point
>   (There is no other rhyme except anoint),
> They well may charge me with—I've no defences—
> Obtaining money under false pretences.

When we too strongly feel the coercions of rhyme we know (if all else, meter especially, is flawlessly handled) that we are reading light verse; whereas coercive rhyme can be one of the blatant signs of poetic incompetence, which may be why some not altogether skillful poets avoid it. But we must turn from this levity to more serious matters.

John Dryden, addressing the earl of Orrery, for whom a model of the instrument, a replication of planetary order invented by George Graham, was made by an instrument maker named Rowley and dedicated to the earl, defends rhyme by approving Sir Philip Sidney's claim that it aids memory and, on his own authority, adds that it discourages prolixity. At a certain early stage in their careers, Eliot and Pound, at Pound's suggestion, applied themselves to the study and imitation of Théophile Gautier as a corrective to the indiscipline of fashionable *vers libristes.* Eliot produced his quatrain poems, while Pound was famously to write:

> The "age demanded" chiefly a mould in plaster,
> Made with no loss of time,
> A prose kinema, not, not assuredly, alabaster
> Or the "sculpture" of rhyme.

"Rhyme" here surely means poetry itself, the whole kit and caboodle, its metrics, stanza form, traditional dignity and reserve, classical grace and decorum. This may be inferred from previous lines, as well as from the poem and doctrines of Gautier's *ars poetica* that Pound means to honor:

L'Art	Art
Oui, l'oeuvre sort plus belle	All things are doubly fair
D'une forme au travail	If patience fashion them
Rebelle,	And care—
Vers, marbre, onyx, émail.	Verse, enamel, marble, gem.
. . . .	. . . .
Statuaire, repousse	Sculptor, lay by the clay
L'argile que pétrit	On which thy nerveless finger
Le pouce	May linger,
Quand flotte ailleurs l'esprit	Thy thoughts flown far away.
Lutte avec le carrare,	Keep to Carrara rare,
Avec le paros dur	Struggle with Paros cold,
Et rare	That hold
Gardiens du contour pur;	The subtle line and fair.

(trans. George Santayana)

(Johann Wolfgang von Goethe, too, in *Lied und Gebilde,* was drawn by the idea of the relation between verse and sculpture.) Stone is resistant, demanding; it lacks the fluidity or limpness of the "prose kinema," the duplicability, hence susceptibility to forgery, of a "mould in plaster," those factory-cast statuettes or bland cinematic tales that "the age demanded." And "demand" is obviously for Pound part of the "supply and demand" language of modern economic parlance, in which art has become merely a servile commodity. The carven skill of Gautier's verses is only emphasized by the brevity of his lines, bringing his rhymes close together, and by the strictness of his form. The likening of verse to sculpture involves not only the challenge, the difficulty, but also the creation of something manifestly durable: the final word of his poem is *résistant.*

The formality here exemplified implies a relation between rhyme and metrical form, a matter about which there is no orthodoxy. Usually, in a stanzaic poem, each line is mated with at least one other line; and if the stanza pattern involves an odd number of lines, the common practice rhymes the odd-numbered final line with one of the previous lines, unless deliberate dissonance is desired, as in George Herbert's "Denial," cited earlier. There is a curious exception to this rule that I think can best be explained musically. In his book on the history of music, Donald J. Grout reports that "Luther himself wrote many chorale verses, for example, the well known *Ein' feste Burg* ('A mighty fortress'); it has never been definitely established that Luther wrote the melody of this chorale (first printed in 1529), though the music is generally attributed to him."[5] The chorale's text is a nine-line stanza, with its first eight lines matched in this rhyming pattern: *ababccdd.* The remaining, final line is unrhymed with anything, either in the original German or in the familiar English translation, which is fairly faithful to the sense and absolutely trustworthy as regards the rhyming pattern. And if we look merely at the printed words, the final line stands out, in terms of word-music, like a sore thumb.

Ein' feste Burg its unser Gott,	A mighty fortress is our God,
Ein gute Wehr und Waffen.	A bulwark never failing;
Er hilft uns frei aus aller Not,	Our helper he amid the flood
Die uns jetzt hat betroffen.	Of mortal ills prevailing;
Der alt böse Feind,	For still our ancient Foe
Mit Ernst ers jetzt meint,	Doth seek to work us woe;
Gross Macht und viel List,	His craft and power are great,
Sein grausam Rüstung ist,	And armed with cruel hate,
Auf Erd ist nicht seins gleichen.	On earth is not his equal.

(trans. Frederick Hedge, 1852)

---

5. Donald J. Grout, *A History of Western Music* (1964), 153.

This curious phonic discrepancy is concealed, or perhaps we may say healed and harmonized, by the musical setting, which recalls the exact notational phrase of music that occurs in the second and fourth lines, thereby producing not only a welcome cadence but an echo, and thus suggesting a rhyme that is, in fact, not there.

Poets have written from time to time about their struggles with rhyme, Ben Jonson (in "A Fit of Rime against Rime") being one of the earlier, and even Chaucer complained (in "The Complaint of Venus") of the "skarsete" of rhyme in English, while in *Satura*, Eugenio Montale, in a poem called "Le Rime," wrote (in William Arrowsmith's translation):

> Rhymes are pests, worse
> than the nuns of St. Vincent, knocking at your door
> nonstop. You can't just turn them away
> and they're tolerable so long as they're outside.
> The polite poet stays aloof, disguising
> or outwitting them (the rhymes), or trying to sneak
> them by. But they're fanatical, blazing
> with zeal and sooner or later they're back (rhymes
> and biddies), pounding at your door and poems,
> same as always.

In the original, the first and last lines truly rhyme (*delle / quelle*), and other lines employ slant rhymes, disguised or outwitted by the poet, or cunningly sneaked by: *supportano / allontana / ardono*. The Italian language simply has more rhyming words than English, allowing it to perform rhyming feats that either would be impossible in English or would sound to us like a tour de force, while quite unstrained and easygoing in Italian. Jacopone da Todi composed a manifestly serious, not to say solemn, poem called "De la incarnazione del verbo divino." It is written in quatrains with the first three lines rhyming with one another, while the fourth line hangs suspended, apparently rhyming with nothing, like the last line of Luther's hymn. But it turns out that the stanza's fourth line rhymes with the fourth line of the following stanza and furthermore, with the terminal line of every ensuing stanza, and there are eighteen of these. The poet, admittedly permits himself three repetitions (*Signore, amore,* and *fiore*), but the effect is persuasive in the redundant manner of Gregorian chant.

This effect is virtually unavailable in English. Multiple rhyme either gives the effect of levity (as in Hardy's "The Respectable Burgher on the Higher Criticism," which parades thirty-six consecutive rhymes of the same sound) or else a sense of nervous obsessiveness approaching hysteria, as in Sylvia Plath's "Daddy." And in "The Ballad of Reading Gaol," Oscar Wilde, through an excess of rhyme, contrives to undermine the very sympathy he must be trying to enlist.

> It is sweet to dance to violins
>   When love and life are fair;
> To dance to flutes, to dance to lutes
>   Is delicate and rare;
> But it is not sweet with nimble feet
>   To dance upon the air.

The labored irony here is due, at least in part, to excessive rhyme and the repetition of words: *lutes / flutes, sweet / feet. Dance* is mentioned four times, *sweet* (a hazardous word) twice. The crude contrast between heedless bliss (of a slightly Bacchanalian kind, with dancing to the accompaniment of flutes; the lutes seem thrown in for rhyme) and hanging by the neck until dead is made grotesquely melodramatic by these chimings, and the ironies are almost adolescent. An 1811 *Dictionary of the Vulgar Tongue* gives "dance upon nothing" as a standard formula for someone who is hanged.

I have found myself put off by the rhymes of one stanza of Edwin Arlington Robinson's otherwise deeply moving and powerful poem "Eros Turannos."

> The falling leaf inaugurates
>   The reign of her confusion;
> The pounding wave reverberates

The dirge of her illusion;
And home, where passion lived and died,
Becomes a place where she can hide,
While all the town and harbor side
Vibrate with her seclusion.

What bothers my ear is the role played in this stanza by rhyme, conjoined to a catalogue of perilous abstractions and more or less mechanically grammatical parallelisms. The four-syllable mating of *inaugurates / reverberates* alternating with the three-syllable mating of *confusion / illusion / seclusion* is conspicuous enough. The parallel construction of the first two lines with the two that follow, down to identical articles and prepositions, identical placement of participles, nouns, and verbs, is so annoyingly efficient and neat that we are prevented from investing any sympathy in the plight of the woman whose unhappy fate is being described, and we are diverted by a sense that approval is being invited in behalf of the symmetries of the language. Such laborious rhyming, enforced upon the reader's notice by other constructive elements, recalls us to Eliot's careful discrimination between heavier and lighter rhymes and alerts us to the serious problem of how much attention rhyme ought to call to itself. There are those poems that rhyme only occasionally and irregularly, of which more in a moment. But because we are now discussing rhymes as obtrusive and conspicuous, a word perhaps ought to be said about *bouts-rimés*.

The story goes that a French poet of no great consequence, named Dulot, reported in outrage to his friends that his home had been burglarized, ransacked, and that some of his most valuable papers were missing, including some three hundred sonnets. No one believed that he could have written so many, and under the pressure of skeptical questioning he admitted that he had worked out only the rhyme-schemes of these and planned to fill in the poems at some later time. This was thought to be quite comic, and it became a fashionable parlor game. Someone proposes the terminal rhyming words of a sonnet, with which none of the other participants have any foreknowledge. Each player is invited to compose a sonnet on the spot, using the rhymes in the exact order in which they have been proposed. Judgment is awarded on the basis of speed and merit, and sometimes the competition is made especially challenging by improbable and far-fetched rhymes. Dante Gabriel Rossetti was reputed to be unusually good at these games, able to produce a respectable sonnet in five or six minutes.

Lighthearted and perhaps frivolous as the game may be, it points to some serious issues. Rhymes are not merely limiting constraints but clearly also suggestive elements that can lend direction to a poet's imagination. If he or she is a bad poet, sooner or later we will feel a sense of bondage by the rhymes. If skillful, our feelings are likely to approve different effects suitable to varied poetic strategies. *Sign* / *dine* is not a striking rhyme until adopted for his purposes by Pope: "The hungry Judges soon the sentence sign / And wretches hang that jurymen may dine." This confrontation of pleasure and execution is not so remote from the lines of Wilde quoted above, but it is far more effective by virtue of its terseness and economy, to say nothing of its smooth incrimination of the justice system, which Wilde's lines make no mention of, at least explicitly. But the illustration of well-deployed rhymes is a thankless task, their fittingness being so integrally dependent on the poetic framework of which they are a part.

Even the degree of integration of rhymes will vary from poem to poem. And with Matthew Arnold's "Dover Beach" and Thomas Hardy's "Last Look Round St. Martin's Fair" we encounter a liberty of rhyming that could have been found as early as the seventeenth century in France but was something of a novelty in English. These are rhymes that occur according to no fixed pattern and at the ends of lines of varying and unpatterned length. After the regularities of the towering Victorians, this might almost be called "promiscuous rhyming." It occurs also in the early poems of Eliot: in "Prufrock," "Portrait of a Lady," and "Rhapsody on a Windy Night," and he would continue this practice right through segments of *Four Quartets*, while varying his style with greater or lesser strictness and attaining a rich variety thereby.

This reference to Eliot's virtuosity of rhyming recalls me to something quoted earlier, in his remarks about Marianne Moore. He speaks of rhyme "which forms a pattern *against* the metric and sense pattern" of a poem, and this contrariety, the more striking in poems of formal regularity, affords a pleasure akin to syncopation, in which internal movements oppose one another in some artistically satisfying way. And I would like to illustrate this with some stanzas of a poem by James Merrill called "The

Blue Grotto." The poem is composed in five-line trimeter stanzas, rhyming *ababa*, and I will confine my comment to the first four stanzas, addressing them two at a time.

> The boatman rowed into
> That often sung impasse.
> Each visitor foreknew
> A floor of lilting glass,
> A vault of rock, lit blue.
>
> But here we faced the fact.
> As misty expectations
> Dispersed, and wavelets thwacked
> In something like impatience,
> The point was to react.

The rhymes of the first stanza are modest and without ostentation. The first line involves enjambment, running smoothly into the second and lightening the rhyming burden of the transitional preposition *into*. *Impasse* is a curious word, a French-English half-breed, subject, accordingly, to a number of pronunciations, one of which, with the dictionary's authority, provides a faultless rhyme with *glass* in the fourth line. But because it appears at the end of the second, we may approach it with a gingerly uncertainty about how it is to be sounded. The approved French pronunciation would rhyme it with *Alsace*, making *glass* as a rhyme sound flat, nasal, and "American." The poet could, of course, have intended just this effect. Indeed, poets have sometimes surprised us by delayed indications of what pronunciations they intend. Here, for example, is a double dactyl by George Starbuck, titled "Said," in which the quasi-literacy of the speaker is surprisingly revealed.

> Said
> Agatha Christie to
> E. Phillips Oppenheim,
> "Who is this Hemingway,
> Who is this Proust?

Who is this Vladimir
Whatchamacallum, this
Neopostrealist
Rabble?" she groused.

Merrill's rhymes in his first stanza, though not simple, are confined to single syllables. But in his second stanza the second and fourth lines offer disyllabic rhymes, and unexpected ones at that. The rhyming of the noun *fact* with the transitive verb *thwacked* and the intransitive verb *react* provides a subtle and important pleasure, amounting to a rule of thumb about rhyming: those rhymes are best which mate different parts of speech, like *into* / *foreknew* / *blue* in the first stanza. Of these first two stanzas we may go on to remark that as a world-renowned tourist attraction, the Blue Grotto at Capri enjoys a celebrity different from Hollywood stardom and more akin to the reverence accorded an operatic diva. Its attractions, spread by word of mouth, travel posters, and postcards, are known to multitudes who have never been there. And such grandeurs are always a challenge when subject to someone's first personal experience. There is always a possibility that what we have allowed ourselves to hope for in imaginative anticipation and what we come up against as "fact" will fail to coincide. And this can mean either that the place or experience is not all it's cracked up to be or else that we ourselves, our perceptions, sensibilities, are somehow at fault. As Edmund White reports of a conversation with David Kalstone, "If I'd say I'd decided I didn't really like Goethe, David would say coldly, 'Goethe is not being judged.'"

Just who is under scrutiny, subject, object, or both, together with the self-conscious posturings engendered by this "test," is a probing part of what this poem is about. The first two stanzas balance upon the fulcrum of reputation and actuality, first felt from the point of view of the visitor, but then, as "expectations / Dispersed," to be replaced by the real thing, we seem to shift to the almost personified, foot-tapping impatience of the place itself, awaiting, like a Metropolitan diva, the tribute of customary ovation; and then, once again refocusing on the visitors' sense of the pressures imposed upon them by the force and majesty of the occasion. Returned by the final line of the second stanza to the viewpoint of the visitors, we are now to examine their individual reactions.

Alas for characteristics!
Diane fingered the water.
Don tested the acoustics
With a paragraph from Pater.
Jon shut his eyes—these mystics—

Thinking his mantra. Jack
Came out with a one-liner,
While claustrophobiac
Janet fought off a minor
Anxiety attack.

The dexterity of rhyming is impressive. The third stanza offers disyllabic rhyming throughout, while the fourth employs it in the second and fourth lines. *Water* / *Pater* is a witty sight-rhyme. But to avoid laboring the matter, it seems to me that Merrill's rhyming in this poem operates like those cutout shapes, fins, or terminal blobs of a Calder mobile, each contributing its own carefully calculated weight, which must be reckoned in achieving the balanced yet flexible effect of the whole. That is, the rhyme is experienced as working within a field of forces that include meter and syntax, line-length, word order, diction, grammar, and tone. Diane gets one line; Don gets two; Jon and Jack share three lines, with Jon getting the larger portion, while Janet is allotted three lines to herself. These disparities are displayed against the formal regularity of the tight trimeter five-line stanzas with their demanding rhyme scheme, each calling for the triple chiming of first, third, and fifth lines, interspersed with the less demanding harmonies of the second and fourth. And this, I think, is what Eliot was admiring in the work of Marianne Moore when he wrote of "rhyme, which forms a pattern *against* the metric and sense pattern of the poem" and which I have characterized as syncopation. Merrill's stanza pattern, made the more demanding by the brevity of his lines, which congest the rhyming words into very close quarters, is imposed upon an amusing catalogue of quirky reactions to the testing sight (or test-site) of the famous grotto, and with psychological insight reveals, like an inkblot test, more about the observer(s) than the observed.

The Music of Forms

—Sounds and sweet airs, that give delight, and hurt not.

I

Esquire magazine published a short piece of mine, introducing the double dactyl, a form of light verse, in 1966. The rules were laid out (two quatrains, with the last line of the first rhyming with the last line of the second; all the lines except the rhyming ones composed of two dactylic feet; the first line a nonsense line like "Higgledy-Piggledy," while the second line must be a name that is two dactyls long; and the second stanza must contain a double dactylic word) and twelve examples were printed exhibiting these rules. The poems published in *Esquire* were about, among others, Marcus Aurelius, Klemens von Metternich, Vladimir Horowitz, and Franklin D. Roosevelt. The readers of *Esquire* were editorially challenged to contribute specimens of their own work in this light-hearted idiom (which, I may add, went on to enlist adoption by W. H. Auden); and, by way of heavy-handed hint, some further double-dactylic names were listed for readers' use (Margaret Rutherford, Arthur M. Schlesinger, Judas Iscariot) as well as some double-dactylic words (heterosexual, incontrovertible, unconstitutional, misericordia), and *Esquire* promised to publish the best of its readers' contributions in a forthcoming issue, the entries to be judged by me.

Reader response was enormous, which was initially gratifying, but it was not long before my more considered reaction was a bizarre mixture of amusement and dismay. Serenely undaunted by ground rules, readers submitted poems about, among others, Fräulein Schicklgruber, Herr Chancellor Hitler, Enrico Caruso, and Alexander Calder, while using such putatively double-dactylic words as *reorganization* and *indefatigable.* Apart from culling the best of that strange harvest, I gave little further thought to the matter until much later, when I was regularly teaching Shakespeare to undergraduates. I quickly found it essential to begin with a lecture on Shakespeare's prose and poetry, his employment of both in his plays, and, under the heading of verse, the lyrics of his songs as well as the role of blank verse in dialogue. Much care was given to discussion of iambic pentameter, and it became my practice to confirm my darkest suspicions about my students' capacity to recognize metrical patterns by asking them, when beginning discussions of *Romeo and Juliet,* where the first line of verse appears in the text, apart from its sonnet-prologue. The play opens with prose dialogue, comic in character but edged with partisan rancor as minions of the Montague and Capulet households meet and taunt each other with increasing boldness that is prudently and comically leavened with a circumspect timidity, until, in line 65, Benvolio, who can see the true dangers of escalation, cries out: "Put up your swords, you know not what you do," the play's first blank verse line, which is responded to in like verse by Tybalt's "What, art thou drawn among these heartless hinds? / Turn thee, Benvolio, look upon thy death."

After a certain number of years I gave up asking my classes this question, which obviously embarrassed them and discouraged me, for it became transparently clear that the overwhelming majority of my students were quite simply deaf to almost all metrical considerations and that my introductory lecture on the topic was purposeless and wasteful. And I reluctantly concluded that there are many who are not so much mystified by meter as completely oblivious to it. There have even been established literary critics who, without the least embarrassment, have acknowledged this deficiency in themselves; so why should I have expected my students to be better attuned to such music?

It was only after many years of bafflement on my part about this metrical numbness in students that I bethought myself again of the readers of *Esquire,* and it dawned upon me that in many cases the names and words they had proposed as double-dactylic (*Fräulein Schicklgruber, Alexander Calder, Herr Chancellor Hitler; reorganization, indefatigable*), while monstrously deformed as regards the dactylic rhythm, which is essentially the

Oom- pah-pah, *Oom-* pah-pah beat of a Viennese waltz, nevertheless contained the requisite six syllables, though without regard to accentual values. And it struck me that there were those who read all poetry as though it were composed as syllabic verse, where, as in some of the poetry of W. H. Auden, Marianne Moore, and Richard Howard, to name only the most prominent practitioners, line length is measured entirely by the number of its syllables.

For a while this led me to account for discrepancies between the First Quarto (1608) and the First Folio (1623) editions of *King Lear,* where virtually the same words in the identical order appear, first, in prose, and later in verse, as though the earlier compositor had no ear for metrical measure. And a later atrocity in the editing of this play tended to confirm my suspicions. Here, to begin with, are the quarto and folio versions of I.iv.275–89.

Leir. It may be fo my Lord, harke *Nature,* heare deere Godeffe, fufpend thy purpofe, if thou did'ft intend to make this creature fruitful into her wombe, conuey fterility, drie vp in hir the organs of increafe, and from her derogate body neuer fpring a babe to honour her, if fhee muft teeme, create her childe of fpleene, that it may liue and bee a thourt difuetur'd torment to her, let it ftampe wrinckles in her brow of youth, with accent teares, fret channels in her cheeks, turne all her mothers paines and benefits to laughter and contempt, that fhee may feele, that fhe may feele, how fharper then a ferpents tooth it is, to haue a thankleffe child, goe, goe, my people?

    Lear. It may be fo, my Lord.
Heare Nature, heare deere Godeffe, heare:
Sufpend thy purpofe, if thou did'ft intend
To make this Creature fruitfull:
Into her Wombe conuey fterility,
Drie vp in her the Organs of increafe,
And from her derogate body, neuer fpring
A Babe to honour her. If fhee muft teeme,
Create her childe of Spleene, that it may liue
And be athwart of difnatur'd torment to her.

Let it ſtampe wrinkles in her brow of youth,
With cadent Teares fret Channels in her cheekes,
Turne all her Mothers paines, and benefits
To laughter, and contempt: That ſhe may feele,
How ſharper then a Serpents tooth it is,
To haue a thakleſſe Childe. Away, away.   *Exit.*

In 1975 Simon and Schuster issued, as one of its Parallel Text Series, an edition of *King Lear* with the folio text on the left-hand side and, facing it, a version intended to appeal to modern readers. The General Introduction explained:

> The purpose of this series is to make Shakespeare fully intelligible to the modern reader. We should have the same immediate response to Shakespeare that we have to any modern writer, without the intervention of notes, commentaries, and glosses. Ironically, non-English-speaking readers of Shakespeare have always had modernized versions in translation, and their Shakespeare has been close to the reader's own spoken language. We English-speaking readers are in some way penalized, and our Shakespeare, after 375 years, has become remote and difficult to understand—a school text that we struggle over. We hope that the modernized texts in the present series will encourage a more spontaneous enjoyment of the plays.[1]

The modernized text of the I.iv passage quoted above is rendered as follows:

> It may be so, my lord.
> Listen to me, Nature, listen! dear Goddess, listen!
> Set aside your normal purpose, if you ever intended
> this creature Goneril to have children!
> Make her womb sterile!
> Dry up her reproductive powers,
> and never allow that contemptible body to have
> a baby to honor her! If she must breed,
> let her child be made of hatred and spite, so that it may live

---

1. *King Lear*, ed. Beatrice Tauss, Parallel Text Series (1975), v.

to be a perverse, unnatural torture to her!
Let her monster transform its youthful mother into a withered hag.
Let endless tears carve deep wrinkles in her cheeks.
Repay all her motherly cares and joys
with laughter and contempt, so that she may feel
how much more painful than the bite of a serpent's tooth it is
to have an ungrateful child! I must go away! away!

I presume that, along with Maurice Charney, general editor of the Simon and Schuster series, there must be others who feel no loss in the dignity of utterance of the original. Yet I can't help feeling that such dignity is conferred by what in this essay I designate as a species of music, and which, while not simply a question of meter, cannot wholly be separated from it. The greatest of Shakespearean actors, such figures as John Gielgud, Lawrence Olivier, and Paul Scofield, as they speak Shakespeare's lines, allow us to hear more than soliloquies or dialogic exchanges of conversation; in them we hear an intricate music of grammar and syntax, the richest of vocabularies daringly deployed, and all this superimposed upon a grid of meter, which itself is the more complicated by virtue of permissible variations of individual feet, as emphasis and dramatic pointing dictate. And these permissible variations, recognized through the template of standard meter, furnish a syncopation, a counterpoint that is lovely in its own right and astonishing in its accommodation of all the other forces of language at work in the plays.

It was Christopher Ricks who very kindly called my attention to, and sent me the text of, an article on the *Lear* texts by Ann R. Meyer which appeared in *Studies in Bibliography* (1994) and which is concerned with the very discrepancies between quarto and folio that I had been fretting over. With scholarship far beyond my reach, Ms. Meyer considered how Shakespeare's play was set in print and by whom. It appears that the quarto edition was set in type by one Nicholas Okes. "It was the first play-quarto Okes had ever printed," Ms. Meyer declares, and she goes on to cite Peter W. M. Blayney to the effect that this quarto "can claim a place among Okes's half-dozen worst-printed books of 1607–1609," noting his further estimate that "there were printers whose worst was worse than Okes's—but not very many, and not *much* worse."

The problems for the compositor included the method of printing signatures, sheets of paper that when folded and cut would produce an eight-page segment of text. This in turn meant printing pages on both sides of a sheet, half of them upside-down, so that when folded they would come out right-side up, thus:

Recto		Verso	
8	1	6	3
5	4	7	2

If, as Ms. Meyer suggests, the play were set by more than one compositor, "or in some cases more than one printing house," a judgment would have to be made along the lines of guesswork about just how much text could be gotten onto eight pages. The supposition of several compositors would make possible simultaneous work on different segments of the text. "If," Ms. Meyer conjectures, "the printer overestimated his copy, he would compensate for error by introducing 'white space' in the text. If on the other hand he had underestimated his copy, he would make adjustments by crowding verse into prose, neglecting proper punctuation, or by leaving little or no space between words and sentences. The quickest and easiest solution, of course, was simply to cut portions of his copy when he had underestimated the number of sheets necessary to print the text accurately and was therefore running out of room. Deletions under these circumstances were not uncommon."

This seems persuasive and has behind it the authority of careful scholarship. Or perhaps I had better say "seemed persuasive" until I tried to reckon with a quarto/folio problem that presents itself in *Love's Labour's Lost.* In that case, quarto and folio agree on the text of the two songs that end the play, *Spring* and *Winter.* Here is what is usually taken, as it is by the editor of the *Arden Shakespeare,* to be the canonical text.

Spring When daisies pied and violets blue
And lady-smocks all silver-white
And cuckoo-buds of yellow hue
Do paint the meadows with delight,
The cuckoo then, on every tree,
Mocks married men; for thus sings he,
Cuckoo;

Cuckoo, cuckoo: O word of fear,
Unpleasing to the married ear!

When shepherds pipe on oaten straws,
 And merry larks are ploughman's clocks,
When turtles tread, and rooks, and daws,
 And maidens bleach their summer smocks,
The cuckoo then, on every tree
Mocks married men; for thus sings he,
  Cuckoo;
Cuckoo, cuckoo; O word of fear,
Unpleasing to the married ear!

Winter When icicles hang by the wall,
 And Dick the shepherd blows his nail,
And Tom bears logs into the hall,
 And milk comes frozen home in pail,
When blood is nipp'd, and ways be foul,
Then nightly sings the staring owl,
  Tu-whit;
To-who, a merry note,
While greasy Joan doth keel the pot.

When all aloud the wind doth blow,
 And coughing drowns the parson's saw,
And birds sit brooding in the snow,
 And Marian's nose looks red and raw,
When roasted crabs hiss in the bowl,
Then nightly sings the staring owl,
  To-whit;
To-who, a merry note,
While greasy Joan doth keel the pot.

 When Dr. Johnson set about to produce his edition of the plays he could tell this was wrong, and he made the appropriate correction. Form itself, made the more formal because these are songs, so the musical score must formally accommodate all the stanzas to an exactly repeated melody, would have told him—though it has not told as much to later editors—that if Spring concludes each stanza with two tetrameter lines, so must Winter; therefore some kind of adjustment must be made. One modern editor solves the problem by concluding the *Winter* refrain with

> To-whit, to-whoo! A merry note,
> While greasy Joan doth keel the pot.

Though this solution furnishes two concluding tetrameters, it leaves unfulfilled the solitary disyllabic equivalent for the antepenultimate "Cuckoo" in each stanza of *Spring*.

Musical settings make demands of their own upon poetry, and in the great Elizabethan era of music devoted importantly to song as solo, as madrigal, as a cappella groups of various sizes, as rounds and catches, there were few poets—and Shakespeare, it may be affirmed, was not one of them—who were indifferent to these demands. Among the most elementary was the requirement that stanzas reduplicate one another formally so that the same musical text can be repeated. The same constraints obtain in modern popular song, sometimes in highly syncopated and closely rhymed passages. Cole Porter is celebrated for his skill in verse as well as music, but I will offer an instance from the team of Rodgers and Hart. In "The Lady Is a Tramp," there is a passage that, with a fine rhythmic sophistication reads:

> I like the free,
> > fresh,
> > > wind in my hair,
> > > life without care.
> I'm broke—
> It's oke.

This pattern in rhyme and rhythm recurs in each of the four stanzas of the song, importantly including the terse, two-syllable couplet—witty in itself, almost epigrammatic—and demanded by, or accommodating itself to, the musical frame in which it is set.

But we need not suppose that we must turn to Lorenz Hart for examples of this formal skill, as though there were no English Renaissance specimens quite apart from Shakespeare. Here is a song from John Playford's *Selectyed Musical Airs and Dialogues* (1653).

> When, Celia, I intend to flatter you,
>   And tell you lies to make you true,
>   I swear
>   There's none so fair—
>   And you believe it too.
>
> Oft have I matched you with the rose, and said
>   No twins so like hath nature made;
>   But 'tis
>   Only this—
>   You prick my hand, and fade.
>
> Oft have I said there is no precious stone
>   But may be found in you alone;
>   Though I
>   No stone espy—
>   Unless your heart be one.
>
> And when I praise your skin, I quote the wool
>   That silkworms from their entrails pull,
>   And show
>   That new-fall'n snow
>   Is not more beautiful.
>
> Yet grow not proud by such hyperboles;
>   Were you as excellent as these,
>   Whilst I
>   Before you lie,
>   They might be had with ease.

There is, moreover, a further ground to suppose Dr. Johnson's emendation was shrewdly correct, and this has to do with the bearing of the two songs on the events in *Love's Labour's Lost*. The play opens with the resolution of the King of Navarre and his courtiers to seclude themselves from the world in order to devote themselves to study, virtue, and self-conquest. No sooner have they pledged themselves to this austerity, albeit somewhat reluctantly on the part of at least one courtier, than the Princess of France, accompanied by a train of noble ladies, appears and, perforce, must be entertained. The resolution of celibate study dissolves with expected speed as well as a certain comic hypocrisy, but the courtship of the ladies by the gentlemen is confounded at the last moment by news of the death of the father of the princess. This in itself demands of her an interval of mourning and makes the further prosecution of courtship unthinkable in the circumstances. The ladies not only resolve to go into mourning for a year, but they impose penances upon the king and his courtiers for breaking the oaths of austerity they had initially imposed upon themselves. There is a lovely and just irony in the imposition, as punishment, of a penalty that was initially self-imposed. The only characters in the play to escape from this term of celibacy are Don Adriano De Armado, a *miles gloriosus,* a braggart soldier, and Jaquenetta, a country wench whom he has gotten with child and must now make an honest woman by marrying her. So there is the further irony that the nobility are condemned for a year to sexual abstinence, while the lower-class characters, who have already indulged in carnal license, need only to solemnize their boisterous activities with wedding vows. And this clearly has a bearing on the songs, or, more accurately, they have a bearing on this curious situation.

The erotic celebration of *Spring* is unambiguous; and while it is edged with anxiety for husbands about the fidelity of their wives, it is richly evocative of the warmth and healthy license of fertility that belongs to the season and to all outdoors. Superficially, Winter seems designed in complementary opposition. It is cold where Spring is warm; it seems inhospitable in its icy discomforts. But if Spring invited the pleasures and liberties of the out-of-doors, Winter can at least recommend the diversions of indoor activities, which, if few, are nonetheless amorous, as the owl reminds us by inviting us all, precisely, *to woo*—which, as the song indicates, is "a merry note," not a chilling or lugubrious one. Johnson, accordingly, concludes Winter's song:

> Then nightly sings the staring owl,
>> To woo,
> To wit, to woo, a merry note,
> While greasy Joan doth keel the pot.

Finally, the flaws in the quarto/folio version cannot be attributed to a compositor's "lack of space" for two reasons: the corrected, Johnsonian version requires no more lines of type than the erroneous one; and, positioned as they are at the end of the play, there could have been little uncertainty about how much space was left in which to set them.

The *Lear* speech quoted above in three versions raises some interesting puzzles. The quarto version (prose) contains a repetition towards the end, "that she may feele, that she may feele," which, in view of what we know about the practices of Nicholas Okes, is likely to be an error. And yet in context the repeated phrase is actually quite moving and seems to emphasize the speaker's desperate emotional turmoil. On the other hand, nowhere else in Shakespeare do we find a like repetition, in which a speaker feels almost unable to continue, as though sobbing were about to overtake him. When we come to consider the "modern" version, we cannot fail to be aware of its clumsiness, its importation of the epithet "monster" for which the original provides no precedent. Nevertheless, one point raised by Maurice Charney seems worth pondering. "Ironically," he writes, "non-English-speaking readers of Shakespeare have always had modernized versions in translation . . . We English-speaking readers are in some way penalized, and our Shakespeare, after 375 years, has become remote and difficult to understand."

So Matthew Arnold also thought and famously declared in the Preface to his *Poems* of 1853.

We must never forget that Shakespeare is the great poet he is from his skill in discerning and firmly conceiving an excellent action, from his power of intensely feeling a situation, of intimately associating himself with a character; not from his gift of expression, which rather even leads him astray, degenerating sometimes into a fondness for curiosity of expression, into an irritability of fancy, which seems to make it impossible for him to say a thing plainly, even when the press of action demands the very directest language, or its level of character the very simplest. Mr. Hallam, than whom it is impossible to find a saner and more judicious critic, has had the courage (for at the present day it needs courage) to remark, how extremely and faultily difficult Shakespeare's language often is. It is so: you may find main scenes in some of his greatest tragedies, *King Lear* for instance, where the language is so artificial, so curiously tortured, and so difficult, that every speech has to be read two or three times before its meaning can be comprehended. This overcuriousness of expression is indeed but the excessive employment of a wonderful gift—of the power of saying a thing in a happier way than any other man; nevertheless, it is carried so far that one understands what M. Guizot meant, when he said that Shakespeare appears in his language to have tried all styles except that of simplicity.

Doubtless it would be impertinent to wonder whether Messrs. Arnold, Hallam, and Guizot would have preferred the Simon and Schuster version of *King Lear.* That new version was, in effect, a translation into a more modern, idiomatic language, nearer the reader's own usage, as Mr. Charney indicated. But is this always desirable? Should Shakespeare sound to us like Edward Albee or Tennessee Williams? Experiments in turning one English to another English have been adventurously undertaken, and it may be worth looking at a stanza of John Donne's before and after such a translation.

Loves Deitie

I long to talke with some old lovers ghost,
   Who dyed before the god of Love was borne:
I cannot thinke that hee, who then lov'd most,
   Sunke so low, as to love one which did scorne.
But since this god produc'd a destinie,
And that vice-nature, custome, lets it be;
   I must love her that loves not mee.

John L. Sweeney rendered this into Basic English, with its severely restricted vocabulary, as follows:

Love's Deity

Talk with some old lover
Dead before the god of love had come to be

Would do my poor heart good. For he,
As full of love when living as I am now
Would not have done what I have done,
Have given love to an unkind, unloving one.
But as this god has made things so,
And ways of men have not till now said 'no',
No other way I see
But to give my love to one
Who has no love for me.[2]

The differences are clear enough. To begin with, Donne's stanza employs sixty words, Sweeney's eighty-four. Donne's meter, with its idiosyncratic liberties in the fourth line, nevertheless keeps to its pattern of six pentameter lines followed by a tetrameter, a pattern adhered to in all four of its stanzas. Sweeney, on the other hand, maintains no fixed form at any point, and, for purposes of providing an unpatterned rhyme, has turned Donne's seven lines into eleven. It is no more than minimal to claim that along the way Donne's music has been lost.

When publishing his translation of that remarkable craftsman and employer of demanding forms, François Villon, Galway Kinnell wrote as commentary, "I decided against using rhyme and meter . . . What is more expressive of a poet than his images? Yet in rhyming translations we can't even be sure the images are the poet's . . . And I wonder, do rhyme and meter mean for us what they meant to Villon? It may be that in our day these formal devices have become a dead hand, which it is just as well not to lay on any poetry." When I first read this, I was somewhat irked by it, until I realized that Mr. Kinnell was wittily and self-deprecatingly acknowledging that to observe the constraints of rhyme and meter is very, very difficult. And the difficulties, moreover, must be met with enough skill to make the reader feel they were not obstacles at all and that the poet was quite free to treat any subject and employ any tone of voice he wished, from the dramatic and serious to the importunities of love, and all with perfect ease. And yet, so much do the standards of formality change that we may wonder what the to-our-ear conventional Michael Drayton, who characterized his poetry this way—

---

2. John L. Sweeney, *Furioso: A Magazine of Poetry* 2, no. 1 (1943): 35.

My wanton verse ne'er keeps one certain stay,
But now at hand, then seeks invention far,
And with each little motion runs astray,
Wild, madding, jocund, and irregular

—would have made of the fourth line of Donne's "Love's Deity." It may nevertheless be pointed out that Mr. Kinnell may be misrepresenting a poet's resources when claiming that his images are what we most treasure in his work or what best characterize it. This would leave nothing to be said in behalf of Wyatt's "Forget Not Yet," Shakespeare's "Farewell, thou art too dear for my possessing," Herbert's "Bitter-Sweet," Dickinson's "Much Madness Is Divinest Sense," as well as major passages of Eliot, Pope, Herbert of Cherbury, and many more.

Here is the first stanza and ensuing refrain of Apollinaire's celebrated (and unpunctuated) poem, *Le Pont Mirabeau,* followed by three translations into English by William Meredith, Richard Wilbur, and W. S. Merwin.

Sous le pont Mirabeau coule la Seine
Et nos amours
Faut-il qu'il m'en souvienne
La joie venait toujours après la peine

Vienne la nuit sonne l'heure
Les jours s'en vont je demeure

Under the Mirabeau Bridge flows the Seine.
Why must I be reminded again
of our love?
Doesn't happiness issue from pain?

Bring on the night, ring out the hour,
The days wear on but I endure.
(William Meredith)[3]

Under the Mirabeau Bridge there flows the Seine
Must I recall

---

3. Guillaume Apollinaire, *Alcools: Poems, 1898–1913,* trans. William Meredith (1956), 17.

Our loves recall how then
After each sorrow joy came back again

> Let night come on bells end the day
> The days go by me still I stay
> (Richard Wilbur)[4]

Under the Mirabeau Bridge the Seine
Flows and our love
Must I be reminded again
How joy came always after pain

> Night comes the hour is rung
> The days go I remain
> (W. S. Merwin)[5]

The Apollinaire poem is distinguished for its music, made all the more intricate by the absence of punctuation, thereby requiring the reader to hesitate even while the poem flows as smoothly as the river, and the effect of reverie is beautifully mixed with uncertainty. Each translator has aimed at this fluidity and pathos, yet their versions are different not only in their music but even in their meaning. In the Meredith version, the speaker seems to feel he is well rid of a love the recollection of which only pains him; he yearns for surcease of memory. In Wilbur's version, the regret is all for a departed love which, for all its intervals of sorrow, had its sufficient leavenings of joy as a compensation now no longer to be had. In Merwin the regret is much like Wilbur's but with this important difference: where in Wilbur joy vanquishes sorrow (a sorrow that could be attributed to the normal fabric of life), in Merwin it comes in oscillation with pain, as though love itself were tainted with inescapable misery intrinsic to itself: if it's joy you want, you've got to expect pain as well, and the pain comes first. It may be worth noticing that Wilbur is the only one who attempts to preserve the French pronunciation of *Seine* by rhyming it with *then*, to which *again* may be made to conform, whereas the other two

---

4. Richard Wilbur, *New and Collected Poems* (1988), 28.
5. W. S. Merwin, *Selected Translations, 1948–1968* (1968), 128.

translators rhyme *Seine* with *pain*, with which *again* may also be made to conform. One further point as regards music: an ear attuned to the French and its literary resources would detect, as Francis Steegmuller pointed out, an echo, in Apollinaire's refrain, of François Villon—music, that is to say, of the most durable kind.

II

It can be no surprise that so subtle and technically expert a poet as Donald Justice, who is also a trained musician and composer, should have addressed this shapelessly extensive topic, the music of forms, in a number of essays. One of them, called "Notes of an Outsider," interestingly and provocatively presents two poems, one in English, one in French, both by Walter Savage Landor and one of them clearly a translation of the other. But the English one is a quatrain, rhyming *abab*, while the other is a couplet. Justice is characteristically shrewd in his conjecture about which came first.

He then goes on to quote a more elaborate Landor poem, which he acknowledges to be beautiful, "and part of its beauty," he says, "at least for me, is its great brevity."[6] Here it is.

> Ternissa! you are fled!
> I say not to the dead,
> But to the happy ones who rest below;
> For surely, surely where
> Your voice and graces are
> Nothing of death can any feel or know.
> Girls who delight to dwell
> Where grows most asphodel
> Gather to their calm breasts each word you speak:
> The mild Persephone
> Places you on her knee,
> And your cool palm smooths down stern Pluto's cheek.

After quoting the poem, Justice engages in the Donald Tovey game that I refer to in my Introduction, in which Gray's "Elegy" was said to be

---

6. Donald Justice, *Oblivion: On Writers and Writing* (1998), 121–22.

trimmed down by cutting an adjective from every line and thereby turning the poem's pentameter metric into tetrameter without sacrificing
much, if anything, in the way of content. Justice experiments in paring
down Landor, who, after all, is one of the sparest of poets. But I would
want to claim that Landor's music, as well as Gray's (the latter being far
more licentious in his profligate use of adjectives), attain by their line
lengths a special music that is essential to the effects of their respective
poems. The slow and mournful pathos of Gray, with rhythms of a natural
yet stately measure that belong to rural and seasonal solemnities of
eighteenth-century poetry, would lose a good deal of its effect if concen-
trated into the more epigrammatic limits of

> The curfew tolls the knell of day,
> The lowing herd wind o'er the lea,
> The plowman homeward plods his way,
> And leaves the world to dark and me.

In the Landor poem what struck me most of all was its employment of
a stanzaic form and music used by Richard Wilbur in a superb translation
he made of Baudelaire's *L'Invitation au Voyage*.

> My child, my sister,
>   dream
> How sweet all things would seem
> Were we in that kind land to live together,
> And there love slow and long,
> There love and die among
> Those scenes that image you, that sumptuous weather.
> Drowned suns that glimmer there
> Through cloud-disheveled air
> Move me with such a mystery as appears
> Within those other skies
> Of your treacherous eyes
> When I behold them shining through their tears.[7]

7. Richard Wilbur, *New and Collected Poems* (1988), 254.

It is curious that the music of Wilbur's translation is actually nearer to Landor than to Baudelaire, the French text being throughout a syllable shorter than its English version:

> Mon enfant, ma soeur,
> Songe à la douceur
> D'aller là-bas vivre ensemble!
> Aimer à loisir,
> Aimer et mourir
> Au pays qui te ressemble!

There is an interesting musical significance to Shelley's "Ode to the West Wind" which cannot be mere inadvertence. Shelley himself has supplied a useful note on the poem's genesis. "This poem was conceived and chiefly written in a wood that skirts the Arno, near Florence, and on a day when that tempestuous wind, whose temperature is at once mild and animating, was collecting the vapors which pour down the autumnal rains. They began, as I foresaw, at sunset with a violent tempest of hail and rain, attended by that magnificent thunder and lightning peculiar to Cisalpine regions."

Shelley's brilliant and innovative form for this poem pays a purposeful, echoing debt to Dante, a native of those very haunts along the Arno, since Shelley's stanza is based, in part, on Dante's terza rima, an homage to the English poet's great predecessor and to the past. But the stanza is also an innovative sonnet, composed of four tercets and a couplet, a form absolutely original with Shelley, and an innovation, therefore, that looks to the future, as the terza rima looked to the past. And the poem itself, beginning with its tempestuous and almost destructive forces of autumnal and extinctive threats, concludes with the confident expectation of a rebirth.

William Carlos Williams avails himself of the same fecund and suggestive music in the opening of his poem "The Yachts," in which the poem, composed throughout in tercets, opens with four lines that observe Dante's terza rima, though promptly and completely abandoning rhyme thereafter. One must ask why the poet so meticulously adopted this fragmentary echo, and I think the poem's submerged symbolism and imagery will explain and justify such allusiveness. The yachts are described as exceptionally beautiful, elitist, privileged, frankly spoiled, "surrounded by / lesser and greater craft, which, sycophant, lumbering / and flittering, follow them," and they have been cared for by crews "solicitously grooming them," like thoroughbreds. They are being readied for a race, and presently they begin. But by the ninth tercet some surprising imagery rises, as it were, from the depths of the water:

> Arms with hands grasping seek to clutch at the prows.
> Bodies thrown recklessly in the way are cut aside.
> It is a sea of faces about them in agony, in despair
>
> until the horror of the race dawns staggering the mind;
> the whole sea becomes an entanglement of watery bodies
> lost to the world bearing what they cannot hold. Broken,
>
> beaten, desolate, reaching from the dead to be taken up,
> they cry out, failing, failing! their cries rising
> in waves still as the skillful yachts pass over.

This violent ending of the poem, Gericaultesque in its ferocity, crops up so suddenly, in a poem that began so smoothly and indeed elegantly with a description of the preparations for and beginning of a modern yacht race, that we are cunningly invited to puzzle about just what is going on in this strange and wonderful poem. At one level at least, it appears to be about class struggle, though perhaps modified as instead the perfect triumph of those favored ones (like film or rock stars) over those whose quotidian miseries are universally taken for granted and never relieved. These yachts have been carefully shielded "from the too-heavy blows / of an ungoverned ocean which when it chooses / tortures the biggest hulls, the best man knows / to pit against its beatings, and sinks them pitilessly." These craft have been exempted from certain dangers, and it could be claimed they are like the spoiled children of rich parents, blandly ignoring the sufferings of the multitudes who lack their means and graces. "Could be claimed," I think, only if one forgets that terza rima opening with its invitation to recall Dante. For it brings to mind the eighth canto of the *Inferno* (lines 30–60), which, in Charles Singleton's translation (1970), presents this terrible scene, in which the "master" referred to is Virgil:

While we were running through the dead channel, there rose before me one covered with mud, and said, "Who are you that come before your time?"

And I to him, "If I come, I do not remain. But you, who are you that have become so foul?"

He answered, "You see that I am one who weeps."

And I to him, "In weeping and in sorrow do you remain, accursed spirit, for I know you, even if you are all filthy."

Then he stretched both his hands to the boat, whereas the wary master thrust him off, saying, "Away there with the other dogs!" Then he put his arms about my neck, kissed my face, and said, "Indignant soul, blessed is she who bore you! He was an arrogant one in the world. No goodness whatever adorns his memory; so is his shade furious here. How many up there now [i.e., in the world of the living] account themselves great kings, that here shall lie like swine in mire, leaving behind them horrible dispraises."

And I, "Master, I should like well to see him soused in this soup, before we quit the lake."

And he to me, "Before the shore comes into view you shall be satisfied. It is fitting that in such a wish you should be gratified."

A little after this I saw such rending of him by the muddy folk that I still praise and thank God for it.

It needs the whole theological structure of Dante's poem to make clear the seeming heartlessness of Virgil and the pilgrim Dante at this point, hostile as they appear to be towards the hopelessly mired and deprived soul of (as we are to learn) Filippo Argenti, who is only one of the vast horde of the tormented, likened by Dante, on the authority of Thomas Aquinas, to dogs.

So the privileged status of the yachts in Williams' poem is ultimately that of the saved, and their scorn for the damned is condoned and legitimized. Yet at the same time, the class distinction is maintained, yachts being by their very nature the pleasure craft of the wealthy; still more do they seem, in their preening aloofness and physical beauty ("they appear youthful . . . fleckless, free and / naturally to be desired"), the film and rock stars whose lives are supported on the adulation of multitudes about whose devotion and condition they are largely indifferent.

A much admired and frequently anthologized poem by Ben Jonson is titled "Epitaph on S. P. a child of Q. El. Chappel," in which the child has been identified as Salathiel Pavy, and the chapel, of course, is Queen Elizabeth's.

> Weepe with me all you that read
>> This little storie:
> And know, for whom a tear is shed,
>> Death's selfe is sorry.
> 'Twas a child, that so did thrive
>> In grace, and feature,
> As Heaven and Nature seem'd to strive
>> Which own'd the creature.
> Yeeres he numbred scarse thirteene
>> When Fates turn'd cruell,
> Yet three fill'd Zodiacks had he beene
>> The stages jewell;
> And did act (what now we mone)
>> Old men so duely,
> As, sooth, the Parcae thought him one,
>> He plai'd so truly.
> So, by error, to his fate
>> They all consented;
> But viewing him since (alas, too late)
>> They have repented.
> And have sought (to give new birth)
>> In bathes to steepe him;
> But, being so much too good for earth,
>> Heaven vowes to keepe him.

The critical commentary on this poem rarely touches on its music, which is subtle and ingenious. Despite its visible appearance of alternating tetrameter and dimeter lines, in which the shorter lines are uniformly given feminine endings, the poem may also be read as composed in quatrains, with a period at the end of each, except for the twelfth line, where we have a semicolon; and the quatrains rhyme *abab*. Nevertheless, the quatrains are not separated by space between them, and we are clearly invited by the poet to read the poem as if it were an entire thing in itself, undivided into parts. The quatrains are identical in form, not only in rhyme but in meter as well; and this entails an abridgment of one syllable at the opening of the first line of each in an acephalic, or "headless," line. This is done with such deliberate and formal exactitude as to supply a curious and notable music, an effect of truncation that symbolically reminds us of the truncated life of the young actor. This is not to say that wherever an acephalic line is used it must invariably refer to some kind of abridgment; Milton makes great use of such lines in "L'Allegro," but he does so promiscuously, in something like random fashion, using the device for surprise and unexpectedness. But in Jonson's case formalities both of verse and of the memorial occasion command, and so lines 1, 5, 9, 13, 17, and 21 all in their ritual order are abridged as, we might almost say, an act of respect to the dead child.

Conventionally, when we speak of "form" in poetry, we fall too easily into discussion of received forms, traditional stanzas, like sonnets, villanelles, rhyme royal stanzas, ottava rima, and quatrains of various kinds. Those who condemn form in poetry are often given to venting their wrath upon these received forms, and often chiefly on the grounds that they coerce the mind, limit the imagination, force language with Procrustean barbarity into set molds. But in fact our greatest formal poets—Donne, Herbert, Campion, Herrick, and Hardy—rarely embrace received forms apart from the sonnet. What they so conspicuously and brilliantly do is to invent forms of their own. This means that with such a poem the poet is free to create whatever pattern and music he cares for; but in each subsequent stanza of that poem the original music and pattern must be religiously observed. And in following a pattern of his own invention, the poet is being as obedient as he would be in writing a sonnet.

III

If Michael Drayton was able to think of his poetry, excellent yet conventional though it be, as "wild, madding, jocund, and irregular," we must remind ourselves how standards of rigor will vary from one period to another. And these standards are by no means merely technical matters, but styles of writing and of experience that reflect upon one another. Modes of feeling themselves go in and out of fashion (a truth which is commonly denied with the platitude that "human nature doesn't change"). Describing the deportment of feeling appropriate to the medieval lover, Maurice Valency reminds us that

> the true lover had also this special virtue, the quality called *mesura*, measure, that inner restraint which governs the appetites and keeps them subject to the intellect. This was both an aesthetic and an ethical concept, and obviously it had some relation to the Greek *sophrosyne* [moderation, prudence]. In the twelfth century it was closely identified with courtesy. "He may boast courtesy," wrote Macabru [celebrated jongleur and troubadour], "who knows well how to keep measure."[8]

Measure is a musical term, and a metrical one, and when Dr. Johnson reproved the poetry of Cowley he observed, crushingly, "To the disproportion and incongruity of Cowley's sentiments must be added the uncertainty and looseness of his measures."

The music of forms requires some kind of regularity, some pattern that allows us as readers to judge proficiency, that engenders expectations which it can then fulfill in some novel way, withhold for strategic reasons, satisfy with dissonances or harmonies that surprise and delight. Our experience of this music is, of course, educated by the reach and breadth of our acquaintance with poetry in general. To begin with, one is able to write a poem because one knows what a poem is—not from dictionary definitions, but from experience. And our experience of poetry is no simple business. In *The Architecture of Humanism* (1974), Geoffrey Scott, addressing common factors in all the arts, observes,

> Every experience of art contains, or may contain, two elements, the one direct, the other indirect. The direct element includes our sensuous experience and simple perceptions of form: the immediate apprehensions of the work of art in its visible or audible material, with whatever values may, by the laws of our nature, be inherently connected with that. Secondly, and beyond this, there are the associations which the work awakes in the mind—our conscious reflections upon it, the

8. Maurice Valency, *In Praise of Love* (1961), 176.

significance we attach to it, the fancies it calls up, and which, in consequence, it sometimes is said to express. This is the indirect or associative element. (55)

I want to quarrel with this formulation of Scott's, while acknowledging that he goes on later in his book to qualify and mute the, as I think, too crude distinction he makes here. What he is meditating upon has to do with the rapidity with which we assimilate a work of art as an aesthetic whole; or, rather, the division of assimilative rates, one more rapid than the other. Our ability to do this will be governed by our experience and the width of our acquaintance in the realms of that art. As Robert Frost has shrewdly and justly observed, "A poem is best read in the light of all the other poems ever written. We read A the better to read B (we have to start somewhere; we may get very little out of A). We read B the better to read C, C the better to read D, D the better to go back and get something more out of A. Progress is not the aim, but circulation." Poems allude to one another formally, and so the breadth of our acquaintance will govern the speed with which we can assimilate poems we newly encounter. And, to explain my objection to Scott's formulation above, I would say that very few works of art can achieve their initial impact in purely sensuous terms. A serious and durable work of art, whatever its medium, will make the sort of demands upon us that invite repeated experiences that will fail to exhaust the work. "It is the lowest style only of the arts, whether of Painting, Poetry, or Musick," observed Joshua Reynolds in his *Discourses on Art*, "that may be said, in the vulgar sense, to be naturally pleasing. The higher efforts of those arts, we know by experience, do not affect minds wholly uncultivated."[9]

It may be claimed that the music of forms goes unheard in two senses. First, in that it makes itself felt subliminally, working upon us in ways of which we are not fully aware unless we put ourselves to the study of the work in question, and examine it with care, tact, and delicacy. It will not dwindle under such examination, though there are some who suspect that it will, such as William Stafford, who observed, "Poetry is one of those things. If you analyze it, it's gone. It would be like boiling a watch to see what makes it tick." Poetry is really sturdier than that; and the better it is

---

9. Joshua Reynolds, *Discourses on Art* (New Haven, Conn.: 1959), 233.

the sturdier it becomes under inspection. Great works of poetry continue to yield new sense of themselves, and prove, to our delight and astonishment, utterly inexhaustible.

But there is a second way the music of forms—its echoic effects, recapitulations, harmonies, and above all its melody—goes unheard: all too often, alas, it falls upon deaf ears.

Acknowledgments

The author and publishers are grateful to the following persons and publications for permission to reprint essays and parts of essays by the author:

"Shakespeare and the Sonnet": to Cambridge University Press, where this essay appeared as an Introduction to the *New Cambridge Shakespeare* edition of *The Sonnets* (1996), edited by G. Blakemore Evans.

"The Sonnet: Ruminations on Form, Sex, and History": to *Antioch Review* 55, no. 2 (Spring 1997).

"Sidney and the Sestina": to the University of California Press, and to Jonathan F. S. Post, editor of *Green Thoughts, Green Shades: Essays by Contemporary Poets on the Early Modern Lyric* (2002).

"Gaze Not on Swans": to Middlebury / University Press of New England, and to Robert Pack and Jay Parini, editors of *Touchstones: American Poets on a Favorite Poem* (1995).

"Technique in Housman": to *Yale Review* 87, no. 4 (Oct. 1999).

"Uncle Tom's Shantih": to *Yale Review* 78, no. 2 and *T. S. Eliot: Essays from the Southern Review*, ed. James Olney (New York: Oxford University Press, 1988).

"Paralipomena to *The Hidden Law*": to Louisiana State University Press and Wyatt Prunty, editor of *Sewanee Writers on Writing* (2002).

"On Robert Frost's 'The Wood-Pile'": to *Crossroads: Journal of the Poetry Society of America*, no. 55 (Autumn 2000).

"Two Poems by Elizabeth Bishop": to Ashley Brown, guest editor of *Verse* 4, no. 3 (Nov. 1987), and to Denis Donoghue, who invited me to speak on "The Man-Moth" at New York University.

"Richard Wilbur: An Introduction": to *Poetry Pilot: The Newsletter of the Academy of American Poets* (Winter 1994).

"Yehuda Amichai": to *New York Review of Books* 47, no. 17 (Nov. 2, 2000).

"Charles Simic": to *New York Review of Books* 48, no. 16 (Oct. 18, 2001).

"Seamus Heaney's Prose": to *New York Review of Books* (forthcoming).

"St. Paul's Epistle to the Galatians": to Alfred Corn, editor of *Incarnation: Contemporary Writers on the New Testament* (New York: Penguin Books, 1990).

"On Rhyme": *Yale Review* 87, no. 2 (Apr. 1999).

1967 by Lesley Frost Ballantine, copyright 1936, 1958 by Robert Frost. Reprinted by permission of Henry Holt and Company, LLC.

A. E. HOUSMAN: "They say my verse is sad," "The night is freezing fast," "He stood and heard," and "Tarry, delight," from *The Collected Poems of A. E. Housman.* Copyright 1936, 1950 by Barclays Bank Ltd., © 1964 by Robert E. Symons, copyright 1922 by Henry Holt and Company. Reprinted by permission of Henry Holt and Company, LLC; various extracts from *More Poems, Last Poems* and "The shades of night were falling fast," reprinted by permission of The Society of Authors as the Literary Representative of the Estate of A. E. Housman.

BRAD LEITHAUSER: "In Minako Wada's House" and "Post Coitum Tristesse: A Sonnet," from *Cats of the Temple* by Brad Leithauser, copyright © 1986 by Brad Leithauser. Used by permission of Alfred A. Knopf, a division of Random House, Inc.

JAMES MERRILL: "Tomorrows" and "The Blue Grotto," from *Collected Poems* by James Merrill, edited by J. D. McClatchy and Stephen Yenser, copyright © 2001 by the Literary Estate of James Merrill at Washington University. Used by permission of Alfred A. Knopf, a division of Random House, Inc.

W. S. MERWIN: translation of Guillaume Appollinaire, *Le Pont Mirabeau,* © 1968 by W. S. Merwin, reprinted with permission of The Wiley Agency, Inc.

EDNA ST. VINCENT MILLAY: "When the Year Grows Old," from *Collected Poems,* HarperCollins. Copyright 1917, 1945 by Edna St. Vincent Millay. All rights reserved. Reprinted by permission of Elizabeth Barnett, literary executor.

EUGENIO MONTALE: "Rhymes," from *Satura 1962–1970* by Eugenio Montale, edited by Rosanna Warren, translated by William Arrowsmith. Copyright © 1971 by Arnoldo Mondadori Editor SpA. English text copyright © 1998 by The William Arrowsmith Estate and Rosanna Warren. Used by permission of W. W. Norton & Company, Inc.

MARIANNE MOORE: "In The Days of Prismatic Color," from *The Collected Poems of Marianne Moore* by Marianne Moore. Copyright © 1935 by Marianne Moore, copyright renewed 1963 by Marianne Moore and T. S. Eliot. With the permission of Scribner, a Division of Simon & Schuster, Inc.; (*British rights*) from *The Complete Poems* by Marianne Moore, Faber and Faber Ltd., publishers.